D1567437

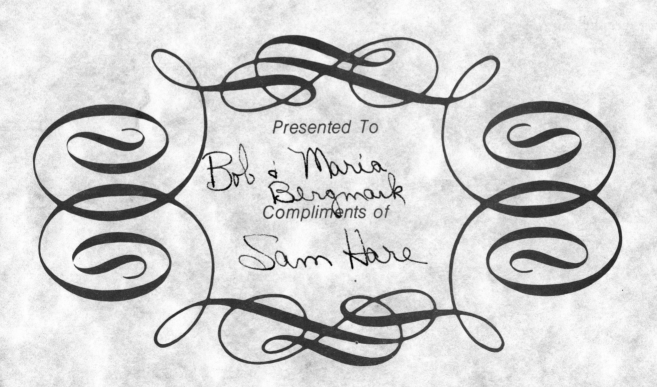

Presented To

Bob & Maria
Bergmark

Compliments of

Sam Hare

SIMI VALLEY

Pictorial Research by Julie Jaskol
"Partners in Progress" by Sharon Makokian
Produced in cooperation
with the Simi Valley Chamber of Commerce
Windsor Publications, Inc.
Chatsworth, California

SIMI VALLEY

TOWARD NEW HORIZONS

An Illustrated History by Linda Aleahmad

Windsor Publications, Inc.—History Book Division
Managing Editor: Karen Story
Design Director: Alexander D'Anca
Photo Director: Susan L. Wells
Executive Editor: Pamela Schroeder

Staff for *Simi Valley: Toward New Horizons*
Manuscript Editor: Douglas P. Lathrop
Photo Editor: Lisa Willinger
Editor, Corporate Biographies: Jeffrey Reeves
Production Editor, Corporate Biographies: Doreen Nakakihara
Customer Service Manager: Phyllis Feldman-Schroeder
Editorial Assistants: Elizabeth Anderson, Dominique Jones,
  Kim Kievman, Michael Nugwynne, Kathy B. Peyser,
  Theresa J. Solis
Publisher's Representative, Corporate Biographies:
  Allison Alan-Lee
Layout Artist, Corporate Biographies: Trish Meyer
Designer: Christina L. Rosepapa

Windsor Publications, Inc.
Elliot Martin, Chairman of the Board
James L. Fish III, Chief Operating Officer
Michele Sylvestro, Vice President/Sales-Marketing
Mac Buhler, Vice President/Sponsor Acquisitions

Library of Congress Cataloging-in-Publication Data:
Aleahmad, Linda, 1947-
  Simi Valley : toward new horizons : an illustrated
history / by Linda Aleahmad : pictorial research by
Julie Jaskol. Partners in Progress / by Sharon
Makokian. – 1st. ed.
  p:208 cm.22x28
  "Produced in cooperation with the Simi Valley Chamber
of Commerce."
  Includes bibliographical references and index.
  ISBN 0-89781-363-4 : $27.95
  1. Simi Valley (Calif.)–Economic conditions. 2. Simi Valley
(Calif.)–Economic conditions–Pictorial works.
3. Simi Valley (Calif.)–Social conditions. 4. Simi Valley (Calif.)–
Social conditions–Pictorial works. I. Jaskol, Julie. II.
Makokian, Sharon. Partners in Progress. 1990.
III. Simi Valley Chamber of Commerce. IV. Title.
HC107.C22S53 1990   90-12961
330.9794'92–dc20   CIP

*The Simi Union Sunday School class poses here in
1899. Courtesy, Simi Valley Historical Society and
Museum, Strathearn Historical Park*

*Previous spread: Montgomery Ranch off First Street
is seen here in its days as a bucolic horse farm.
Watercolor by Dee Hodson*

Contents

To Nancy Bender and Pat Havens, both of whom so clearly express
the spirit of Simi Valley. Pat's dedication to the valley's history
has kept the richness of the past vividly alive,
while Nancy's forward energy keeps our imagination open
to the prospects ahead. It is this blending of past and future
that makes Simi Valley such a stable community.

This watercolor illustration of a blacksmith shop at Strathearn Historical park brings back nostalgic memories of the crafts and trades common to people of long ago. Watercolor by Dee Hodson

Preface

This photo from the Austin family's album provides a good look at the kind of clothing worn by children in Simi's early days. Courtesy, Simi Valley Historical Society and Museum, Strathearn Historical Park

History is a flow, a blending of one event into another. Sometimes the flow is so imperceptible that we do not recognize it until we can stand back and look at how far we have come.

Each moment is a vital thread of the history we weave. The longer one lives in a community, the more one participates in its growth, the richer the weave that is created. Indeed, if any one thread were missing, it would alter and weaken the overall pattern. Thus, history belongs to all of us.

It has been an enriching experience writing this book—sometimes a challenge to unravel the threads even temporarily. And while this book does not presume to be the final word on the development of this valley, I hope the reader will gain an appreciation of the interweaving of people and events which creates a strong community.

My sincere appreciation to those many who so graciously shared their time and memories with me, be it an afternoon of reminiscing or straightforward, pertinent facts. I also thank those certain few who may not, as yet, know much of the valley's history, but do know how to give a needed word of encouragement.

As the heritage of the past meets the energy of today, creating the drama of the future, know that each and every one of us has a role to play.

I
Keepers of the Key

From all viewpoints Simi Valley enjoys a landscape rich in texture, nourished by a gentle history, blessed by the whims of nature. The unique arrangement of vast, fertile lands surrounded by singularly distinctive mountains has enabled the valley to progress at its own pace and on its own terms, not unlike the tortoise that paced along, with little attention from bystanders, only to win the race.

Early inhabitants, living close to the land and extending arms of welcome, set the tone for the character of this bountiful valley. But long before the Spanish or Americans arrived, long before even the Chumash Indians are known to have been here, what is now known as Simi Valley was simply a stretch of land tossed and turned by the dictates of nature.

The Santa Susana Mountain range slopes southward into the valley. This and the Simi Hills comprise the main mountain structure surrounding the valley. The Simi Hills are said to contain the thickest Tertiary Period rock in North America, if not the world. Composed of a single geologic structure called the "Chico Formation," rising nearly 1,500 feet from the valley floor, the Simi Hills boast a thickness of 6,000 feet and are calculated to be well over 80 million years old, a product of the Upper Cretaceous Period.

Geologist Dr. Albert Hirschi, onetime resident of Simi Valley, believed the mountains to consist of a series of sedimentary rocks alternating with volcanic rock and solidified molten materials, a process that produced the granite mined extensively in the Santa Susana Park area and shipped by rail to other parts of California, most notably as railroad culverts between Simi Valley and San Luis Obispo.

During the Miocene Epoch some 7 million to 25 million years ago, the ocean extended as far inland as the Central Valley, leaving only tips of mountains visible, like stepping-stones across a vast lake. Mighty evidence of this process of nature was the deposit of 1,500 to 3,000 feet of marine sediment in the northeastern part of the valley, in approximate alignment with what would later become Tapo Canyon Road. Known as the Gillibrand Oyster Shell Mine, this gift of nature provided a lucrative industry beginning in 1925. It produced nearly pure calcium for use in medicines, in feed for chickens to strengthen the shells of their eggs, and in an oil-absorbent cleaning agent. It

This is a view of the untouched Simi Valley land-scape as it must have looked when the Chumash lived there. Courtesy, Ventura County Museum of History and Art, from Views on the Simi

is the only known deposit of such quantity to exist in the Americas.

Although the riches of oil eluded early speculators who would soon learn that the richness of the land lay in its fertile soil and abundant harvests, some diatomaceous shale was found in Tapo Canyon. In 1921 the California State Mining Bureau reported four producing leases: Tapo Canyon and Scaraba operated by Pan American, and the Union and Century leases operated by the Century Oil Company of California.

Not only did nature provide an abundant variety of geological formations to study, but it also supplied abundant resources for human habitation. It was to these riches that the Chumash Indians were led. Carbon 14 tests indicate that the Chumash lived in the Simi Valley as a separate and distinct cultural group as long as 3,000 years ago.

The first written information about the Chumash people is found in diaries from the 1542 Juan Rodríguez Cabrillo Expedition. But perhaps more enlightening is data gathered by famed Indian anthropologist John Peabody Harrington, a member of the Harrington family of Simi Valley, who studied the Chumash culture extensively. So intense was his work that it led to the honor of working full-time for the American Bureau of Ethnology at the Smithsonian Institution. Upon his death in 1961, among the 800,000 pages of notes turned over to the Smithsonian were 60 boxes devoted exclusively to the Chumash Indians. Thanks to the legacy of this man, rather than becoming a forgotten people, the Chumash will be remembered and their place in local history will become clearer.

Although the Chumash lived a simple life, existing on acorns and sage seeds, recent discoveries indicate that, in fact, their culture reflected a sophisticated understanding of the stars. Cave drawings take on new significance in light of Harrington's research. A pertinent example is the pictograph at Burro Flats on the North American Aviation, Inc., property in the Santa Susana Mountains. One of the few left in the country, the drawing, which shows figures representing the heavens and elements of nature, is painted with mineral pigments mixed with milkweed in red, black, orange, white, pink, and blue. Some of the pigments were prepared by grinding, as shown by three small depressions used as paint mortars in the earthen floor of the cave shelter.

Much of Harrington's understanding of the Chumash resulted from direct conversations with Santa Cruz Island resident Fernando Librado, who was 109 years old when Harrington was able to track him down in 1912. With vivid detail, Librado recalled the spiritual and cosmological belief system of his people, that of a threatening universe of aggressive, supernatural beings vying for control. Most frightening was said to be the time of midwinter, when, it was feared, "the sun might choose not to return from its journey to the south." It was believed that from this full circle would come renewed warmth, food, and prosperity.

It is likely that the cave drawings at Burro Flats were derived from this philosophy, as it is considered to be the setting for a winter solstice ritual. If the cave paintings are indeed an early example of dealing with the mysteries of the heavens, it is very appropriate that they are located on property belonging to those who still deal with those same mysteries. Although the cave site is not now open to the public, a reproduction of the pictograph may be seen at the Strathearn Historical Park.

The original painting is located along the back wall of a sandstone shelter about 16 feet long and 4 feet high. A small natural arch allows light to shine on the painting. An archaeologist at the San Diego Museum of Man has said that he witnessed "a striking play of early morning light over the painted images. It reached a climax when a thin streak of light crossed the eyes of a red-painted horned figure—perhaps a sky being or a priest wearing a mask." Such figures appear on the pictograph at Burro Flats. Those who have seen this beam of light believe the painting was deliberately positioned to mark the exact occurrence of the winter solstice on December 22.

Studies indicate that human activities around Burro Flats took place primarily from 1500 to 1800, the peak years of the Chumash culture. It is considered to have been a site to which they journeyed rather than one on which they lived.

The Chumash are known to have established permanent villages at other locations, most notably at the far western end of the valley, where the Strathearn Historical Park now sits. Known in the Ventura dialect as Shimiyi, meaning "village," it is likely that it was from this source that Simi got its name. The village of Ta'apu was located by the Tapo Creek in Tapo Canyon with perhaps a smaller one located on a marshy *cienaga* a little further north. At the eastern end of the valley among a forest of oak was a village, the name of which in Chumash meant Hummingbird's Nest. This property is still known by this anglicized name.

Above and Left: Rafael Solares was a Chumash Indian who was photographed by a visiting Frenchman in 1878. A headshot of him is shown here along with a portrait of him wearing the ceremonial costume of a shaman. These and other photos of Solares are on display at the Musée de l'Homme in Paris. *Courtesy, Santa Barbara Museum of Natural History*

It appears that only a few hundred Indians lived in this area at any one time as the Chumash were a migratory people who followed available food supplies. Residents of this valley traded with the coastal villages, exchanging beads made of bones or seashells, and, possibly, salmon and steelhead caught from the Arroyo Simi for sea otter pelts, tar, and other varieties of fish. No doubt, flea-size sage seeds, an abundant food source in the area, were also traded along with blackberries from the hills.

Mike Kuhn, senior planner for the City of Simi Valley, has studied the Chumash culture for many years. He states:

They lived, developed, and adjusted within their limited long-distance tradings to a lot of visiting between villages. They would host or be guests at feasts or celebrations where tribes with surplus food would share it with those who had less.

Generally the Chumash were a very peaceful people who only became territorial when protecting their oak grove from infringement by another family. Extensive white oak forests in parts of the valley

Roy Rogers and Trigger may have gone "Down Dakota Way" in the movies, but in actuality, the "happy trails" wound along the Simi Hills. Courtesy, Corriganville Preservation Committee

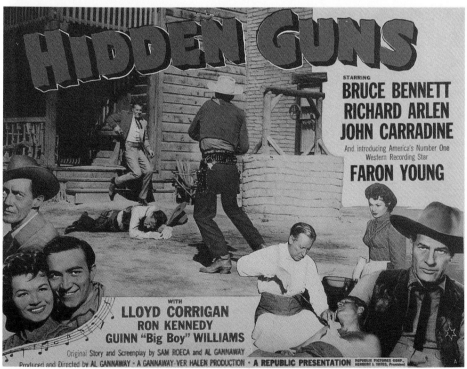

Left: The expansion of Corriganville in the 1940s coincided with the flood of inexpensive shoot-'em-ups Hollywood was releasing. Courtesy, Corriganville Preservation Committee

Facing page: Shown here is a detail of the Strathearn home, the centerpiece at Strathearn Historical Park. Watercolor by Dee Hodson

Each Chumash family generally had its own hut, made of poles lashed together, then covered with canes or grass. As seen in this photo of a replica, each hut was about 20 feet across. Released by Carol A. Bidwell

would have provided well for the Indians, who removed the bitter taste from the acorns by sifting them through sieves made of woven grasses, creating a bland mush.

By several accounts, the Chumash were a handsome people. A naturalist named Martinez, on a botanical expedition in 1792, offered this description:

The dress and adornment of the women was graceful. From the waist down they usually wear two very soft pieces of buckskin, the edges of which are cut into fringe and ornamented . . . One of these skins is worn in front, one behind. From the waist up they wear a [cape of] fox, otter, or rabbit fur . . . They adorn their heads tastefully with necklaces and earrings. Their hair is worn in bangs cut short and combed forward. They trim it daily by singeing it hair by hair with a piece of pine bark so that no hair protrudes.

The men were usually naked. Some had their nose cartilages pierced. All had their ears pierced with two holes through which they hung finger-size tobacco pouches.

Early Spanish explorers were impressed with the Chumash Indians' bathing habits. Each village contained a sweat house called a *temescal,* which was heated sufficiently to cause profuse perspiration whereupon the Indian would scrape his skin with sweat sticks and run from the hot spot to fresh water for thorough cleansing.

The Chumash were first-rate basket weavers, and baskets were an integral part of their culture. They were used for food preparation, eating, trading, ceremonial activities, and as cradles. The Chumash even lived in inverted basket-style domes of interwoven grass. When a Chumash woman died, her gravepost was decorated with baskets. Spanish explorers were very impressed with the well-constructed coil baskets. Pedro Fages, a soldier with the de Anza expedition in 1776, noted:

In their manufactures, these Indians . . . are more finished and artistic than those of . . . San Gabriel . . . The women weave nearly all their baskets, pitchers, trays, and jars . . . The tools of these skillful artisans are only two, the most simple ones in the world, the knife and the punch.

While the women were skilled in basket weaving, the men constructed seaworthy canoes that would rival those of today. Harrington recorded Librado's amazingly detailed recollections from the time they first met in 1912 until the Indian's death in 1915. In 1914, working from Librado's memory, the two men were able to reconstruct the celebrated *tomol,* a traditional open canoe ingeniously formed of planks sewn together with leather and caulked with asphalt. Typically such a boat would be 22 to 27 feet long, capable of seating 10 to 15 men. These canoes were all the more remarkable because they were built with only stone age tools. Canoe making was not a trade which just any member of the tribe could practice. An interested Chumash would have to apply to the Brotherhood-of-the-Canoe. If he was admitted, he would pay a required fee and then be introduced to the secrets of canoe making. (The *tomol* made by Harrington and Librado is currently on display at the Santa Barbara Museum of History.)

It was not all work for the Chumash. Ceremonies were always a welcome occasion. The forerunner of the American Thanksgiving was the *hutash* ceremony, which celebrated the acorn harvest of late

Left: Candaleria was one of the prominent Chumash basket weavers of the Sespe. Courtesy, Ventura County Museum of History and Art

Below: The Chumash were known for creating baskets like this one, woven in 1821 at the Mission San Buenaventura. Courtesy, Ventura County Museum of History and Art

These Chumash children were taught Christian doctrine by an elderly missionary who sought to replace their Chumash culture with European ways. Courtesy, Ventura County Museum of History and Art

summer Held in major towns, the *hutash* ceremony drew people from all over to celebrate, trade, and play. They always managed to include their favorite activity—gambling—in the day's events. A popular game was *tikauwick,* similar to field hockey but allowing 200 to 300 players on a team. The victorious side would give half of its winnings to the chief of the village hosting the celebration. Kickball, marbles, and dodge rock were also popular activities.

Although the primary Indians in this area were the Chumash, studies indicate a Fernandeso Shoshone site may have existed at the east end of the valley. The Fernandeso Shoshones are generally identified with the Chatsworth area. However, the site in the study uncovered 33 small arrow points, 23 of which were identifiable as the triangular type used by the Shoshones; one was identifiable as Chumash. It is speculated that they occupied the site just before the Spaniards began to settle the area.

Little disturbed the peaceful existence of the Chumash for well over 200 years following Cabrillo's 1542 expedition along the coast, other than the arrival of the Viscaino expedition in 1602. Then, in 1769, the transit of the planet Venus was to occur, and astronomers thought the best viewing advantage would be off the coast of Lower (Baja) California. King Carlos III of Spain did not trust the motives of other European countries planning scientific expeditions. Not wasting any time, he quickly made plans to claim the land of Upper California through colonization. To that end, the first mission was founded in San Diego on July 16, 1769.

Spain had conceived a commendable plan. A chain of missions would be developed to educate the California Indians with Christian doctrine and prepare them to assume citizenship so that they could acquire title to the lands around the missions. Strategically placed presidios would serve to protect all those within their jurisdiction. Unsavory persons would be confined. Many were sent to Sonoma, the last established mission, which was founded in 1823. In the meantime, until the Indians could assume ownership, land grants were issued on a temporary basis to Spanish soldiers.

With this plan in mind, periodic expeditions were sent forth to implement the mission system. Thus it was in 1769 that military leader Don Gaspar de Portolá, along with his diarist Father Juan Crespi, headed north from Mexico (then held by Spain) to settle Upper (Alta) California. The first known reference to Simi was made in Crespi's diaries as the expedition returned in January 1770, suggesting it passed through the Santa Susana Mountains over what would later be the stagecoach trail.

In 1776, while the United States was fighting for its independence from Britain, Spain was continuing its plans to colonize the California area. Juan Bautista de Anza led an exploring expedition north from Mexico. Included in his entourage was a soldier named Santiago Pico. This expedition moved even closer to Simi Valley when it camped near Triunfo in the Russell Valley (two miles southeast of Thousand Oaks).

Juan Bautista de Anza leads 240 soldiers and settlers the length of California to settle San Francisco. The trek, which skirted Simi Valley, included a soldier named Santiago Pico, who in 1795 received 113,000 acres of grazing land from Spain. The land grant became known as El Rancho Simi. Courtesy, University of California Extension Media Center, Berkeley

As expeditions continued, the mission system progressed. In 1795 Father Vincent de Santa Maria of the San Buenaventura Mission, founded in 1782, reported in a letter dated September 3 to his "Most Venerable and Esteemed Fr. Presidente":

. . . in order to find the best location between this mission and San Gabriel . . . I have to report that on August 16, at twelve o'clock at noon I set out from this Mission . . . accompanied by Ensign Don Pablo Cota, Sergeant Don Jose Maria Ortega, and four soldiers. We arrived at the Rancheria of Cayeguas, distant from the Camino real two leagues to the north. We stopped at the Parage del Conejo at four in the afternoon and passed the night there. On the seventeenth we reached a valley which is called Simi, at about nine o'clock. In the middle of the valley, we came upon a small pool of water in a dry arroyo which crosses the valley halfway. Here we stopped at ten o'clock. At three in the afternoon the ensign, sergeant, and two soldiers and I went to reconnoiter a place which said soldier Jose Antonio Lugo claimed to have seen and which, he said, had water and land. Going toward the north of our camp at a brisk pace, we reached the place at 4:30 p.m. After examining everything, we found the water to be not abundant, the valley very narrow and dismal, the soil salinous, and consequently unserviceable. We returned to the camp galloping and arrived there at half past six in the evening.

Historians surmise it was Tapo Canyon that they had explored. Simi was passed over as a mission site in favor of the diocese of San Fernando Rey Mission, to which Simi would belong.

In 1795 Governor Diego de Borica of Spanish California bestowed the largest land grant in Santa Barbara County (which still included Ventura County). As it turned out, this grant was one of only three made by Spain. Conejo and Refugio were the others.

Various sources state that the 113,000 acres of grazing rights went to Patricio, Miguel, and Francisco Javier Pico. However, more recent study indicates El Rancho Simi went to their father, Santiago Pico, in partnership with Luis Peña, a soldier of the guard in Ventura. According to translations of mission records at the Los Angeles Museum of Natural History, Santiago Pico petitioned for Los Angeles while on expedition with de Anza. Since it was preferred that he take Simi, he requested that his sons be allowed to live on the property. Historians speculate that the brothers would have been too young to be qualifying veterans able to secure a grant for themselves.

In the tradition of large Spanish families, Santiago Pico had two other sons as well. They were José Delores, who sired the line of Picos known in Northern California, and José Maria, father of Andrés Pico (associated with San Fernando) and Pio Pico, who became governor.

Originally known as San José de Nuestra Señora de Altagracia y Simi, El Rancho Simi stretched from Simi Valley westward to what is now Moorpark. As only grazing rights had been granted, very little was done with the land for some time.

It is not known just when the Simi adobe was built on El Rancho Simi. Mission San Fernando Rey records from 1797 indicate that Santiago Pico was living in Simi, as he was named godfather at various baptisms. Yet the records of the 1795 expedition of Father Vincent de Santa Maria through Simi make no mention of an adobe. However, the Picos would have needed a place to live. It is very plausible that the adobe-brick structure (which archaeologists have determined to have been one room larger than the existing portion at Strathearn Historical Park) would have

This is the earliest known photo of the Simi adobe, taken in 1900. Archeologists have determined that the adobe was 100 years old by then. The adobe still stands today at Strathearn Historical Park. Courtesy, Simi Valley Historical Society and Museum, Strathearn Historical Park

been built by 1800. Some sources mention adobe construction in the 1820s, but it is more likely this refers to reconstruction following an alleged raid on the adobe by a group of San Diego Indians.

It may be that the adobe at Tapo was established in the 1820s. Thompson and West, in the 1883 edition of *Santa Barbara and Ventura Counties,* speak of the Tapo Rancho, stating:

[The rancho] *has been established for sixty-odd years . . . It lies in the northeastern portion of the Simi Rancho, of which it was once a part . . . it contains 14,000 acres. From a vineyard which has been planted 40 years superior wines and brandy have been made.*

It is known that in 1816 there were a number of people living at the Rancho Simi adobe. With the threat of attack to the California coast by South American revolutionaries, the call went out through the region for a complete accounting of men and arms. Santa Barbara presidio records, as well as those of the missions, specify that Simi had three male civilians with one rifle, one lance, and one sword. They also claimed one *invalido,* probably Miguel Pico, who had been a soldier at Santa Barbara Mission. It is assumed that there were also women and a number of children.

The population on El Rancho Simi no doubt saw a slight, temporary increase in 1818, when a number of people moved inland from San Buenaventura in anticipation of a coastal attack by the French privateer Hippolyte Bouchard. When the coast seemed clear, the temporary guests resumed residency at the mission and life continued at a peaceful pace with little else but sheep-herding to pass the time. However, this must not have provided much satisfaction for the Picos. Because the wool and mutton trade at the time was very limited, there apparently was insufficient reason for them to be bothered with this business. In 1816 Patricio Pico notified the San Fernando padres that the mission sheep would no longer be welcome on Rancho Simi. (The last of the mission sheep were seen in 1819.)

In 1821, as Mexico (New Spain) was fighting for independence from Spain, which it gained in 1822, the Pico brothers petitioned for and received a renewal of their grant from the last of the Spanish governors, Pablo Vicente de Sola. In flowery language, they made their plea:

. . . Your Excellency, these are the places and the leagues of this place, which your excellency conde-scended to let us ask for in allowing us to present this paper, since this said Rancho was given by his Excellency, Governor Diego de Borica, who is happy with the God, in the year 1795. We ask and duly pray your Excellency to be so good as to grant us all the succession of said Rancho, so that we may all unite in brotherhood as long as His Divine Majesty may be please; and thus, your Excellency, we hope from your pious heart, you may grant us as we ask. Your humble subjects, who duly kiss your hand.

The property continued in the hands of the Picos, although by 1829 some interest was develop-ing by an outsider who felt that Rafael Pico (most likely the son of one of the brothers) was not caring adequately for the property. The complaint came from a high-enough source to generate a letter from Mexican governor Echeandia commanding Rafael to explain himself, which he has-tened to do. He stated that he had just made a contract with the San Gabriel Mission to stock El Rancho Simi with 600 head of cattle.

In 1834 José De La Guerra y Noriega (sometimes referred to as Noriega, sometimes De La Guerra), commander of the Santa Barbara Presidio, attempted to buy El Rancho Simi from Rafael Pico. De La Guerra's son-in-law, Alfred Robinson, an agent for a New England shipping company, had little regard for Rafael and may have been behind the rumors of Rafael's ineffectiveness. Nevertheless, the deal did not go through until 1842, just after Manuel and Patricio Pico had the grant once again reconfirmed.

Having retired from military service, De La Guerra finally acquired the property at age 63 on

This image of José De La Guerra y Noriega appeared in a book called El Gran Capitan, *written by Father Joseph A. Thompson and published by the Franciscan Fathers. The book extolled the peaceful, productive reign of De La Guerra on Rancho Simi. Courtesy, Simi Valley Historical Society and Museum, Strathearn Historical Park*

José De La Guerra y Noriega, one of the richest men in California in the 1850s and 1860s, ran his Simi Valley holdings from this adobe in Santa Barbara. The two story addition at right is believed to be De La Guerra's counting house, where he kept all his gold. Courtesy, Ventura County Museum of History and Art

April 25, 1842, adding it to his already vast holdings that ranged from San Luis Obispo to the Los Angeles County line, including his most recent acquisition, Rancho El Conejo. For El Rancho Simi, he paid $800 cash, $219 in goods, and closed out a $2,000 debt the Picos had with San Gabriel Mission, perhaps a result of Rafael's cattle contract with the mission.

As De La Guerra and his entourage traveled to Simi, the landscape they encountered was very much like that described by Alfred Robinson when he visited the valley a few years before. In "Life in California," his narrative of trading up and down the California coast, Robinson writes:

. . . The clear heavens; the bright moon; the beautiful country stretching far away into the blue distance, and basking in the moonlight; the deep silence, unbroken save by the footfalls of our horses, or the cries of some wild night bird; all formed a scene of such rare beauty that the impression still lingers in my memory. At midnight we reached the "Rancho de Simi" some fourteen leagues from the Mission. The good people who inhabited this lonely spot we found were fast locked in sleep, so that we were obliged to take up our quarters upon the ground in the open air . . . We slept soundly in spite of the rudeness of our beds, and awaking at daylight much refreshed, pushed on for Los Angeles, which we reached at noon.

The legendary pastoral days had eluded Simi until Captain De La Guerra took ownership. He had arrived in California in 1801 at the age of 22, already well along in his military career. He was confident, sophisticated, and, by all accounts, a shrewd businessman.

William Heath Davis, author of *Seventy Five Years in California* and a business associate of De La Guerra, offers this insight from his business dealings with De La Guerra in 1842 and 1843:

On these occasions Noriega [De La Guerra] took me to the attic of his house in Santa Barbara, where he kept his treasure, the room being used exclusively for that purpose. There was no stairway, the attic being reached by a ladder, which was removed when not in use. In this room were two old-fashioned Spanish chairs, and ranged round were twelve or fifteen coras—strong, compactly woven baskets, of different sizes, made by Indians, the largest holding perhaps half a bushel—all of which contained gold, some nearly full . . . I was astonished to see so much coin in the possession of one person in a country where the wealth consisted mainly of horses and cattle. The old gentleman said that the attic was the safest place to keep it. I asked him how he managed to collect so much gold, and he replied that it was the accumulations of all the years he had been on the coast. The Spanish soldiers, when they were paid off, spent their money freely, and he had supplied them with what they wanted, having carried on a store of his own.

Davis goes on to explain that the attic may not have been such a safe place after all. Legend has it that some of the sons were not as aboveboard as their father. Since the ladder was kept out of reach, they would gain access to the attic hoard by climbing to the roof from the outside and removing a few of the tiles. Then, "reaching down into the baskets with an improvised pitchfork, they drew out as many coins as they thought it advisable to take."

Don José De La Guerra developed a vast sheep and cattle-raising enterprise. From his Santa Barbara home he would make periodic visits to Simi to review the cattle, participate in sheep-shearing activities with the help of shepherds from Piru and Camulos, and oversee grape harvesting and wine making at his Tapo vineyards.

By 1858 De La Guerra had moved the base of his El Rancho Simi operation from the Simi adobe to Tapo Canyon. The mission system had ceased to exist. The few remaining Chumash lived on ranchos, helping as they had been trained. The presidio was a thing of the past. California was now the 31st state of the Union, following the signing of the Treaty of Hidalgo on February 2, 1848, which established the Rio Grande as a natural border between the United States and Mexico. Under this treaty the United States was to honor all property titles previously granted by Mexico provided certain conditions were met. De La Guerra, recognizing the growing importance of the area due to the proximity of the Gold Rush, hastened to file his deed with the General Land Office of the United States. He received a decree of confirmation to all of El Rancho Simi in 1854.

While some sources say the move to Tapo was due to a fire set by Indians, there is no evidence to support this and much circumstantial evidence to the contrary. It is more likely they made the move to a more dependable water supply since the Tapo Creek at the time was thought to be substantial enough to be a perennial stream. It was here that Simi's agriculture began with orchards and flowers growing profusely by the Tapo Alta with several acres of mission grapes.

The life-style of rancho days was one of generous hospitality and simplicity. As many as 50 guests might descend on a rancho unannounced to stay a week or even a month. The adobe floor was earthen, but the master bed boasted white crocheted bedspreads (and sometimes a surplus of fleas). Beef, beans, and tortillas with homegrown peppers were the diet of the day. Dairy products were rare as no one seemed to want to milk the cow.

The Spanish men had such a proficiency with horses that few could surpass them in horsemanship. Horses were always available and saddled at the door, at the ready disposal of guests. When a don was to take a lengthy trip, he would take several of his horses with him. As one tired, he discarded it and continued his journey on a fresh horse.

Legendary accounts tell of the grandeur of the De La Guerras riding up and down the land in their state carriages accompanied by six outriders, outfitted in livery of silver and blue. In later years they traveled from Santa Barbara by oxen-drawn wagon in a cavalcade of 50 to 60 people. Beds and cooking equipment were brought along for leisurely overnight stops along the way.

While travel was done in style, education was of little importance. It was the thinking of the day that the teaching of the Christian doctrine would suffice. As a result of the Spanish Inquisition, very few books even existed in coastal communities. Don José De La Guerra was one of only four public people to have a noteworthy library. Even if education had commanded a higher status in the scheme of things, little money was in the public treasury to fund schools since taxes were paid in hides and tallow.

Hides and tallow from the cattle brought revenue to the ranchos. The Mexican cattle hides generally sold for about two dollars. With the tallow and processing, the whole animal might bring about four dollars. De La Guerra's annual sales amounted to $50,000 to $100,000, suggesting a substantial cattle estate. Trade was done through the missions, which, in turn, dealt with sailing ships seeking leather for the New England shoe factories. When De La Guerra died in February 1858, he left his vast holdings, including El Rancho Simi, valued at $200,000, to his four sons: Pablo, Francisco, Antonio Maria, and Miguel.

Although Janet Scott Cameron, in corrected copies of *Simi Grows Up,* suggests the De La Guerras inhabited the Tapo adobe in 1858, there is some confusion as to just when the Tapo adobe was built. A map discovered by Robert E. Harrington dated "June or July 1859" depicts the Ventura County ranchos with Simi written as "Sime." The Simi house is shown with the inscription

"Francisco de la Guerra y Noriega." A cross is drawn nearby. This cross, which sits atop Mt. McCoy at the western end of the valley, is believed to have been placed there originally by the missionaries as a guide to the Simi adobe stopover. A dotted line marks a trail to the "Noriegas Tapo," but no house is indicated there. Several mountain trails are shown, and "Main Road between San Fernando and San Buenaventura" is inscribed at the point of the Santa Susana Mountain pass, suggesting this route may, in fact, have been part of the original El Camino Real.

By the 1860s circumstances did not bode well for the De La Guerras. The feisty young sons apparently did not inherit the business acumen of their father. With the closing of the mission system in 1846, trade to the east coast had diminished. The Gold Rush had slowed to a trot and so had the demand for beef products.

To fulfill their escalating debts, the De La Guerra brothers mortgaged a portion of their holdings to Isaac Cook in May 1861, having been denied a homestead petition filed earlier by Francisco's wife. In October of that same year, further property was mortgaged to Gaspar Orena, a brother-in-law. When the De La Guerras defaulted on their loans, Cook began foreclosure proceedings. A November 17, 1861, court decision decreed the De La Guerras would have to sell enough of the property to satisfy the indebtedness. Under this judgment the property was sold to Cook, who in turn sold it to Levi Parsons.

While the Civil War raged on, the De La Guerras fought to keep their heads above water when they were struck by a drought of astronomical consequence during 1863 and 1864. El Rancho Simi lost by death or forced sale nearly its entire stock of cattle and sheep. By Santa Barbara records, 190,000 of the 200,000 cattle listed on the tax roll died.

Circumstances finally stabilized when, on June 29, 1865, following lengthy court proceedings, El Rancho Simi was conferred to the De La Guerras and heirs by President Andrew Johnson. This was a retroactive decision on the homestead claim made earlier under the 1851 Land Act (Homestead) "but with the stipulation, that in virtue of the 15th section of the said Act, the confirmation of this said claim and this patent, shall not affect the interest of third persons."

With the death of Francisco De La Guerra in 1878, the Spanish period in the valley drew to a close, leaving behind a legacy so substantial that the Simi adobe was named California Historical Landmark No. 979 in 1989 (thanks to the efforts of Strathearn Historical Park director Pat Havens).

Gone, too, were the Chumash Indians. Learning the ways of the missionaries had weakened their own cultural skills, making it difficult to survive outside the realm of the missions once they stopped operation. Exposed to diseases brought by the white man, their physical stamina had also weakened.

These early inhabitants left behind a spirit of hospitality and appreciation of the land that would open the door for future residents.

Simi retained its rural beauty for many decades after the Chumash Indians celebrated the solstice and gazed at a night sky full of stars. In this photo, settler M. Poindexter explores a creek in an oak grove 50 or 60 years after the Spanish period in the Valley had come to a close. Courtesy, Ventura County Museum of History and Art

II

And Mortimer Park Makes Four

As seen in this photo circa 1900, Jim and Bert Strathearn (center) pose in a field with friends Mr. Shaw and Hugh Reed, looking more like dandies than settlers in rural Simi. Courtesy, Simi Valley Historical Society and Museum, Strathearn Historical Park

As the Chumash population waned and the dust churned up by the Spanish vaqueros began to dissipate into thin air, the valley entered a new era of development often called the American Period.

Simi had been a rather well-kept secret, with passage to the south limited to sturdy legs and steady horses following well-worn Indian and mission trails over the Santa Susana Mountains. A new road was about to open new doors.

While the first transcontinental stagecoach company, the Great Overland Mail Route of Butterfield and Company, was thriving elsewhere in California, stage travel had bypassed the valley. Inspired by the success of Butterfield's stage line, the Legislative Council of Los Angeles approached the officials of Santa Barbara in 1859, proposing that the two counties cooperate in developing an alternate route to the existing Coastal and Inland routes, thereby linking the two counties. Soon sandstone was flying as the stage road was blasted along the Santa Susana mountainside. In 1861 the Santa Barbara-Los Angeles stage route opened. The Coast Stage Line ran its six-horse stagecoach from Santa Barbara through Ventura, Los Posas, Cañada de Quimada, and Santa Susana over the pass into Los Angeles County until 1874.

As it happened, completion of this stage route was very timely. The Coastal Route was in such a state of disrepair that it was soon necessary for stages using that route to divert to the newly created alternate route. Thus the Butterfield Line ran daily across Simi Valley, carrying passengers and mail, then connected back with the main route near present-day Pacoima. Five years later, when repairs on the Coastal Route were complete, the Butterfield Stage returned to its original route. Settlers in the Simi Valley then had to make Saturday trips to Conejo for the mail.

The new stage line brought not only mail, but, more importantly, it also provided access. Until then most trade and communication had taken place with towns and villages to the north and west. The valley's new stage line made possible an economic and cultural exchange with the rapidly advancing Los Angeles area. Travel was no longer limited to foot and horse; now it could be by stagecoach or wagon. For the valley this would mean new markets for exchanging goods and easier access to supplies and materials. It would mean people could enter the valley.

A ride in a stagecoach, like this in 1887, was described by a Ventura newspaper editor: "Get up at midnight and crawl into an old, rickety stage without cushions, or with a few as an apology for cushions, inside not swept out and dusted in a month, spend 12 hours on the road, often without breakfast, and pay 10 cents a mile for the privilege." Courtesy, Ventura County Museum of History and Art

The first to do so was Charles E. Hoar, who arrived in 1872 from Massachusetts. Like many of the settlers to follow, Hoar was a man of education and class. Following graduation from Harvard, he had been working with the railroads, which were making their big thrust westward. When he returned to Massachusetts two years later to wed his school sweetheart, he discovered she had married a mutual friend. He reportedly scurried to Simi, putting as much distance as possible between himself and the object of his broken heart. He never married, and his only concession to affairs of the heart was, according to some accounts, an annual drinking bout that would last for days.

Upon his arrival, Hoar lived with Bud Taylor at the eastern end of the valley, which was sometimes called the "Roblara." Taylor, who had arrived in 1866, recalled for Janet Scott Cameron in *Simi Grows Up* his first memory of the valley when "the eastern half was covered with oak trees; the flats were covered with elderberries, and the north-part with cactus."

Hoar continued to live with Taylor until his house burned down, sending Taylor to Nevada. Hoar then purchased 10 acres hidden in the northeastern hills of the valley. Still known as Hummingbird's Nest, the property at the time belonged to the Pucillos, a mother and son who stayed on as hired help.

By 1870 the high times for the De la Guerras had come and gone. However, they still retained 1,400 acres on the Tapo and sheep-grazing rights throughout the valley floor. Most of the holdings that they had lost through gambling or lengthy court battles were purchased by Thomas Scott of the Pennsylvania Railroad at 65 cents an acre.

Anticipating the discovery of oil, Scott soon formed the Philadelphia and California Petroleum Company. In 1879 he hired Thomas Bard (who would later become a United States Senator) to oversee his holdings. He had seen Bard in action with the Commissary in Washington, D.C., in 1865 and was very impressed with his initiative and style.

Initially they rented the valley to grazers. As yet, the only broken ground in the valley was the Evans place on Erringer and Royal where the first crop was raised—60 tons of hay (the only rust-free crop in Ventura County in 1876). Evans' success was not without cost. His partner lost his life when he lost control of his team and a harrow was dragged over him. Horses were so abundant that some had to be shot to control the population. At the same time, the area was experiencing a severe drought.

When Thomas Scott determined that oil was nearly nonexistent on the vast Rancho Simi acreage he had purchased, he instructed Bard to lease the land for farming and grazing. Rent would be one-fifth of crops raised. Hoar took the eastern end of the valley while Bates and Brown Company leased the western end, all of which was given over to sheep grazing. In turn, Hoar, Brown, and Bates sublet the land to farmers to raise dry-farming crops of hay and grain, charging them likewise one-fifth of their crop, as well as the stubble to be used for their 13,000 sheep.

By 1877 Eli Barnett had taken over Evans' operation. J.Y. Saviers was farming everything north of the Arroyo Simi.

Thomas Scott died in 1882, leaving Bard to dispose of his holdings. With the Philadelphia and California Petroleum Company now defunct, Bates, Brown, and Hoar were offered the valley floor at one dollar per acre. Hoar returned to New England to get the funding for his share but, upon his return, learned that Bates and Brown had decided not to take the offer. Instead they went to Ventura and Hoar continued to sublet the land.

At this time there were only three or four families living in the vast valley. N.B. Cornett, originally from Missouri, arrived in 1884 to take over Eli Barnett's operation, which was threatened with foreclosure by mortgage holder Pete Brown. Samuel Miller Woodson Easley raised bees in Happy Camp Canyon past Moorpark, then known as Little Simi. Reportedly, in one year his bees

Pictured here in the late 1800s, Charles E. Hoar, Simi's first settler, reclines by the fire on a Simi campout. Courtesy, Ventura County Museum of History and Art

The Scarab Oil Well pumped oil from the earth just north of Oak Park in 1915. Courtesy, Simi Valley Historical Society and Museum, Strathearn Historical Park

produced 112,000 pounds of white sage honey which sold in Port Hueneme for five cents a pound. Easley was to become the first acting county clerk when Ventura County separated from Santa Barbara County in 1872.

For these families, education was very important. They had come from civilized eastern communities, bringing with them a taste for culture and knowledge.

Thus, Easley and Cornett hired an itinerant schoolmaster to teach their children in exchange for board with the Cornetts and a small stipend from Easley.

Life in the quietly beautiful valley was mellow, but this was soon to change. The valley's pace was about to be stepped up a notch.

Thomas Bard now owned nearly all of the Simi Rancho land. In 1882 he had purchased the Tapo Alta in a sheriff's sale held to satisfy judgment against the beleaguered De La Guerras. It

Thomas Bard became the biggest landowner in early Simi and is still the only U.S. Senator Ventura County has ever produced. Courtesy, Simi Valley Historical Society and Museum, Strathearn Historical Park

became increasingly evident that the land was not going to provide him the liquid riches he and his former associate Scott had anticipated. However, being the astute businessman that he was, he quickly recognized the true wealth of his holdings and developed an enterprise that was to be the real estate deal of his career. The *Los Angeles Tribune* called it the "largest individual transaction consummated in this county."

Following the liquidation of the Philadelphia and California Petroleum Company, Bard formed the Simi Land and Water Company in 1887 with R.W. Poindexter as secretary. Hoar still had two years to go on his lease, which he relinquished in exchange for additional acreage for Hummingbird's Nest along with the stipulation that the company could install a two-inch-diameter pipeline from the springs on his property to the hotel the company was constructing. Further, he was offered first option to purchase any of Simi Land and Water Company's unsold property, once a certain amount of time had passed, at just $60 an acre. He did just that, purchasing several hundred acres of land west of Erringer and south of Royal, where he subsequently moved and began raising hogs that he shipped to the stockyards in Los Angeles.

Simi Land and Water Company built an imposing three-story hotel with a red tile roof on a knoll where Simi Valley High School now stands. Nine rooms on the second floor with one inadequate bathroom awaited travelers. The reception room was on the first floor, along with a commodious dining room, pantry, and huge kitchen run by a Chinese cook. Charles B. McCoy (who would later own the property upon which the landmark McCoy Cross sits) was local manager of the 96,000 acres of the Simi Land and Water Company, handling sales and running the hotel. In addition, he managed the farming operations, which consisted of all of the unsold land. Ranch hands bunked in the third-floor quarters.

The enterprise of Simi Land and Water Company appeared to be a substantial success. Company letterhead of August 1891 boasted "23,260 acres sold in 11 months." Lured to the valley were many of the personalities who would build the framework for the community of today. These stalwart pioneers brought a sense of camaraderie, of neighbor helping neighbor, a sense of self-propelled destination that has remained to this day.

First to respond to Bard's ads were a group of eight doctors from Illinois who had formed the

Mr. and Mrs. Charles B. McCoy peruse a document in a grassy field in the late 1880s. Charles was the manager of the Simi Land and Water Company, and he ran the Simi Hotel. Courtesy, Simi Valley Historical Society and Museum, Strathearn Historical Park

Above: Guests lounge on the wraparound veranda and the brush-covered grounds of the newly built Simi Hotel in the 1890s. Courtesy, Ventura County Museum of History and Art

Right : These men began construction on the Simi Hotel as seen here in this 1887 photo. The hotel was built on a knoll where Simi Valley High School now stands. Courtesy, Ventura County Museum of History and Art

California Mutual Benefit Colony of Chicago. They had sold fellow Chicagoans on the health benefits of Southern California in an elaborate, flowery brochure titled *Ventura County and the Valley of the Simi—The Garden of Southern California—With a Description of SIMIOPOLIS the property of the California Mutual Benefit Colony of Chicago.* Pretentious were their claims, and pretentious was the proposed name of the development.

Coincidentally, the railroads played right into their plan. A railroad rate war was developing with rates from the Midwest reportedly as low as one dollar, drastically reduced from the customary $125. The doctors played the railroad to their advantage, claiming they had been able to attain prime land at bargain prices since the railroad, though not yet built, would be passing right by the proposed colony.

"Remember the railroad is coming," a brochure proclaimed, "and then our property goes up. It is a second chance for poor or rich to get a home in the finest climate on earth cheap, and make a fortune at the same time. Call for particulars."

Not only did the clever doctors in Chicago think the valley was special. From the *Rural Californian,* Los Angeles, June 1888:

We allude to the Simi Valley, a vast and fertile tract, covered with waving grain and containing some of the largest fruit trees in the State, yet by reason of its being off the usual lines of travel, and having as yet no railroad, we presume that not one in a hundred of all Los Angeles population have ever seen, or have any more accurate idea of this lovely valley, than if it were a thousand miles away.

Meanwhile, a thousand miles away, the California Mutual Benefit Colony of Chicago, realizing only a handful of houses existed in the valley, decided to ship prefabricated houses from Chicago to their new home in Simiopolis. Twelve houses were sent by rail, then brought by wagon from Saticoy to Simi, where they were reassembled in a two-square-mile nucleus south of Los Angeles Avenue between First and Fifth streets.

Like the houses they would inhabit, adventurous young Midwesterners boarded the train November 15, 1888, and headed to San Fernando, California. From there they caught the private stagecoach run by Simi Land and Water Company, where, careening and sliding, they were taken on a harrowing ride down the Devil's Slide through the Santa Susana Pass, where they stopped at the

Right: Pictured here in the early 1900s, these horse-women pose in front of one of the prefabricated houses provided by the California Mutual Benefit Colony of Chicago. This may be the Montgomery house, with one of Wayne Montgomery's daughters on horseback, on the left. Courtesy, Simi Valley Society and Museum, Strathearn Historical Park

Below: Charles A. and Anna Havens pose with their sons Lester and Charlie in 1900. Great-great-granddaughter Pat Havens is president of the Simi Valley Historical Society. Courtesy, Simi Valley Historical Society and Museum, Strathearn Historical Park

foot of the Santa Susana Mountains at Larry's Station for refreshments and a change of horses. Then on they continued, entering the Simi Hotel along a palm tree-lined circular driveway from the stagecoach road, the forerunner of Los Angeles Avenue.

They had arrived at their dream, full of hope, having left friends and familiarity behind. They had been promised bargain prices, fertile soil, and an abundant supply of water. And, indeed, upon their arrival they found abundant water, only it was not seeping from the ground. Rather, it was pouring from the sky.

Anna Havens, whose husband Charles was nephew of C.G. Austin, Jr., one of the original colony members, described her January 1889 arrival to the valley:

After one night in the San Fernando Hotel we went on to Simi to the lovely home which was supposed to be waiting for us. It was not plastered and a cow was tied in the front yard where they had told us there would be a beautiful lawn. The first night there it rained and it was necessary to put up an umbrella over the foot of the bed to keep dry. It rained steady for three weeks.

Despite the precarious beginnings, soon a community was developing. The tongue-tripping name of Simiopolis was dropped after six months and became simply Simi or, as it was affectionately called by the residents, the Colony.

A few months later the January 1890 *Overland Monthly* described:

Descending the ridge, we saw the surveyors of the new railroad working near the base of sandstone cliffs. Turning down a dusty road we passed a salt grass flat on whose upper border there huddled a singular collection of buildings. They were the exact counterpart of one another, with steep roofs, walls cut up into sections, and doors and windows set with painful individuality. A few of these homes were deserted but the rest had newly-made blower and grass plats, all watered in common from an artesian well. There was something uncanny about this lonely village with its mathematical likeness and precision, and its utter absence of suburbs.

By 1890 approximately 20 additional families had moved into the valley. They purchased land directly from Bard, often replacing renters who were moving on. The presence of many of these early settlers may be felt in the community even today: J.C. Scott (who took over the Barnett place), Fitzgerald, Appleton, Montgomery, Strathearn, Haigh, Gillibrand, Havens, Adrian Wood, and W.C. Woods.

Prominent among the first settlers was Robert Perkins Strathearn, who arrived in Simi in 1889 with his wife, Mary Lamb, and two children, Robert Perkins, Jr., and James Lamb. Strathearn left a flourishing wholesale tea business in Scotland when his doctor advised a change of climate. Because he knew people there, he chose Santa Barbara over Australia, eventually working his way down through Piru. He reportedly chose Simi because the symmetrical trees suggested there would be no strong winds; the chaparral and weeds indicated fertile soil.

Initially he settled his family into the De La Guerra adobe, which was situated on the 14,000 acres he had purchased from Bard. It was a matter of expediency to bring this roofless adobe, where a Basque sheepherding family named Jauregui had been living, to a suitable condition instead of building a new house. It was not long, however, before it became necessary to enlarge his home. Fortunately for history, he added the two-story home to the existing adobe, thereby leaving the valley a structure of unparalleled historical significance. Strathearn developed one of the largest beef cattle herds in the county, providing him with much clout in the community. The Strathearns had seven children, one of whom, Robert Perkins, Jr., became a well-known political cartoonist, spending 10 years with the *Los Angeles Express*.

Right and far right: These photos of prominent early settlers Mary Lamb Strathearn and Robert P. Strathearn show their "foreignness." As settlers in Simi Valley, they retained the culture of Scotland, their native land. Courtesy, Simi Valley Historical Society and Museum, Strathearn Historical Park

The Strathearn home, shown here in 1895 when David Strathearn was an infant, became the centerpiece of Strathearn Historical Park in the 1960s when the Strathearn family donated 6-1/2 acres to the city. Courtesy, Simi Valley Historical Society and Museum, Strathearn Historical Park

Edward Clayton (Gillie) Gillibrand arrived in the valley about the same time. He and wife, Ellen, along with her brother, Jack Hesketh, took up residence on the Tapo Alta. Unlike the Rancho Simi adobe, the Tapo adobe was uninhabitable. Gillibrand migrated from England rather than follow in the family business, Gillibrand & Calloway Silk and Cotton Spinners. He had a luxurious adobe home built for him in the canyon, which he and his wife decorated with fine china, linens, and furniture imported from England.

He also had a cattle operation offering an arena for talented cowboys. As one resident recalls, "almost any day one could look up to the mouth of the Tapo Canyon and see a streak of dust coming across the open space. This meant the Gillibrand cowboys were coming to town." The cattle business gave way to an extensive operation of gravel and oyster shell, which was ground up in appropriate sizes for use as fertilizer, chicken or cattle feed, or making tiles. When Gillibrand died in 1925, he was buried in the family vault in the side of the mountain, remaining close to the land he loved so much.

The Gillibrand family relaxes with their dogs at home in this late nineteenth-century photo. Edward Clayton Gillibrand, his wife Ellen, and her brother lived in an adobe home on the Tapo Alta, which they filled with fine furnishings from England. Courtesy, Ventura County Museum of History and Art

With the advent of the Colony came organized commerce. Storefronts sprouted up right along with the dry-farming crops. John Sawtelle set up shop on Los Angeles Avenue at Third Street just across an old rickety bridge. It had a feed store and a dry goods store connected by a boxcar with shelving, which he had purchased in Los Angeles and, removing the wheels, brought to the Colony by wagon. "Honest John" would drive weekly to San Fernando to pick up supplies, often charging his customers two or three times the going prices. His was the only store for some time. But by 1907 competition had arrived with the W.S. Kier store, a replica of which is at the Strathearn Historical Park, and the Montgomery store. Blacksmiths, an ice house, barbers, and a saloon filled out the business section. Dora Beach opened a dry goods store immediately west of Sawtelle's. It still stands today. Manuel Banaga, Jr., whose father was caretaker of the McCoy ranch, has operated the Simi Valley Barber Shop from there since 1958.

By 1891 the California Mutual Benefit Colony of Chicago had dissolved, but not before the stalwart pioneers had commandeered an empty colony house at the northeast corner of Pacific and Second for use as a church and school.

Intent on providing an education for the children of the Colony, the Simi School District was created February 4, 1889, with Easley, McCoy, and Hoar appointed trustees. On February 20 an election was held at the home of N.B. Cornett, whereupon the three were officially elected. School opened in the rent-free Colony house on April 18 with the teacher receiving $60 a month. The residents considered this a temporary solution to a permanent need and were soon at work to secure a "real" school.

An excerpt from the *Hueneme Herald* dated June 6, 1889, reads:

Dr. Cutler, Postmaster of Simiopolis [he held the position for two years before returning to Chicago] *was in town Monday. He reports everything on the Simi is flourishing. Grain looks first-rate. Now some twenty houses in the Colony. Vines and trees which were set out are in splendid condition.*

As for the new schoolhouse, the Chicago Company donated a block in Simiopolis for such a purpose; bonds are to be voted . . .

Above: Pictured here in the late 1880s, Honest John Sawtelle's store was Simi's first supermarket, offering everything from books to hay to medicine. Courtesy, Simi Valley Historical Society and Museum, Strathearn Historical Park

Right: Seen here is the W.S. Kier store at the corner of Los Angeles Avenue and Fourth Street. The photo serves as the best view of the bustling Simi business district around 1910. Courtesy, Simi Valley Historical Society and Museum, Strathearn Historical Park

Nine days after the article quoted above was published, on June 15, 1889, an election was held for a 10-year bond of $3,000 at 8 percent per annum to build a new schoolhouse. The balloting was conducted at the Simi Hotel between sunrise and 5 p.m. The bond passed unanimously 7 to 0.

The new school opened in September 1890 with Miss Northcutt as teacher. Situated on Third Street, a half block back from Los Angeles Avenue, the new school was complete with horse shed and outdoor privies for its 20 students.

At the same time the early settlers needed nourishment for their mind, they also craved spiritual fulfillment. Thus, the Colony house served as church on Sundays, offering services to Protestant and Catholics alike.

When, in 1898, the services under the Reverend Warrington became too Methodist, the Presbyterians, of whom there were a substantial number, decided to form their own church. They met temporarily at the elementary school until they built a church building on Pacific and Third.

Because this was a rural parish for both of the Protestant churches, preachers were not always available. Soon citizens were alternating between the two churches, depending on which one had a preacher that week. Often, it fell to Fred Howland to lead the services as he had done when he first came to Simi to plant the first eucalyptus trees, holding services at his home on the 80 acres at Erringer and Royal he had earned for the planting. Mrs. Printz and Carrie Willard also served as leaders.

When money became tight in 1908, the Presbyterians closed down their church and once again attended services with the Methodists. In 1911 St. Rose of Lima Catholic Church assumed ownership of the abandoned Presbyterian church.

A Methodist church was built in 1912 right beside the Colony house, which then was remodeled into a parsonage. Money to build the church came from a sizable memorial donation and the stipulation that the church be called Edmund W. Keen Memorial Methodist Episcopal Church. It remains a mystery just who Edmund Keen was.

The Colony was establishing a pattern. Homes and businesses encompassed the area of First and Fifth streets. A solid business community was developing with dry goods stores, a butcher shop, an ice shop, a post office, a saloon, and a couple of blacksmiths. Many of the amenities of civilized society were now available. The dry hillsides were given to cattle ranching, while the fertile valley became the province of the farmers.

The time was ripe for successful farming and cattle ranching. The promised railroad was about to be a reality. The railroad through the valley, first proposed by Bard in 1888 when he offered 60 feet of right-of-way, would be the final link in the Southern Pacific main coastal line from Los Angeles to San Francisco.

Construction of the track through the base of the Santa Susana Mountains began in 1900. Blasting passage through the mountain was a challenge that was met head on. The 7,369-foot tunnel built through the mountain was considered one of the engineering marvels of the time. The bridge and culverts were constructed from sandstone excavated from the local quarry.

It took four years and one million dollars to complete the 10-mile strip, with much of the work performed by Mexican labor. Local resident Lucy Chavez recalls that her father, Atilano Ferrer,

This view from around 1900 shows Simi Public School after it was enlarged. It was originally built in 1890 for $3,000–including furnishings. Courtesy, Ventura County Museum of History and Art

was one of those who helped lay the tracks. Recruited in El Paso by Southern Pacific, he became part of the ambulatory camp that moved from state to state laying rails. The final nail found him in the Simi Valley, where he moved his family in 1905.

Also, with that final nail driven in 1904, the valley became as connected to the outside world as was any major city. Farmers would now have not only a new continental market, but an international market as well.

In anticipation of the completion of the railroad, a two-story, wood-frame depot was built at the turn of the century immediately east of Tapo Street. This location was chosen over the Colony because it offered flat land, which would make loading and unloading freight easier. Perhaps more importantly, the location was offered to the railroad at no cost while they would have had to pay for any right-of-way in the Colony.

The train station included a section house, boxcars to be used as sleeping quarters, assorted warehouses, oil-loading racks for the limited oil production in the Tapo fields, and a public spur. A large waiting room with a potbelly stove and natural pine benches along the walls welcomed travelers. The shipping and receiving portion of the building opened up at boxcar height to allow easy transfer of goods between the train cars and the loading dock. A three-bedroom apartment on the upper level provided housing for the stationmaster, who handled telegraph and post office services in addition to ticket sales. At one time, Federal Express Service brought large mail-order packages to the Santa Susana station, named after the Santa Susana Mountains.

As to where the name Santa Susana originated, Father Senan, in an 1804 letter to the governor, wrote: "The distance between the missions San Fernando and Mission San Buenaventura by way of Santa Susana and Simi is reckoned to be 22 leagues . . . believed to have honored Saint Susana, Roman virgin and martyr of the 3rd century."

With the train station as the cornerstone, the town of Santa Susana began to develop. The Southern Pacific Warehouse, a red-frame building, opened to store the farmers' produce until it was sold and ready for shipment by rail. Businessmen opened storefronts. Forward-looking citizens quickly formed a new school district.

The S.P. Warehouse, located where Winfield Lumber would later stand, served as a school that

first year, 1901, with J.S. Appleton, Frank Henderson, and Joe Horner as trustees. Annie Shyrock was the teacher. One year later the district built a school on Tapo Street 500 feet south of Los Angeles Avenue to serve all students east of Sycamore. The one-room schoolhouse was complete with bell tower, windmill, well, and sheds for the students' horses.

As the town came into being, most of the surrounding area belonged to a group of men constituting the Oxnard Company. Ernest Erbes, who was renting the property, persuaded his brother-in-law, Theodore Beesmeyer, to leave his lucrative work in Hollywood, grading the streets that would become Hollywood Boulevard, Sunset, and Vine. Theodore and his wife, Lydia Erbes Beesmeyer, arrived in 1907, taking up residence in the old Simi Hotel, which would be vacated by Ernest Erbes, who could now go to his ranch in Conejo, confident he was leaving his Simi operation in good hands. The original hotel register found by the Beesmeyers indicated they moved into the hotel 24 years to the day it had originally opened for business. Charles B. McCoy, the original manager of the hotel, had left in 1898 to purchase the Cañada Verde on the far western end of the valley. While the Beesmeyers lived there, the hotel was again open to guests or transients. It was customary for newcomers to live there while their own homes were being built. When it was finally torn down, the lumber was used to build smaller ranch houses in the area.

Horace J. Crinklaw arrived in Santa Susana about 1905, purchasing 130 acres, mostly south of Los Angeles Avenue. His was one of the earliest storefronts, a small dry goods store near the curve of tracks on Los Angeles Avenue. The post office was moved to this store from the train depot in 1907. Robert Harrington, in *Early Days in Simi Valley,* recalls the teasing Crinklaw would receive from his wife, Eva, when he eagerly approached the post office anticipating a letter from a "friend."

Horace Crinklaw put up a number of buildings, including his home on Tapo and Los Angeles. Most impressive, however, was the two-story Crinklaw Building constructed with granite that Crinklaw hauled in his four-horse wagon from the quarry south of Santa Susana Park. The upper floor, which also included hotel rooms, was offered as a meeting place for plays, dances, and showing movies. The lower floor housed two stores, run by the partnership of Whipple and Riave, offering general merchandise including axle grease, buggy whips, and horseshoes. The Crinklaw Building stood until the earthquake of 1971.

In 1910 the Oxnard Company disbanded, with each partner receiving a portion of the land. To Ferd Roussey went the section northwest of the train station, which he sold to R.M. Wright, Sr. Although the Wrights and the Crinklaws kept their property boundaries, their families joined forever when young Bob Wright married one of the Crinklaw daughters, Lou. Lou Crinklaw Wright would later become the first honorary mayor of Simi Valley.

It was 1912, the year the Crinklaw Building went up, a symbol of steadfastness, stability, and prosperity. Charles E. Hoar died that year, having seen a great many changes wrought to the sparsely settled valley he had discovered only 40 years earlier. Now there were two distinct towns with a friendliness that recognized no boundaries. There were now two schools where there had been none. Religion was flourishing. A second wave of agriculture was shaping the valley, bringing it of identity and prosperity. That year, the valley had its first car, purchased by Fred Fitzgerald, which he took out only on special occasions.

A car in the neighborhood presented special problems. Accustomed to driving in the center of the road with his wagons, Fitzgerald was wont to do the same with his car, causing the horses he passed to shy at the new contraption. The matter was taken before the judge, who determined vehicles should be kept to the right of center whenever possible.

Santa Susana continued to grow, enjoying agricultural success spurred on by abundant crops and railroad access. In 1917 a three-room brick school, the largest yet, was built on Los Angeles Avenue just east of Peppertree Lane. Lou Crinklaw Wright was a teacher there. The building later served as the American Legion Hall.

Simi Valley has depended on the automobile for decades. This circa 1920 photo reveals the pride this early resident had in his car. Courtesy, Simi Valley Historical Society and Museum, Strathearn Historical Park

Just down the road to the west, another community was developing, namely the Community Center. With the breakup of the Oxnard Company, Ferd Roussey purchased the land in 1910 for $150 an acre. By 1923 he was subdividing the land, offering it at $800 an acre, unimproved. The school district purchased 12.5 acres for a new high school. One acre was proposed for a new Methodist church. The Simi Valley Woman's Club, formed in 1914, purchased an acre to house a clubhouse.

Community Center was an appropriate name. The spirit of the purchases was to provide amenities from which the entire community could benefit. Wayne Montgomery, son of Melville, bought lots north of School Street on which to build housing for teachers since there was no place available for them to rent. The quaint little bungalow units are still standing. Because the availability of lumber supplies was very limited, Montgomery went north and purchased a lumber mill to meet his building needs.

The Community Center was zoned against commercial buildings. Nevertheless, seeing a need, Manuel Alvarez bought land immediately west of the Roussey tract and started a grocery store that flourishes to this day, now called Green Acres. Following Alvarez's death, the store was run by Bill Luna and family. Alvarez also constructed the building that currently houses Town and Country Sports. Longtime residents will recall the years Holbrook's served the community. During war years, it served as a cannery with everyone bringing fruits and vegetables to be canned and then exchanging with one another.

The Community Center was bound on the north by Los Angeles Avenue, on the east by Blackstock, named after a Colony schoolteacher who later became a judge, and on the west by Sequoia.

In 1922 the trustees of Simi School District and Santa Susana School District joined forces to establish a high school at a point between Simi and Santa Susana. Before then, many of the local

The Reverend Ralph Lee poses with his family in front of the cornerstone of the Simi Valley Community Methodist Episcopal Church in the 1920s. Courtesy, Simi Valley Historical Society and Museum, Strathearn Historical Park

young people had attended Los Angeles High School. According to Phyllis Beesmeyer Vanniman, Simi Valley parents would rent apartments in Bunker Hill to house their children while school was in session. The Community Center was chosen for this much-needed school, which was dedicated in the fall of 1923 with Wayne Montgomery, I.V. Brown, J.F. Fitzgerald, and Walter Osborne as trustees. The first graduating class of 1924 matriculated two students. Today Apollo High School stands on that site.

Soon thereafter the Simi Elementary School was built, the first unified school on the lower grade level. The school is still in use today.

Joining in the spirit of a unified community, the Methodists decided to build a church that could accommodate all Protestants in the valley. Under the spiritual leadership of the Reverend Lee, the task was soon accomplished. The Simi Community Methodist Church was indeed a community effort. A 2 percent assessment was placed on all property. Even absentee landowners contributed to the building of the church. On February 19, 1928, the commanding building at 3050 Los Angeles Avenue was dedicated, debt-free, having done so with only 33 actual members.

The fourth development of the valley was the Knolls, originally called Mortimer Park. In 1924 Louis Mortimer and his wife discovered this lovely area at the foot of the Santa Susana Mountains when they were forced to make a detour through Simi due to construction work on the Conejo Grade. They were real estate people who thought they knew a good opportunity when they saw it. They believed the rustic atmosphere would appeal to city people. Consequently, they purchased 1,787 acres from the California Commercial Club and divided it into 18 tracts. In 1941 the name of the area became Santa Susana Knolls due primarily to the efforts of the Knolls Garden Club, which was also responsible for naming many of the valley's streets.

Accomplishing much in this valley was the Simi Valley Woman's Club. This organization was not confined to one of the communities of the valley, but rather, included many caring and talented women throughout. Their activities were a reflection of the concerns of the times.

The first meeting took place in 1914 at the Crinklaw home. One of the first orders of business was the Santa Susana grade. Determined to do something to repair it, they reportedly packed picks, shovels, picnic baskets, and husbands and headed for the grade, intent on removing or covering the worst offending rocks.

When the county supervisors got wind of their ploy, they insisted they would take care of the road. And indeed they did, for in 1915 the third Santa Susana Pass Road, a two-lane affair, was put through.

In 1922 they purchased the old Fraternal Aid Hall from the Colony. When, following World War I, the insurance company collapsed, the property was auctioned for back taxes. The club's successful $580 bid got them a clubhouse complete with chairs and a piano. They moved it onto the one-acre lot they had purchased on Church and School streets in the Community Center, where it stood for many years until it was condemned by the fire department.

At one time it was a botanical showplace as Dr. Albert Hirschi and his wife, Irene, a member of the club, were very generous in their donations of flowers and trees to beautify the lot.

Always in step with the times, in the 1920s the women were encouraging other women to vote, supporting a world court, and doing battle against the "narcotic evil." They protested a prison site in Simi Valley and kept abreast of world events with knowledgeable speakers. They were the force behind the establishment of Oak Park in the 1930s, at about the same time they sponsored the Junior Woman's Club.

When the country was dealing with World War I, this group of women did its part. It purchased liberty bonds, sent a library to an army encampment, volunteered for the Red Cross, conducted aluminum drives, and donated money to a hospital in Belgium. It pushed for electricity in the schools and churches, amenities that had only recently become available in the homes.

The Simi Valley Community Methodist Episcopal Church was built in the 1920s at 3050 Los Angeles Avenue. It still stands today. Courtesy, Simi Valley Historical Society and Museum, Strathearn Historical Park

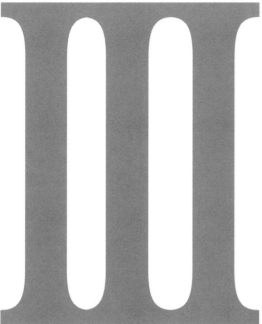

III

Apricots, Oranges, and a Cup of Sugar, Please

As pictured here in an early 1900s photo, the cowboys of the Gillibrand cattle operation prepare to brand a steer. Ranching out of Tapo Canyon, the dashing cowboys were an integral part of Simi's colorful past. Courtesy, Simi Valley Historical Society and Museum, Strathearn Historical Park

Ａs the four clusters of homes and businesses developed, the larger expanses of land on the hills encircling the valley were given to cattle ranching. Largest of the ranches was that owned by the Strathearns. The vast acreage, extending past the northwestern end of the valley to Little Simi (Moorpark) and Happy Camp Canyon, was strategically located. When the railroad was extending the track, Robert P. Strathearn astutely granted the right-of-way through his property with the stipulation he could have a cattle siding at the tracks for loading and unloading cattle. His request was granted along with the option to flag down the passenger train whenever he needed it, a service he often used.

Strathearn Siding, located just below where Marie Callender's restaurant now stands, served the Simi Valley and Moorpark. Ranchers would bring their cattle to load onto the trains through chutes. Guiding the cattle through the sided ramps was not always easy. On one occasion, the cattle were so spooked by the train, the runaways were scattered all the way to Somis.

Although the hills were too dry for farming the barley, beets, and apricots flourishing on the valley floor, the cattle ranchers who claimed the hills were just as dependent on a good crop. Only for them, the crop was calves. They had to keep culling the cow herd, getting rid of older, non-bearing cows. Periodically, a new strain of bull would be introduced to keep the blood lines vital. Just as rain was vital for farming crops, it also was important for growing food for the cattle. In one year of severe drought Strathearn was forced to grind cactus to feed his herd.

One of the longtime cattle ranchers was Frank Runkle, who arrived in California from Pennsylvania at the age of 19 and worked in Saticoy for a few years before moving to the valley in 1904. He hired on for a few years with the Kujwaski & Goldsmith Ranch, which encompassed the Sinaloa area, Bridle Path, and the west side of Madera Road. In 1910 he purchased extensive acreage in the southern hills of the valley, known as Tract "B" of Simi Land and Water Company. There he formed the FR Cattle and Farming Company, where he ran beef cattle with the help of two of his sons, Jim and Ralph. He also had mules and raised his own horses. (The Runkle mules were often seen on the big screen, hired out to filming companies. One film required that they trek all the way to Sedona, Arizona.)

Right and far right: Leyland (right) and Clayton Gillibrand (far right) were among the young men who cultivated cattle in the early days of Simi settlement. Courtesy, Simi Valley Historical Society and Museum, Strathearn Historical Park

George, Dave, and Isa Strathearn were the three youngest children in the Strathearn family. Courtesy, Simi Valley Historical Society and Museum, Strathearn Historical Park

Horses gather at the trough at Strathearn's cattle ranch, which was the largest in Simi. It extended past the northwestern end of Simi to Little Simi and Happy Camp Canyon. Courtesy, Ventura County Museum of History and Art

Hereford cattle stand patiently at the Montgomery Feed Lot on Sinaloa Road. Courtesy, Simi Valley Historical Society and Museum, Strathearn Historical Park

Their horses were generally sent to the less expensive pastures of Bishop to "grow out." When the animal was three or four years old, it would be returned to the home ranch in Simi. Jim Runkle recalled with wry amusement the phone call he would get from his father, who had gotten the horses as far as San Fernando. It was then Jim and his brother Ralph's chore to get up at 4 a.m. and ride over the pass to San Fernando to drive the horses back to Simi over that challenging road. Sometimes there would be as many as 60 horses to guide back.

In the interest of economics, the cattle ranchers would also drive their cattle up to Bishop in the Owens Valley, particularly during dry times. Frank Runkle rented acreage from the City of Los Angeles when it first purchased the Owens Valley, running his cattle up there for many years. Likewise, the Strathearn Cattle Company ran its stock up there.

During the heyday of ranching, the packinghouses would come out to the Simi Valley to look at the "crop." In later years, when the packinghouses no longer offered the service, ranchers would take their stock to the Union Stockyard in Los Angeles to place it on consignment.

Melville Montgomery owned a feedlot at the end of Sinaloa, property which had once belonged to Goldsmith and then Charles McCoy. Here cattle could be fattened up before being shipped to market. The feedlot was just one of many enterprises in which Montgomery engaged. He had been a passenger on the third train to come all the way from Missouri. Arriving in California, he spent a year in Ventura, settling in Simi in 1890. He married Lorena Lloyd, whose father was enjoying great success in Ventura with oil and cattle. Soon after his arrival in the valley, Montgomery created competition for Sawtelle, Kier, and Dora Beach's dry goods store when he opened his store in the Colony, a general merchandise and meat market on Fourth and Los Angeles. He later constructed a brick store across the street. In 1914 he left the retail business and took up farming on his ranch, which extended on either side of Erringer. There he raised apricots, walnuts, and grapes. It was in later years that he took to cattle ranching, operating the feedlot.

Montgomery had five children, one of whom, Berenice, married David Lamb, son of Robert P. Strathearn. David Jr. reminisced that the two family heads were like the Hatfields and McCoys. Strathearn was a staunch Republican, Montgomery a devout Democrat. According to family legend, neither would attend their child's wedding, not wanting to be in the company of the other. But whatever their political differences, they had a mutual concern for the growth of the valley. Both

Above: This J.S. Appleton photo shows the closeness and camaraderie of many early Simi families. In this shot, Mr. and Mrs. Nealy Woods sit in the back seat, Charles Blackstock is on the hood, Mrs. Shyrock is at the wheel, Mrs. Appleton is behind the car, and Mr. Shyrock is at the crank. Courtesy, Simi Valley Historical Society and Museum, Strathearn Historical Park

Left: Marcellus Ephraim Jones was the midwife who delivered many of the babies born in Simi Valley. Courtesy, Simi Valley Historical Society and Museum, Strathearn Historical Park

During the heyday of ranching, the western end of Simi Valley had several ranches and farms where fences like these were used to corral sheep and other livestock. Courtesy, Ventura County Museum of History and Art

Barley was introduced to the Valley in 1887 and remained the main crop until competition from the San Joaquin Valley edged out the market in the early twentieth century. Here teams of horses haul grain out of Tapo Canyon. Courtesy, Simi Valley Historical Society and Museum, Strathearn Historical Park

families were very instrumental in directing that growth, whether on their own or through the values they instilled in their children, values and concerns that were evident in the majority of the families who developed the valley.

While cattle ranching meant long, dusty hours of work and weeks on the road driving cattle up and down the state, perhaps the highlight of the business was the roundup. A vivid demonstration of neighbor helping neighbor, ranchers and their families from around the valley would gather at the appointed ranch for a sweaty, muscle-testing day of vaccinating and branding cattle.

Having worked from early morning, the ranchers eagerly ate their noon meal. Thick barbecued steaks would be served along with a plentiful array of food prepared by the women. An hour's rest in the shade and the men would be back at the task at hand. Sometimes as many as 200 might attend a roundup. It was a favorite excuse for children to skip school. The event lured many of the film industry "ranchers." Joel McCrea, James Arness, and Peter Graves were frequent participants in the Runkle ranch roundups.

Just as there were times of plenty, there were lean years, too. The Depression hit many of the ranchers hard. During those years, Frank Runkle had gone to Arizona to purchase cattle at $65 a head. After running them for a year on rented acreage in Oxnard and feeding and watering them, he suffered severe losses when he could only get $45 a head in the current marketplace. Security Trust National Bank of Oxnard came to the ranch to serve papers, intent on foreclosing on the 2,800 acres. Fortunately Franklin Delano Roosevelt had initiated a loan program for farmers and ranchers with a 3 percent interest rate.

"Apparently it was a very new program because when my father went to pay it off, the loan officer didn't quite know what to do. I guess my father was the first one to pay it off," Jim Runkle mused.

The Strathearn operation found itself in similar circumstances when the Bank of Italy, now Bank of America, threatened to foreclose when $3,000 was owing on their 12,000 acres. Berenice Strathearn, however, was able to save the day with money of her own.

Whatever the challenges, the ranchers met them head on with determination, ingenuity, and a

The bean thresher of the Mahan threshing outfit on the Berywood Investment Company Ranch was operated by a steam engine which had to be moved by horses. Fourteen wagons and 26 mule and horse teams were needed to do what two people could do today. Courtesy, Simi Valley Historical Society and Museum, Strathearn Historical Park

willingness to work. The cattle ranches held their own until well into the 1970s.

While the ranchers raised cattle on the hillsides, farmers experimented with crops on the valley floor. The early settlers had begun with dry grain farming, beginning with the Evans crop of hay on land sublet from Hoar, Bates, and Brown.

When Eli Barnett introduced barley in 1887, it became a mainstay crop for a number of years. Its growing pattern lent itself well to the agricultural temperament of the valley.

Because barley was sown annually in the late fall, just before the heavy rains, and harvested at midsummer, it required no additional watering. This was an important factor in a vast dry area where irrigation had not yet been introduced and natural water was not as plentiful as promised. Additionally, the stubble left from the harvest provided the sheep with forage for grazing.

By the end of the decade, most of the valley was used for dry farming except 2,000 acres of woodland-grassland in the eastern end used for pasturing sheep. All the oak trees in the east end had been removed by 1910 to make way for farming. Japanese workmen cleared the land in exchange for the valuable wood.

Combine harvesters led by 26-mule-and-horse teams were a common site across the valley floor. As the sacks aboard the harvester were filled with grain, the sack sewer would sew them shut. When five sacks of grain had accumulated, a lever would be pulled to release the sacks through a chute to the ground. Later the piles of sacks would be gathered. Eventually, steam-driven threshing, heading, and cleaning equipment was used in the farming operation. Several hundred men were hired to operate the equipment and haul grain to Port Hueneme. This was generally a three-day round trip requiring a stopover at the American Sugar Beet packinghouse in Camarillo.

From 1887 to 1895 the annual production of barley averaged about 100,000 tons, one-third of the county's production. Gradually, as competition from the grain belt in San Joaquin edged out the valley barley market, acreage and production began to drop. But the small landowners were now becoming very adept at the farming life. They were ready to irrigate, eager to experiment with specialty crops. It was a promising time. The railroad was imminent, offering new markets and access to seasonal workers.

Thus, just before the railroad tracks were laid, the valley introduced deciduous fruits. This

Arnold Appleton, the eldest Appleton boy, stands by a coyote he killed. Local boys earned bounties for killing coyotes that menaced livestock. Arnold later became president of the historical society. Courtesy, Simi Valley Historical Society and Museum, Strathearn Historical Park

marked the beginning of intensive, serious farming in the Simi Valley. Prunes and apricots prospered in the southern portion of the valley plain. Production was limited and experimental at best, however, until the turn of the century when irrigation began on a larger scale.

Irrigation itself was not new; the De La Guerras had used it on a limited basis. By 1895 each ranch house had a pumped well that ran to a depth of 80 to 50 feet to meet their livestock and domestic needs.

The earliest use of groundwater for irrigation was for the prunes and apricots. The drought had proved the necessity to change from dry farming, which was dependent on the elements of nature, to irrigation farming, which afforded the farmers some measure of control. As the need to supplement groundwater became more apparent, Fred Fitzgerald became the first to drill solely for irrigation. By 1912, 500 acres were under irrigation, but normal rainfall could reliably revive the water tables.

N.C. Woods, who was farming what used to be the Howland place, planted the first crop of prunes—an 80-acre orchard in the south central valley. Soon the valley was producing 100 tons of dried prunes annually, most notably the French prune. The area near Erringer and Royal proved the most beneficial for producing these fruits. The well-drained, loamy soil made for the most prolific artesian well.

Woods' success with the first commercial orchard prompted other small farmers to follow suit. Soon there were several individually owned orchards ranging in size from 40 to 80 acres.

The farmers enjoyed even greater success with the apricot, which required less irrigation than the prune because of its growing season. Apricots could be harvested in early July before the sum-

Joe Appleton, complete with long curls and white dress, was the youngest Appleton boy. He became a county supervisor for the Simi area in the 1960s. Courtesy, Simi Valley Historical Society and Museum, Strathearn Historical Park

mer heat demanded irrigation, unlike the prune, which could not be harvested until the heat of September.

Dried prunes and apricots were shipped to Europe where the demand was high. Unlike Americans, who preferred fresh or canned fruit, many people overseas—particularly Germans—enjoyed dried fruit. At the height of the overseas market demand, the Simi Valley was shipping nearly 500 tons annually, netting the farmers 5 to 10 cents per pound return on their crop.

Apricot orchards on the south side of the valley included the Camerons, Appletons, and Harringtons. Nearer the center were the Wright ranch and the Currier ranch. It was breathtaking to see mile after mile of white apricot blossoms in bloom. But when the bloom was off the orchards and harvest time had arrived, trays of drying fruit spread out as far as the eye could see. Women worked in the pitting sheds, removing the pits by hand as they stood under makeshift shade.

The Harrington ranch, where apricot pitting took place, was 80 acres east of Fourth Street on the south side of Royal Avenue, which, family legend has it, was named by E.A. Harrington, who

Leading citizen Robert E. Harrington supervises the resurrection of the white cross on Mt. McCoy in 1921. Courtesy, Simi Valley Historical Society and Museum, Strathearn Historical Park

felt his colt, "Queen," should travel a royal path. Others believe the name honors the royal apricots that grew so abundantly in that area.

The Harringtons, who had come from New England through Santa Barbara to Simi in 1907, had two sons. Unlike his brother, John Peabody, whose Indian work took him elsewhere, Robert Harrington put his energies into the community. He and his wife, Ethel, gave much of their time to the care and nurturing of young people. For 10 years they ran the Harrington Home for Boys on their ranch. The boys raised food for the ranch and were involved with 4-H. This led to the Harrington Home Dairy, where 25 cows furnished milk for his ranch and surrounding communities for a number of years. Ethel Harrington implemented a hot lunch program in the schools, insuring that all the students received a nutritional lunch. It was Harrington's Sunday school class that resurrected the cross on Mt. McCoy in 1921.

Apricot harvests flourished until World War I curtailed the shipment of fruits to Europe. Consequently, a major marketplace for the farmers was curtailed. But, once again, the farmers used seeming adversity to look to the future. They began experimenting with other orchard crops discovering that the soil, air, drainage, and water supply were perfectly conducive to growing walnuts and oranges. Soon much of the valley was planted with fruit trees.

Although citrus was on the verge of becoming the major crop of the valley, farmers were asked by the federal government to plant castor beans during World War I. The oil extracted from the plant could be used as a lubricant for planes. Remote though the valley was, Simi could celebrate when the school bell rang throughout the valley on Armistice Day in 1918, since it knew it had played its part in achieving victory.

The Tapo district was particularly well suited for the new crops, producing a quality that gained the farmers a favorable reputation that served them throughout the valley's agricultural days. The Valencia orange, which relied on the frost-free climate of the Tapo, became the valley's most important commodity.

The earliest planting of a citrus orchard, however, was at the northwest portion of Erringer and Cochran when C.G. Austin, one of the original Colony settlers, grew one acre of Washington navels relying solely on natural rainfall. Thus, these oranges, which could be harvested before the frosts of winter, proved successful on the valley floor. But, with the development of irrigation, growers promoted the summer-ripening Valencia in the Tapo, leaving room throughout the basin for walnuts.

With the success of the Valencia orange, a railroad spur was laid from the train station to the Tapo Citrus Packing House, built in 1917 on Alamo (where the city hall complex now sits). With this shift in the agricultural pattern, the Tapo area became a natural magnet for development.

The Patterson Ranch Company of Oxnard had purchased 12,500 acres from A. Berheim, the part of the Rancho Tapo that Bard had sold him. Patterson ranched the land until 1911, when the company no longer needed the wide expanse. Under the leadership of the company's manager, John Roup, the land was subdivided, creating Subdivision I (bounded by Tapo Drive on the east and Lemon on the west) and Subdivision II (which extended to Sycamore). Lots of 5 to 15 acres were offered with established fruit and walnut trees. In addition, for the asking price of $457 per acre, the purchaser would own shares in the Tapo Mutual Water Company and have the hope of discovering oil (since wells existed within a few rods of the tracts). Early residents of this tract included Dr. Albert Hirschi, James Callahan, and Joe and Jon Schreiber. In fact, many German families settled in this area. Once oil was known to exist, Edward L. Doheny purchased the remainder of the Patterson ranch but enjoyed only a small success in his quest for oil in that area.

The Tapo Mutual Water Company was incorporated by local residents, who further expanded it, drilling more and deeper wells, installing electric deep-well pumps, building large reservoirs, and laying 222 miles of concrete pipe.

Throughout the 1920s, while the major ranch holdings in the western end of the valley remained intact, the central and eastern portions of the valley experienced more subdivision.

Kadota Fig Farms encompassed 320 acres owned by W.F. Loomis, which he had purchased from Justin Petit of the defunct Oxnard Company. His vision was to offer single-acre parcels complete with fig trees and facilities for pigeon farming. Although he had been successful with a similar operation in San Fernando, his asking price of $2,800 was too exorbitant when compared with Community Center property going for $1,000 per improved acre. Those few who did purchase the property, however, found it to be a sound investment, although the idea of the pigeon farm never did fly.

The Santa Susana Development Company subdivided the land surrounding the Simi Hotel in 1922. The hotel was torn down to make way for the proposed farmsteads on the 720-acre La Placentia tract. Although water seemed sufficient at the time, the supply could not meet the long-term needs of such a project.

Simi was hitting its stride. Crops were well established and had found a commanding niche in both the national and international marketplace. There was a network of solid citizens working for the combined good of the valley. Many of the amenities of prosperous, progressive living were now provided.

By 1917 Southern California Edison was supplying some electricity. The first power line was in,

*This photo captures a high-
spirited moment on the
Austin Home Ranch.
Courtesy, Simi Valley
Historical Society and
Museum, Strathearn
Historical Park*

but power was not yet available to the homes because there was such a distance between them. The Strathearns and Crinklaws, however, received electricity in consideration of the right-of-way they granted through their property. By 1922 electricity was available throughout the valley.

The telephone found instant reception, connecting neighbor to neighbor, friend to friend. Initially the only phone to exist in the valley in 1897 was in the Sawtelle store. Residents could only use it to make long-distance phone calls. By 1909 service was available but members of the Colony had to keep up their own lines. Rose Printz operated the first switchboard in her Colony home. Party lines might accommodate up to 12 phones. One pioneer recalled that when the telephone lines went in, everyone on Royal Avenue was on one line. When someone got a call they could hear "click, click, click" all the way down the line as everyone listened in.

By 1920 there were 70 phones, increasing to 557 by 1950 when Bessie Printz, daughter of Rose Printz, and her exchange were handling 2,000 calls a day. Four years later a dial central office was constructed in Los Angeles.

In 1930 the valley had its first official library. Previously, a corner of the Crinklaw building housed books gathered by the Woman's Club as early as 1917. The new library, located on Los Angeles Avenue just north of the elementary school, was the only freestanding library in the county. All other libraries shared space with an existing enterprise in their community. It was a testament of the values of the residents that the neighborhood raised funds to increase the size of the lot to 50 feet from the originally planned 25 feet. They then donated the lot to the County of Ventura. Additionally, they raised $50 to purchase supplies not provided in the county budget. The library is now a part of the Strathearn Historical Park.

The Simi Valley Woman's Club was in full swing, providing a creative outlet for the women of the area. In 1928 the Simi Valley Lions Club was formed, suggesting that some of the energy that had gone into forging a new frontier could now be channeled into the more subtle areas of community development.

The Simi Community Methodist Church Brotherhood Suppers were a popular event on Friday evenings. For a minimal price and a potluck dish, one could enjoy an evening full of heartfelt camaraderie and fine local entertainment.

Longtime resident Jackie Bunker remembered the days when each ranch had its own basketball team. And native Lucy Chavez (whose father arrived in 1905, having worked his way west laying railroad tracks) has fond memories of playing on an all-Mexican women's baseball team. It was grand fun traveling to Canoga Park, Camarillo, and Moorpark for games. A corresponding men's team was known as La Cruz Azul.

Of course, not everyone felt the need for regular social activities. As Jim Runkle described, for some that was still a luxury:

You get up about 4:30. Go out and feed the horses and the mules, curry them off and harness them. Come in about 6:00 a.m., eat breakfast and leave for the fields. You quit about 11:30. Start to unhook your team, bring them in, feed and water them. Have dinner as they called it. Then back to work. 5:00 and you come in, unharness the animals and feed them again.

Whatever it took, the valley was on its way to developing a strong sense of identity. As Jackie Bunker said of those developing days, "We felt very exclusive—very secluded—and we liked it!"

IV

Visions and Visionaries

It is an intriguing paradox of Simi Valley that the residents could feel so secluded and select while all around them the hillsides were teeming with life that was very much connected to the outside world.

Perhaps most notable was Corriganville, on the eastern end of the valley. As a result of the massive filming done there, the craggy terrain of the Simi Hills will forever be the Old West in the minds of millions of filmgoers around the globe.

According to lines by D.L. Scott, Corriganville became the place "where Tarzan swung and horse thieves hung." Ray Corrigan, whose stunt work earned him the nickname "Crash," purchased 2,000 spacious, wide-open, rugged acres in 1932 to serve as home for his family and parents. His $15,000 find proved beneficial for a multitude of people.

By 1937 he was renting out the canyons, hills, and oak forests to Hollywood studios. The idea caught on with the movie moguls, who found the 35-mile distance very appealing. While Los Angeles was rapidly developing (thanks in part to that very same industry), Simi still held the allure of wilderness. Inspired by the warm reception of the studios to his property, Corrigan began to expand. He decided to offer filmmakers an entire town.

He appealed to his Hollywood connections, offering the opportunity to construct any type of building they would choose. The only condition was they leave it intact when they were finished using it. In exchange, they would have exclusive access to that set for two years.

It was an industrious endeavor, to be sure, but soon a full-fledged Western town was created. A road was developed, walls were dug, and trees were removed. Columbia Studios even put in a lake, which it used for the filming of *The Adventures of Robin Hood.* Eventually Corrigan installed a tram system for his visitors. In all, 45 different set locations were constructed, connected by 11 miles of trail, creating a complete 190-acre Western town.

In 1949 Corrigan opened the "World's Most Famous Movie Ranch" to the public. Many of the sets that had served the moviemakers so well now doubled as a special function of a Western-theme amusement park. The Old West newspaper office actually printed the *Corriganville Gazette,* a 10-cent quarterly that highlighted events at the movie ranch. The cafe sold 5-cent salami

Roy Corrigan poses with visitors at Corriganville, the movie ranch he opened in 1949 on his 2,000 acres in Simi Valley. Courtesy, Corriganville Preservation Committee

Right: Roy Corrigan resists the charms of an unidentified dance-hall girl while stuntman Ricky Silva looks on. Courtesy, Corriganville Preservation Committee

Below: "Wagons West" inhabited the streets of Corriganville in 1952. Courtesy, Corriganville Preservation Committee

sandwiches; cold drinks were available at the saloon.

One of 10 amusement parks in the country, Corriganville was open daily during summer months and weekends the remainder of the year. Visitors could tour the movie sets or watch live performances staged on the streets by the stable of stuntmen who lived at the park. Performers attired in period clothes lent an authentic air to the Old West atmosphere. Guests could indulge in pony, horseback, or stagecoach rides, purchase Indian crafts, practice their aim at the shooting gallery, take in a rodeo performance, or visit Boothill Cemetery, all for an entry fee of $1.25. Lucky guests might actually see their favorite movie stars filming on the set.

Many careers were launched amid the pounding hooves and flying dust of Corriganville. Steve Gillum, currently the coordinator for the Western stunt show at Universal Studios, cut his teeth as a stuntman at Corriganville, performing in rodeos from the age of 12. In a recent interview he recalled: "It was pretty spectacular watching a movie being filmed right in front of you. I remember one day we did 20 different shows for an audience of 20,000 people and the traffic was backed up all the way to the old Santa Susana Pass Road."

Simi Valley resident Hi Busse was at one time a feature of Corriganville. A member of the Frontiersmen, the second-oldest country western band, right behind the Sons of the Pioneers, he was still entertaining many years later when the band performed at the first annual Barn Dance and Pioneer Rendezvous, which was sponsored by the Simi Valley Historical Society.

The list of stars who filmed movies at Corriganville reads like a who's who of Western classics. More than 3,500 movies were also filmed at Corriganville, including *Fort Apache* and *Diamond Trail*. Visitors might well have seen Shirley Temple, John Agar, James Garner, Mickey Rooney, Henry Fonda, Glenn Ford, Richard Boone, Clint Eastwood, Doug McClure, Tom Mix, Gene Autry, and Clark Gable. Here Howard Hughes filmed his famous *Vendetta* starring Jane Russell, and Errol Flynn robbed from the rich in *The Adventures of Robin Hood*. John Wayne roamed the

The Simi hills rise above Corriganville's western street in a scene repeated in thousands of western movies and television shows. Courtesy, Corriganville Preservation Committee

grounds in *The Durango Kid.* When Roy Rogers and Dale Evans sang "Happy Trails to You," it was the trails of Santa Susana they clip-clopped along as they sang.

Corrigan himself was not just an entrepreneur. He was very actively involved in stunt activities, performing in 107 films of his own. Additionally, he doubled for Johnny Weismuller in his famed Tarzan role. When he was done with swinging from the trees for that role, he played ape roles for Abbott and Costello and the Three Stooges. He also doubled for Clark Gable in *Mutiny on the Bounty,* and may be best known for paving a path to the breakfast table as the first star to eat Wheaties.

When television came along, Corriganville was right in step with the times. Many of the well-loved Western serials were filmed here.

When the Lone Ranger heartily exclaimed, "Heigh Yo Silver!" from 1949 to 1958, it was away into the Simi Hills that he galloped. When Rin Tin Tin sprung from a high cliff onto an unsuspecting criminal, it was the craggy rocks of Simi's east end from which he lunged; 164 episodes of

Film crews shot Death Valley Rangers *at Corriganville in 1943. Courtesy, Corriganville Preservation Committee*

"The Adventures of Rin Tin Tin" were filmed at the former set of *Fort Apache.* Seventy-two episodes of "Sky King" were filmed at Corriganville, and the list goes on—"The Adventures of Kit Carson," "Gunsmoke," "Have Gun Will Travel," "Fury," "Flicker," "Annie Oakley," "The Gene Autry Show," and "Hop-Along Cassidy."

Curiously, while the hills of Simi spelled W-E-S-T to so many people worldwide, the residents of the valley paid little attention to the comings and goings of Corriganville. They simply went about their own business while the flurry of guests would swoop down on the little corner of the valley. As many as 10,000 a day, in its heyday, would take their day of delight and return over the rugged Santa Susana Pass to Los Angeles County, fairly well ignoring the community of Simi Valley.

As progress began to infringe on the natural beauty of the place, and wide-open expanses began to be a thing of the past, the Western movie faded into the proverbial sunset. The impending freeway would separate the dramatic Rocky Peak Road from the remainder of the filming acreage.

"Crash" Corrigan continued operation of Corriganville until 1965, when he moved his family off the property. He sold it to Bob Hope for a reported $2.8 million. Seventy stuntmen who called Corriganville home were displaced.

Within a year the park, renamed Hopetown, was closed. In 1969 it met its final demise when a fire razed the classic Western town. Auspiciously, only the wishing well was left standing.

When Griffin Homes purchased the property from Hope, intending to build homes, purists cried, "Preserve the memories; preserve the environment!" When the Simi Valley Cultural Association staged a successful Western film festival as a fund-raiser in 1985, interest in reviving the movie ranch was renewed. Following many negotiations and much public outcry, 190 acres of the property were dedicated to the Rancho Open Space Conservation Agency as a regional park.

The banner for re-creating the Western theme park was taken up in 1988 with the creation of the Corriganville Preservation Committee. Advocates wish to secure a place in history for the "one truly American art form—the Western movie." The motto of the committee is "Save the Past for the Future." According to proponents, there is no one single Western film museum honoring the Western film industry in the entire country. As Western landscapes give way to highways and homes, the need to preserve a rapidly disappearing facet of American culture becomes more obvious and urgent.

Estimates run about $5 million to restore the park, adding a Western film museum and theater. Plans call for riding trails that would become an integral part of the development of a regional equestrian/hiking trail system. Promoters of the revival of Corriganville, as it is once again named, include Guy Madison, Dale Robertson, Peter Fonda, Dennis Weaver, Ernest Borgnine, and Iron Eyes Cody.

The world's concept of the Old West has not been limited to the craggy rocks of the eastern hills. The northern hills, too, have etched a fond picture in the hearts and minds of many through the TV series "Little House on the Prairie." The rolling prairie is not in Walnut Grove, but, rather, in Simi Valley, tucked behind the hills north of the freeway. The hills of Laura Ingalls' childhood suggest a time of tranquility and character, qualities very reflective of the Simi Valley community.

As lifetime resident Phyllis Beesmeyer Vanniman remembers, the area could well have been called Walnut Grove in its own right for it was once peppered with black walnut trees. However, when J.P. Getty purchased this portion of the Patterson ranch, the walnut trees were cut down and the burls shipped to Italy to be used in jewelry and music boxes. Getty purchased the property in the 1920s and held onto it until Texaco purchased it along with adjacent property formerly owned by Doheny. When Texaco had problems with their Pennzoil product, it sold the land to the Big Sky Ranch Company owned by Ray Watt.

While the 11,000-acre property belonged to Getty, he sublet about 2,000 acres for farming to the Newhall Land and Farming Company. Another large portion was given over to cattle. The remainder served as scenery for a wide range of familiar and futuristic films.

Movie mania was not confined to Corriganville. A portion of the Gillibrand ranch was turned into a movie set and dude ranch in a quest for fame and fortune. Here Ralph Leyland "To" Gillibrand (left) and Philip Walton "Bo" Gillibrand (center) entertain a visitor from Los Angeles. The three are in costume. Courtesy, Simi Valley Historical Society and Museum, Strathearn Historical Park

Right and far right: The annual open house at Big Sky Movie Ranch offers visitors the sights and sounds of shoot-'em-up westerns of yesteryear. Along with daredevil horseback riding and gunplay, the ranch puts on an arts and crafts show in a secluded, rustic setting. Photos by Mark Hawker

Left: The television series "Little House on the Prairie," based on the Laura Ingalls Wilder novels, was filmed in the northern hills of Simi on land that now belongs to the Big Sky Ranch Company. Photo by Mark Hawker

Nearly 500 acres, Big Sky Ranch is now operated by Don and Debi Earley, who oversee the farming and cattle operations and handle all the aspects of the Big Sky Movie Ranch, including maintenance of the sets and property and negotiations with the film companies. Flanked on the front by the bold, barren bluff, White Face, extending to Madera and Easy Street, portions of the property run all along the northern slopes of Simi Valley to Brown's Canyon by the Los Angeles County Ventura County line.

The scenery that for residents so well represents home is likely to be any town or any country to movie and television viewers around the world. Even a Japanese McDonald's commercial was filmed in these hills. And many of the stars from Corriganville have found their way over to Big Sky Ranch. James Garner did a Mazda commercial. James Arness filmed "Gunsmoke" here in the late 1950s and early 1960s. Although the series has ended, the house still stands surrounded by a white picket fence. The house itself is painted a different color on each of its four sides to allow it to resemble four different homes. The barn still stands, red as always. The set so long used for filming scenes where the white hat wins has also been used to film scenes of "Dallas."

"Little House on the Prairie" was filmed on the property for years. A school, houses, and even a pond were created for the town of Walnut Grove. The house was sent up in flames as part of the final segment in the series. The barn was moved in sections to the Strathearn Historical Museum in 1985 to serve as a reminder of Simi Valley's film history.

James Arness, who owned land in Simi Valley, starred in "Gunsmoke," a television series filmed at Big Sky Ranch in the late 1950s and early 1960s. Courtesy, Viacom Enterprises

"Father Murphy" lived his TV life at Big Sky. "The Yellow Rose of Texas," a short-lived series, featured Sam Elliot and Cybil Shepherd. The popular soap opera "Days of Our Lives" filmed an elopement segment in 1986. The updated version of "The Miracle Worker" was filmed just near the set of "Little House on the Prairie."

Simi Valley took on an international flavor with the filming of the Australian-based story "The Thornbirds." Carroll Vanniman, who was farming that acreage at the time, sublet his land to the filming company temporarily. "That was my best year in farming," he joked.

Modern-day filming has included the first episode of the TV series "Quantum Leap" as well as the futuristic horror film *Pumpkinhead,* directed by Stan Winston, who won an award for his special effects in *Alien.*

Eddie Murphy's castle in *Coming to America* still stands tall and proud, intriguingly out of place in the vast, dusty expanse of the tripas area to the north.

The Earleys currently live in the house that the Vannimans previously (and before them, Johnny Hare, who was supervisor for the Patterson ranch operation) called home.

Current plans for the vast acreage include developing a Beverly Hills-type residential layout of 1,523 homes complete with three golf courses. The format is called the Whiteface Specific Plan.

Marafuji American now owns 1,700 acres (once Watt Industries property) from Anderson to Tapo Canyon which will be developed into 364 homes and two of the golf courses. Lowe development owns 1,200 acres to the west, intended for the third golf course and a senior citizen housing project.

With this industrious development in the works, farming has begun to wane, and most of the movie ranches have gone the way of silent films. Land is now more profitable as a development. The rolling hills of the 497-acre movie ranch are not to be developed. Big Sky is still an attractive area for the film industry. Because it is well within the studio zone, it is cost-effective for the studios who will not have to pay mileage. The president of Watt Industries, recognizing the value of Big Sky Movie Ranch, calls it "the last great movie ranch in Southern California."

Although the major portion of filming has been done in these two movie locales, various other areas of Simi Valley have also found their way to the screen.

Rancho Simi Community Park became the setting for a My Little Pony commercial in 1989. One thousand stemless chrysanthemums transformed the park into a blooming meadow.

The Burger King on Cochran was apparently the standard when it was used in a commercial for the national chain. Another business, Hiatt's Hallmark at Sinaloa Plaza, was featured in Hallmark's nationwide Halloween promotion.

A Victorian home on Longbranch was chosen by Dutch Boy Paints from Cleveland to highlight the value of painting one's home. The commercial, aired in the summer of 1990, featured the house painted in a variety of colors to emphasize the details of the structure and styling.

The Strathearn house and ranch were used to shoot *The Louis Pasteur Story* in the 1930s. *Green Light* also was filmed there. In the 1940s the industry was back to film *Adventure* with Clark Gable and Greer Garson. Parts of the house were also used in the Jack Lemmon film *Days of Wine and Roses.*

The Three Amigos, with Steve Martin, was filmed at the southern end of Sinaloa Road. In November 1977 *Harper Valley PTA* was very much a part of Simi Valley. John Candy lent the valley notoriety in *Who's Harry Crumb?* when scenes in the movie referred to the "Simi Valley Game Farm."

Nearly all of the western end of the valley got into the act when *The Doberman Gang* was filmed in 1972. The movie began at the Valley Diner on Los Angeles Avenue, a popular eatery for locals. About 80 percent of the film was shot at locales around town, including the junkyard and Larwin Square. Nearly all the extras in the movie were local residents. The robbery occurred in the Bank of A. Levy, where all but the teller were Simi Valley residents. This was the movie where resident Jay Paxton got to utter his famous lines "Give 'em the money." In a very telling way, the only scene filmed outside the valley was one that required surveillance from a high-rise building. That scene was filmed in Encino.

Simi Valley has not only given its live scenery to the film industry, but also, with the coming of Dream Quest Images to the area, special effects are now a substantial product of the community. This special effects firm is rapidly bringing Simi Valley prestige within the film industry. Its efforts and talents earned an Oscar in the 1990 Academy Awards for special effects, surpassing *Back to the Future II.* The 10-year-old firm has done special effects for a number of commercially success-ful movies, including the remake of *The Blob, Scrooged* (starring Bill Murray), *Big Business* (with Bette Midler and Lily Tomlin), *Short Circuit II, Exorcist III,* and *National Lampoon's Christmas Vacation.* The company also worked on the popular Disneyland attraction, "Captain Eo," featuring Michael Jackson.

Legendary pioneer film director Raoul Walsh made 140 movies, including The Thief of Baghdad *and* What Price Glory *and is credited with discovering John Wayne. In 1964 Walsh retired to a ranch in the northeastern hills of Simi where he wrote his first novel, a western. Courtesy, The Academy of Motion Picture Arts and Sciences*

All of their endeavors have not been commer-cially oriented. In 1990 a "Drug-Free America" film was shot at Sycamore Plaza. Special effects called for a drug pusher to turn into a snake.

Legends that were created in the hills were so often transcribed to celluloid. Some of the leg-ends remained on the screen; some were living, breathing men like Raoul Walsh. His career spanned 52 years, dating back to D.W. Griffith's 1915 production of *Birth of a Nation,* in which Walsh played John Wilkes Booth. He was one of the legendary pioneer directors, putting James Cagney through his paces in six films. All in all, Walsh made a total of 140 films, several of which he wrote himself, such as *The Thief of Baghdad.* He also did documentaries, at one time riding with the notorious Pancho Villa to get actual footage of him during one of his raids.

Walsh is credited with discovering John Wayne and with giving Rock Hudson his first break. His story of the United States Marines, *What Price Glory,* was one of his fondest accom-plishments. His last film, *The Distant Trumpet,* was made in 1963.

He retired shortly thereafter, in 1964, to a modest ranch in the northeastern hills of Simi Valley. At the age of 84 he wrote his first novel, *The Anger of the Just Ones,* a western. An eyepatch worn over one eye following an automobile accident became his trademark, lending character to this already larger-than-life figure. Walsh died in January 1981 at the age of 93.

While Walsh's life was primarily dedicated to the big screen, Murray Harris has spent the major portion of his life promoting newspaper cartoon strips. With the help of his wife, Bea, Harris has brought national attention to Simi Valley with this seemingly obscure lifelong interest, developed when he was a political cartoonist with the *Boston Globe* during World War II. His car-toon collection, which includes the original artwork of "Krazy Kat," is one of the most extensive private collections in America, dating back to the beginning of the art form. He has been invited to exhibit this collection in a number of museums around the world. About 30 of his pieces have

In this 1977 photo, folk artist Grandma Prisbrey poses before the Doll House, one of the 15 buildings she constructed from bottles and other found objects. The Doll House contained around 600 dolls Grandma saved from the town dump, some of which can be seen behind her, mounted on a surf- board. Photo by Amanda Devine, courtesy, Preserve Bottle Village

toured the country for two years in a Smithsonian Institution exhibit. Additionally, Harris is one of the original members of the Museum of Cartoons' Hall of Fame selection committee.

His talents and interests, however, have not been confined to the cartoon format. He has done portraits of every vice president of the United States up to and including Dan Quayle, using an opaque maroon watercolor applied on acetate with a pointed-tip brush. This collection hangs permanently in the Presidential Museum in Odessa, Texas, where 25,000 visitors a year enjoy his works. The series has been named "Second-in-Command: The Harris Collection of Vice Presidents of the United States." Bea Harris has written biographies of the vice presidents planned for a miniature book format, a strong area of interest for her.

Understandably, art is a matter of personal taste. While some works of art are readily recognized as aesthetic and contributing to the higher essence of man, other works of art are subject to debate. The latter has been the case with "Grandma" Prisbrey's Bottle Village at 4595 Cochran Street in the Kadota Fig area.

In 1956, at the age of 60, Tressa "Grandma" Prisbrey began making "little homes" from discards found in the dump. While developers were beginning a whirlwind of stucco housing in the valley, she was creating her own development of cast-off items.

Prisbrey was a collector extraordinaire. It all began with an impressive collection of 17,000 promotional pencils she had accumulated during political campaigns. When the cement blocks she planned to use to build storage proved too expensive, she quickly rebounded and began using discarded bottles, which were in abundant supply.

She made daily treks to the dump in her old Studebaker pickup, gathering not only bottles, but

Seen here is a view of the inside of one of the structures in Grandma Prisbrey's Bottle Village. In 1965 at the age of 60, the self-taught artist began to build miniature homes from found materials. By 1976 she had completed her project, which consisted of 15 structures on her property at 4595 Cochran street. During her lifetime she conducted tours of the site, which is now closed for reconstruction. Photo by Mark Hawker

often the beginnings of a new collection. Six years later the industrious woman had the foundation of her village—13 houses, 2 wishing wells, a water fountain, planters, 2 shrines, and a mosaic walkway embedded with thousands of household discards. Such an elaborate undertaking, and all it had cost was the price of cement, sand, roofing paper, two-by-four studs, and time.

There was much whimsy incorporated in the development. She built one house two feet into the ground so she wouldn't have to reach so high to put on the roof. The commanding Round House, 23 feet in diameter, was constructed of brown beer bottles with the necks outward, creating an imposing prickly surface. A garden of doll heads impaled on sticks lent a macabre tone. One wall was built entirely of television picture tubes. Blue milk of magnesia bottles caught the rays of the sun, glistening underfoot as one walked the path through the Lilliputian village.

The complete project, built over a 20-year period, utilized more than one million discarded bottles. Prisbrey was 79 years old and had run out of space. The 40-by-300-foot confines of her property were her only parameters for knowing she was done. Had she had more room, it is likely she would have built more structures.

Soon the village was open for tours with "Grandma" as tour guide. Listening to her feisty tales and thoughts was as entertaining as viewing the strange little village she had created. As she wrote in a small pamphlet she sold for a dollar to her visitors:

Around all the buildings I have cactus beds. I don't care much for cactus myself but I don't have a green thumb and if I forget to water the cactus they would just grow anyhow . . . They remind me of myself. They are independent, prickly, and ask nothing from anybody.

Many in town, however, felt she did indeed ask a lot, terming the primitive folk art an eyesore. Despite the opinion of local residents, the structures have garnered interest and recognition from far and near. Photographs of Bottle Village have been displayed in major exhibitions throughout the world.

It is conjecture just how much of an artist "Grandma" was. A group of local artists who believe her work is indeed art formed a nonprofit committee in 1979 and have charged themselves with restoration of the village and, ideally, the purchase of the property.

The committee still has much work ahead of it. While the dream is to purchase the property, the demanding reality is the need to reinforce the masonry. Restoration estimates currently run as high as $250,000.

The structure, currently closed to the public due to safety concerns, may be crumbling, but its status is permanent. The county named it Landmark #52 in 1979. In 1984 Bottle Village was designated State Historical Landmark #939. Inscribed on the plaque is "One of California's remarkable 20th century folk art environments."

Tressa "Grandma" Prisbrey died October 5, 1989, leaving behind a one-of-a-kind legacy. Some consider her work to be a time capsule and her a historian, a native recorder of the present. Perhaps indeed, like those a hundred years before her, she was a pioneer, using materials at hand, working with the resources available, tirelessly creating something from nothing.

Not all impact on Simi Valley was so visual, so concrete. The hillsides of the valley have long rung with the visions of the spiritual, those who look to the unseen. Such was Pisgah Grande, a Pentecostal colony in Las Llajas Canyon. In 1908 Dr. Finis E. Yoakum, a prosperous Los Angeles doctor, had a life-changing accident in which he was gored in the chest and lungs by the shaft of a runaway wagon as he gallantly tried to stop the stampeding horses.

Yoakum took his pain-racked, scarred body to Mt. Pisgah near his home. There he prayed to God, forsaking all his worldly goods in exchange for his health. When he, in fact, experienced a miraculous recovery, he took to the back streets of Los Angeles, preaching his new dedication to God, relinquishing his man-taught medicines for the certainty of healing prayers.

Soon the down and out were responding to the preachings and teachings of this neatly bearded, white-haired man of God. His followers, thereafter known as Brothers and Sisters, were offered meals and a bath in exchange for a generous serving of the gospel according to Yoakum. As word spread of his teachings and the numbers increased, he was receiving donations from around the world. Soon the "family" outgrew the mansion the Brothers and Sisters had built for Yoakum and his wife in Arroyo Seco, where he had also run a home for delinquent girls, Pisgah Ark. He also established Pisgah Gardens in the San Fernando Valley for those afflicted with tuberculosis, cancer, and mental difficulties.

In 1914, just six years after his calling, he discovered 3,200 acres in the Las Llajas Canyon of the Santa Susana Mountains between Tapo Canyon and Hummingbird's Nest. He purchased the "Garden of Eden" from Jack Hesketh, brother-in-law of Edward Clayton Gillibrand, for $50,000. It was perhaps prophetic that Yoakum found his way to Las Llajas, for the name given to the canyon by the Spanish padres meant "the scars."

With the bounty of the land, Yoakum and his disciples were able to create a self-sustaining community complete with a post office and a little red schoolhouse.

Running springs and acres of fertile land for gardens and orchards provided all the food needed by the vegetarian community. With the honey from the bees and milk from the goats, their meals were complete. In fact, over 350,000 meals a year were served family style in the spacious dining hall.

Approximately 300 searching souls called Pisgah Grande home. Each family lived in its own brick house, complete with fireplace built from bricks manufactured on the premises from native materials. Each brick bore the Pisgah brand. Followers without a trade soon learned to be brick-layers and carpenters. They cut building stone from the sandstone formations and dug clay from the hillsides for processing into lime, which became part of the mortar used for laying the brick.

Homes, a post office, an imposing prayer tower set high on a knoll, a printing office, and mission headquarters were all made from the materials at hand.

This building was part of the Pisgah Grande colony, founded in 1914 in Las Llajas Canyon. Each of the bricks in this building bears the word "Pisgah." Courtesy, Simi Valley Historical Society and Museum, Strathearn Historical Park

Under the eye of God, Pisgah Grande flourished. Wrote Beverly Les in the *Ventura County Historical Society Quarterly,* "Children skipped to school; geraniums lined the path; prayer and song rang through the hills." The valley residents first approached the colony with skepticism. But as trust began to develop, the Brothers and Sisters would often wander down into the valley along the road Yoakum and his followers had created. Valley residents would sometimes be invited to Pisgah Grande activities.

The Beesmeyers and Crinklaws often counted on the residents for seasonal help in their farming operations. Lydia Beesmeyer made clothes for at least one of the Sisters.

In her book, *Simi Grows Up,* Janet Scott Cameron recalls the occasion when she and Mildred Brigham, along with Jessie and Marian Strathearn, were invited to the colony. Upon their arrival to the colony, nestled in the lush green hills, they discovered they had been invited to a "Coronation in the Heavenly Kingdom" or, in other words, a funeral service. The daughter of the deceased sang a hallelujah song, rejoicing in her mother's death, according to the philosophy of the group.

When Yoakum died in 1920, Pisgah Grande died with him. His two sons, Finis and Charles, moved the operation to San Bernardino and later to Pikesville, Tennessee, where a Pisgah Home still exists. Many of the Brothers and Sisters were absorbed into the community as they had proved themselves to be upright citizens under Yoakum's tutelage.

Gilbert Beesmeyer, cousin of Theodore Beesmeyer, purchased the property. The 3,223 acres were sold to E. Tropp in 1924 for $500,000. Tropp named it La Quinta. The millionaire real estate man had planned big improvements for the property that were never realized. Cecil Miller of Oxnard began using the property as a ranching operation, converting the buildings to his own use. It later became part of the Runkle holdings before it was sold to Bob Hope, the current owner.

The remote, unspoiled hills surrounding Simi beckoned many who wanted to be near the powers of the Creator. The Eleven Club was another such entity. In 1926 it settled high up Alta Vista Road in one of the subdivisions of Mortimer Park, later known as Santa Susana Knolls.

Although accommodations were very rustic the first year, with tent living and lanterns for lights, eventually the members were able to build beautiful homes and gardens secluded behind iron gates.

By 1933 there were 74 members of the "country club" and church. Intended as a weekend retreat for Los Angeles residents, the Eleven Club had sunken grounds, a playground, a tennis court, and a swimming pool. An oval-shaped ravine on the side of the hill created a natural amphitheater called The Bowl. A clubhouse was erected on the Round Hill, where they held meetings, supposedly in a darkened room before a golden throne.

The philosophy of the Eleven Club, led by the Reverend May Otis Blackburn, was based on the seven-day creation of the world. Group members believed that there was only one grand "week," which kept repeating in a continuing cycle; after "Sunday" life circled back to the first and only "Monday." From there the club's teachings apparently expanded into complicated numerical calculations of the concepts of the world. Their bible was a work called *The Great Sixth Seal of the Church of the Divine Science of Joshua, the Branch, the Headstone of the Corner.* The group's creed read:

His full creation is in the seven stars of the Great Dipper. The North Star holds the quality of the four directions at one eternal, powerful, magnetic point. If one would see the word of God visibly manifested, he should look at the North Star.

Much rumor surrounded the group. Many viewed them as a "superstitious club" and a "cult." The children, however, were accepted at the local school. Residents recall only that they all wore bracelets, and that the boys had unusual names such as Zela, Zola, Zuman Lee, and Geneva.

The Eleven Club's views on death were suspect. A scandal involving the death of Blackburn's daughter, in which the group was rumored to have preserved her body, reportedly forced Blackburn and her followers to Oregon.

Not far away, as the Eleven Club was relocating, further into the Knolls area in Box Canyon was the WKFL Fountain of the World (Wisdom, Knowledge, Faith, Love), which proclaimed to be one of the world's outstanding humanitarian organizations. The facility became a training ground for 144,000 who professed to embrace all religious concepts and all races of people, following their philosophy, "Love ye one another."

One had to be accepted into membership, which required signing a Declaration of Faith. All worldly goods were to be denounced and donated to the foundation to be shared equally by all. Master Krishna Venta led the group, the lives of whose members were to be dedicated to complete service to man.

Members wore long, flowing, multicolored silk robes and long, flowing beards; they wore no shoes. No doubt they were a strange site for this steadfast farming community.

All members were trained in first aid to better serve. It was in attempted service that the group first came to public attention. When members tried to help a downed airplane, their cumbersome robes caught fire. They were forbidden to assist with fires in the future.

Like others before them, they used the materials at hand to construct the buildings they needed, working primarily in stone, the most readily available resource.

The group's existence in this area was short-lived. On December 11, 1958, 12 years after they had begun, two disgruntled ex-members, suspicious of the Master Krishna's transactions, blew up the monastery in a heated dispute. The Master was killed along with his assailants. But all was not lost; Krishna's wife had already escaped to Alaska, taking a nucleus group with her.

Portions of the arches of the WKFL Fountain of the World still stand. While the World Foundation was taking flight, another religious establishment was putting down roots that exist to this day.

In 1947 Santa Susana became the full-time home of the Brandeis Institute, a center of worship and study for the Jewish culture.

When, in 1941, Supreme Court Justice Louis D. Brandeis could no longer contain his concern that college-educated youth were leaving Judaism, he began to see the need for an institution that would instill cultural understanding and pride. He decided to offer an alternative, to create a magnet for scholars around the world.

Working with Shlomo Bardin, a Russian-born Jew, Brandeis founded the institute, merging higher education with a recreational camp. The offerings are three-fold, based on the concept of American summer camp, Danish folk school, and Israeli kibbutz.

The first facility was established in Amherst, New Hampshire, followed by ones in North Carolina and Pennsylvania. Only Santa Susana, a year-round facility, remains.

Brandeis and Bardin purchased the 2,200 beautiful, rolling acres with their commanding view of the valley for $150,000 in 1947. Then, in 1973, James Arness, whose property was nestled between Brandeis and the Runkle ranch, donated 900 acres. Only about 60 acres are developed; the remainder are left open for the benefit of those who attend the institute.

The institute boasts an architecturally striking building—the House of The Book—where many of the weekend adult activities are held. Completed in 1973, it was intended to be the first building of a prep academy. This was a dream of Shlomo Bardin as yet unrealized. The building has been registered as a county historical landmark.

Shlomo Bardin died in 1976 at the age of 78 and is buried on the grounds. The following year the learning facility was renamed Brandeis-Bardin Institute to honor this well-loved man.

The background of the property was not always so intellectually based. It once belonged to Eddie Maier, a millionaire whose money came from the beer he produced in his two-story brewery that took up half a city block in Los Angeles. In this area his Brew 102 was fairly well known. Like many breweries, he offered more than one choice. An ad from 1906 proclaims, "There's health and nourishment in every glass of Pilsner Imperial Select."

Maier had purchased the property from Jack Haigh, uncle of Gerald Haigh, the author of *Straw Roads.* Haigh had used the land as a stock ranch. Maier used it as a lavish getaway. The house Maier built, which later became the administration building for Brandeis, was one of the first luxury homes in Simi Valley. It was equipped with stables, a swimming pool, a dancing pavilion, and quarters for the baseball team he sponsored. There were the usual cattle pens and beautiful peach trees. Gerald Haigh recalls pens of monkeys and a couple of buffalo.

A popular legend recalls the days when Eddie Maier entertained lavishly. It was not uncommon for a convention of Masons, weary from train travel, to be treated to frosty beers as they trekked along the tree-lined road up to the Maier home, since buckets of ice and brew lined the pathway.

There has been the visual word, performed on screen; the promised word, sent from the powers above; and the written word. The vision of the written word has been expressed by those who have created it and by those who have presented a medium for those creations.

In 1910 the area's first newspaper was published in Moorpark by George A. Stewart to serve the entire Simi district, which included Big Simi and Little Simi (Moorpark). Annual subscription to the *Moorpark Star* was $1.50. In 1912 he sold the operation to J.M. Brackett, who changed the name to the *Moorpark Enterprise,* considered the forerunner of the current *Enterprise.* Two years later the *Moorpark Enterprise* was taken over by the Reverend William H. Fulford, a circuit preacher who then sold it to Cal Hoffman in 1920. Following a series of owners, John Jenkins purchased the paper in 1965 along with the *Simi Valley Sun,* merging the two papers into one formidable newspaper that has served the community's needs ever since. It has grown from a one-day-a-week publication to a full-service, seven-day operation.

The Simi Valley *Advertiser* was the first licensed paper in the Simi Valley-Santa Susana area. It appeared in September 1951 with editor Ernest G. Buckner, known to many as Buck, a third-generation newspaperman who had come to the valley to recover from a nervous breakdown. He began the operation in a one-room shack he built on his Barnard Street home, printing with a small hand press he had brought with him. Ten years later he added news to the weekly advertising sheet. Alma Stark was originally the editor, but became a columnist with a byline when Amy Mekkelson took over her position.

When Buckner went into partnership with a friend, Frank Schroeder, he expanded his building and got a linotype machine, eliminating the need to travel to the San Fernando Valley. He also bought a fully powered press to replace the semiautomatic one he and his staff had been using. By 1966 the *Advertiser* was incorporated into the *Enterprise-Sun-News.*

In 1947 Wayne Montgomery, Jr., published a mimeographed paper he put together in his real estate office located on Los Angeles Avenue. *The East Wind,* a community service publication, lasted a year or two.

Another short-lived but feisty paper was the *Simi Valley Mirror,* published in the 1970s by Jim Whitehead. It was a noble attempt to offer an opposition view on controversial issues. It was eventually sold to Dan Schmidt, who had previously owned the *Moorpark News.* As he had a noncompete clause in his sale contract, he operated the newly acquired *Simi Valley Mirror* in Simi until the clause expired. Then he moved the operation to Moorpark. In late 1989 the paper was acquired by the *Enterprise,* which also owned the *Moorpark News,* converging the two papers into the *Moorpark News and Mirror.*

The valley is home to many established screenwriters and authors (including the only female member of Bob Hope's writing staff) and a strong camaraderie exists within the writing community. Several of these accomplished writers meet regularly at one of the city's longest-operating restaurants, Millie's Country Kitchen (formerly Alphy's).

At one time Simi had its own full-color, full-fledged magazine. It began simply as a newspaper print magazine named *Simi Today.* Publisher/editor Charlotte Jackson operated the advertising format with some copy that gave businessmen an outlet to express their side of issues in the late 1970s. In 1984 Robert and Janice Lease bought the magazine when Jackson moved to Hawaii. Soon they rapidly expanded the format, bringing it from black-and-white newsprint to full-color glossy. The name changed from *Simi Today* to *Today* and, finally—in the burgeoning trend to reach all of Ventura County—to *Gold Coast Today.* It became a high-style representation of the valley and helped launch many writing careers. When the financial demands of putting together a high-quality monthly became too much, the magazine ceased publication.

Relax magazine began in 1986, and circulation is increasing. Published by Ted Ottinger, it is a newspaper-format monthly publication offering readers a look at leisure activities in and around the area.

Also keeping citizens abreast of activities is Comcast Cablevision, which operates under the sanction of the city. Each Monday evening, city council meetings are broadcast over their own channel 19. In addition, an ongoing community bulletin board tells of forthcoming community events. Formerly Group W (and before 1982 known as Clarity TV), the company became known as Comcast in 1986.

There have been a number of attempts to establish radio stations in the valley. When Bob Russell could not broadcast from a radio frequency in 1979, he did the next best thing—he broadcast over cable. He operated KCME-FM from his home while he awaited acquisition of his own

Above and center: Supreme Court Justice Louis D. Brandeis (left) and Shlomo Bardin (center), a doctoral student at Columbia University, were interested in experimental educational methods for teaching cultural and moral values. In 1941 they founded the Brandeis Collegiate Institute in order to educate college students about Jewish identity and culture. Courtesy, Brandeis-Bardin Institute

Right: Built in 1947, the Brandeis-Bardin Institute is located on 3,100 acres in Simi Valley. The institute claims as its purpose the enhancement of the Jewish people, and offers numerous courses in varied subjects such as Jewish folk art, dance, and music. Photo by Julius Shulman, courtesy, Brandeis-Bardin Institute

on-air FM frequency. None, however, became available. He sold the operation in 1989, and the new owners moved "99 Rock" (90.3 FM) to Hollywood. In 1982 Ron Lewis also made an attempt with a cable radio station, 96.1 FM KQSV.

Manual Cabranes was successful in his bid for radio air space. KWNK 670 AM broadcasts from a radio tower in Tapo Canyon. He was in the right place at the right time and was able to take advantage of the FCC, which allowed clear-channel stations to be licensed. After three or four years of negotiation, Cabranes received authorization November 1, 1984, to operate at one kilowatt 24 hours a day. The station operates under a limited partnership, with Cabranes as the general manager and Robert C. Landegger as the limited partner.

Simi Valley residents have sought to express themselves not only through visual art and the printed page, but also through the performing arts. In fact, theater has been a mainstay of the valley's cultural expression from the days of the first American settlers. Lou Wright organized the well-received Simi Community Players in 1917. When the musical cantata *The New Minister* was performed at the Colony Methodist church in 1921, the performers played to standing room only, turning away more than six farm machine loads of people.

Fifty years later Mike Monahan founded the Horizon Players, a community theater group that initially staged its productions in a warehouse on Easy Street. Later the group moved to the old movie theater on High Street, now the home of the Moorpark Melodrama. They held their performances there until they were forced to leave when the owner doubled the rent. With no other location available to perform, the group disbanded in 1982.

For three years the valley had no theater. In 1985 Marilyn McCormick, originally of the Horizon Players, founded the Theater Guild of Simi Valley, thus ending that three-year drought. Again the limitations of performing platforms made the going rough. The Theater Guild was soon transformed into SAVE (Stage and Video Education Theater), making it the oldest theater organization in the community. David Newcomer has served as artistic director and Sid Haig has directed several productions under the auspices of both SAVE and the Theater Guild of Simi Valley.

When this group has found it difficult to find a stage where people could come, they have taken steps, instead, to bring the production to the people, taping original stage shows for airing on KADY-TV, often using scripts written by community members.

The urge is strong for theatrical expression in Simi Valley. Adding to the list of theater groups is the Santa Susana Repertory Company, a semiprofessional theater company with hopes of gaining full professional status. Cofounded by Victoria Morris and with David Ralpe as artistic director, the company has gone to innovative lengths to present its craft. To call attention to the group, the performers donned costumes and made the rounds of local businesses, staging scenes from *Man of La Mancha.*

When the facility on Stearns and Los Angeles Avenue failed to meet fire codes, in the nick of time (and money), the company had to make a quick decision for presenting its ready-to-go performance of *Man of La Mancha.* The solution was a circus tent in the parking lot. What could have been a disaster turned into a feather in their cap. The *Los Angeles Times,* impressed by the initiative of the company, gave rave reviews.

The Santa Susana Repertory Company spawned the Soap Box Players, headed by Kevin Traxler. The group originally began as a summer performing group, but it currently enjoys independent status, performing one or two shows a summer. They have had to go out of the valley on occasion to stage some of their productions due to the limited venues available in Simi.

The need for performance space has not gone unrecognized. The Simi Valley Cultural Association, composed of volunteers, has worked for several years to bring a stage to town. The city has donated land in the Civic Center site in anticipation of this long-awaited event. The city also authorized money for a feasibility study. While plans for the performing arts center have gone from a maximum seating of 2,000 down to a modest plan accommodating 750, the association has amassed all its ingenuity to develop funds for the building or locate an interim facility that could be adapted to the needs.

At this time the spirit is willing, but the money is tight. The association has held a number of fund-raisers generating some start-up funds. Their very first effort was a Western Film Festival, which was also instrumental in the revival of interest in Corriganville.

Two songs have been written to honor Simi Valley, songs that seem to have fallen by the way-side. In 1978 Jim St. Ours wrote the words and music of a song titled "Simi Valley." St. Ours, once a member of the management staff of the city, penned the song to commemorate the city's ninth anniversary. Much earlier, in 1960, Denna Hardin Merrifield wrote "My Simi Valley." Merrifield created the song during a family vacation, capturing the mood of the valley in the 1960s. Both songs pay tribute to the natural beauties of the valley.

Simi Valley was also commemorated in a poem, "Simi," written by Mildred W. Brigham for the Simi Valley Women's Club.

All visions and artistic expressions need not be written, performed, or painted. Modern-day Simi Valley is seeing its share of creative scientific expression as well.

On June 10, 1979, the *Gossamer Albatross,* a human-powered aircraft designed by Paul MacCready, crossed the English Channel. The creation of this unique aircraft exemplifies the pioneering spirit to never give up no matter the setbacks.

MacCready is president of AeroInvironment, Inc. He found himself in need of money when a friend defaulted on a $100,000 loan he had cosigned. Auspiciously, Henry Kremers, a British industrialist, offered $100,000 for the first man-powered plane that could actually fly. For a winning glider pilot from way back, this was an inviting challenge.

For the purpose of the competition he first made the *Condor.* He gained worldwide attention for this first plane that could fly without an engine for at least two hours. The plane was later placed in the Smithsonian Institution right alongside the Wright Brothers' first plane and Charles Lindbergh's *Spirit of St. Louis.*

Next, MacCready updated the concept of the *Condor.* He needed a lighter craft for pilot Bryan Allen to make the crossing, but one strong enough to endure the strong gusts of wind over the channel. This time the dangling carrot was $200,000.

Thus, the *Gossamer Albatross* was born, with lighter and sleeker wings. The crossing would take about three hours. The *Albatross* had a 96-foot wingspan, two feet longer than a DC-9 airliner. Using pedals, the flight across the 23-mile channel took two hours and 49 minutes, an extraordinary achievement.

In 1981 the *Solar Challenger* became the first sun-powered plane to cross the English Channel. It was built to prove that the sun can power large aircraft. However, although it was possible, it was not economically feasible. The aircraft was able to attain heights of 30,000 feet, but in crossing the channel it was only able to rise as high as 11,000 feet. It was never flown after that, but it did tour the country in a Smithsonian exhibit.

By the 1980s the creative, scientific community seemed to have turned its attention to the automobile. The Sunraycer, a solar-powered vehicle, won a 1987 cross-country race, speeding along a 2,000-mile route in Australia in a solar vehicle competition.

Latest in MacCready's parade of scientific wonders is the electronic car. In 1990 the Impact, a solar-powered car, was introduced. AeroInvironment, Inc., did the structural design for the body. General Motors expects to put the car on the market in 1994. In designing the body, AeroInvironment incorporated some of the technology it had developed for the Sunraycer.

As Simi Valley moves toward its new horizons, it is rich with the culture of the past and the visions of those who are planning for the future.

V The Great Divide

The valley continued about its business, growing and harvesting lush crops of apricots and walnuts. Unfortunately, it was not as secluded as its residents wished to believe. Although it was a community developing on its own terms, it could not escape the effects of major international events. Thus, World War II reached its long, bony fingers even into this valley, clutching and carrying away many of the community's young men. Some were reported missing in action and later discovered to be interred in German or Japanese prison camps. Some received distinguished service medals.

While the young men were fighting on foreign battlegrounds, the folks back home were doing their part for the war effort. Men and women alike served as air raid wardens, scanning the skies with binoculars, alerting Los Angeles if a suspicious plane was spotted overhead. All became rather adept at identifying the planes. Women would stand watch during the day, men at night.

Gasoline was rationed and many residents took to riding bicycles to conduct their local business. When cars were used, it was most often in car pools.

Vegetables and fruit were also pooled and brought to the cannery on Los Angeles Avenue in the Community Center to be processed and distributed co-op style. Saccharin was commonly used as a staple during the war years—though not in Mrs. Phelps' chocolate cake. Everyone contributed their sugar coupons to the Susana Knolls resident so they could enjoy her delicious cakes at the Brotherhood Suppers.

When meat became scarce, farmers' wives could count on walnuts to provide protein, grinding them into mock hamburger meat. Often these walnuts would be harvested by the local high school boys, who were dismissed for two weeks each harvest to bring in the crops since local help was so limited with everyone off to the war.

Many of the crops grown in the valley were sent overseas to soldiers serving on the western front, little realizing what a care package from home they were receiving. The produce was sent under the supervision of Lee Havins, who arrived in the valley in 1942. It was part of his military service to oversee the fruit pickers. He soon opened a small grocery store on Tapo Street just south of Los Angeles Avenue. Nearly 20 years later, in 1961, when Vons was scheduled to be built

Above: Al Main, the district commander of the American Legion, helps dedicate "34 Susan 8" Aircraft warning station at 5th and Pacific streets in the 1940s. Al Gardiner stands behind him and Pete Hovley stands at the end of the porch with his arms folded. Courtesy, Simi Valley Historical Society and Museum, Strathearn Historical Park

Right: Women pause from their labors at the Tapo Citrus Packing Association House in 1937. They are, from front to back, Betty Osborn, Jessie (last name unknown), Alma Timmons, Etta Ward, Uretta Turner, Minnie Turner, unknown, and Hattie Hansen. Courtesy, Simi Valley Historical Society and Museum, Strathearn Historical Park

on Tapo Street, he converted the business to a restaurant, El Gallito.

Following the war, the agricultural climate of the valley began to change. As apricots began to drop in price, farmers began pulling them out to replace them with Valencia oranges. Ernie Volz was actively farming during that transition time. He had arrived in the valley as an infant in a horse and buggy in 1918, a year after the Tapo Citrus Packing Association House was built. He lived within walking distance from the packinghouse in a small, 860-square-foot house on the southwest corner of Tapo Canyon and Avenida Simi. In the mid-1930s, when his dad died, Ernie assumed charge of the farming operation. He was 19 years old, just out of high school.

Ernie grew up as the area around him grew. He recalled the days when cattle and sheep were driven up and down Tapo Canyon. As a young boy, he dreamed of growing up to be a cowboy, inspired by the Gillibrand cowboys and their awe-inspiring rope and lasso tricks as they tried to round up a stray steer or two. He recalls trampling over hundreds of beautiful packing labels—little appreciated then, now collector's items—so heedlessly strewn about the packinghouse grounds.

With the drop in apricot prices, Volz, like those around him, went from the golden fruit to oranges, trying to keep in step with the times and a few steps ahead of the bills. Farmers were often at the mercy of the citrus companies as to the flow of their cash. Volz preferred selling his crop to Cal-Fame, which bought for cash. This was in marked contrast to Tapo Citrus, wherein the farmer had to wait until the end of the year to see his profits.

Likewise, the businessmen would be paid once a year. Neil Havens recalls the days when Bill Luna owned Green Acres market. Customers would be billed monthly based on detailed receipts

kept in Velveeta boxes under the counter. When a customer paid the bill, he would receive a free pie as a thank you. When times were tough it was not unusual for him to carry the account into the next year, if necessary. It was a time and a rhythm that required trust on everyone's part, and it was a manifestation of that trust that developed such a camaraderie among the local citizens. As Ernie Volz said, "It was a time when farmers helped each other and a handshake was a guarantee."

In the same spirit of neighbor helping neighbor, residents recall when Seaside Oil Company of Santa Barbara would work until midnight filling up tractors and trucks to save their customers the one-half cent per gallon increase that would become effective the following day.

By the 1950s Valencia oranges had largely replaced the other crops, becoming the single most important crop of the valley. Simi Valley's orange crop accounted for nearly 3 percent of Southern California's orange production.

Near the end of the decade, 1,900 acres were given to Valencia oranges, planted on large land-holdings and moderate farms, while 2,800 acres were set in walnuts. The walnuts were handled through the Simi Valley Walnut Growers Association, which had been established in 1921. In 1929 a modern plant replaced the original packinghouse, which was located on Valley Fair west of Riave's store. At one time the association was processing more than 1,800 tons of walnuts a year. However, although walnut production remained steadfast and plentiful, it never commanded the price that the citrus enjoyed. The packinghouse ceased operation in 1960.

A record harvest in 1958 produced 692,545 boxes of oranges, equaling 371 boxes per acre. But by 1967 the Tapo Citrus Packing Association House, used by every citrus grower south of the Santa Clara River, had closed its doors. Closed, too, were the labor camps located beside the packinghouse that provided housing for the immigrant workers. Other such labor housing existed in the valley, including some further up Tapo Canyon on the Patterson ranch. Neil Havens described the labor house on his father's property as complete with beds, redwood walls, well-stocked wood-piles, electricity, and showers. And of course, all the ranches had their bunkhouses for their cowboy staff.

The crops had been flourishing; life had been flourishing. But just over the horizon lurked change, major change, just waiting for the right circumstances. And they came—high taxes, low water tables. Soon the farmers had little choice but to sell their land. Developers were right there with a hearty handshake and escrow papers.

Developers are often presented as vultures waiting for the kill. But, in fact, many see them-

The orchards of Simi stretch to the horizon in this wide-angle photo. Courtesy, Ventura County Museum of History and Art

Right: Seen here in the mid-1940s the Knolls Methodist Church was located in a picturesque, pre-smog rural Simi landscape. Courtesy, Simi Valley Historical Society and Museum, Strathearn Historical Park

Below: The Reverend Thomas A. Grice leads the dedication service of the new Knolls Methodist Church in the mid-1940s. Courtesy, Simi Valley Historical Society and Museum, Strathearn Historical Park

selves as businessmen trying to fulfill a need. Once Simi Valley was discovered, it became an obvious solution to the high-priced housing in the San Fernando Valley. Land was less expensive. Consequently the developer could offer housing at a more affordable price. Unfortunately, before it was all over, Simi Valley housing became a little too affordable.

One of the first developments was the Pride tract, built by Tom Bowles between First and Fourth streets at Royal Avenue. A three-bedroom, two-bath home on the tract, which was constructed in 1956, sold for $11,995 with a $25 fee to secure it.

Paul Griffin of Griffin Homes remembered his first look at the sleepy community of Simi Valley:

I was looking for Tommy Bowles' Pride tract. He had told me how well it was doing so I drove into the valley. Although I lived all my life in San Fernando Valley, I had never been there before. I drove down over the pass, down Los Angeles Avenue, which was just a two-lane highway. There was just a field. There was hardly nothing there. I stopped at a little real estate office on the edge of Los Angeles Avenue and asked if he knew where the Pride subdivision was. "I never heard of it." When I found it, it was a mile away from him across the field on Royal.

I drove over and saw the demand for housing. The people really wanted to come to the country and buy houses. That was the first time the development community became aware of Simi Valley.

From that point until 1970, Simi Valley would be a magnet primarily for families seeking their first home.

Griffin began his first subdivision (the community's third) just down the street at Sinaloa and Royal. Jack Rosenberg of JBR Development built the valley's second subdivision next to Griffin's on Royal, west of Sinaloa.

The housing picture began to change drastically when Larwin Company moved into the valley. The first project it developed was south of Royal, west of Erringer, rapidly followed by a succession of others. During those early years it was credited or discredited (depending on one's viewpoint) with building more houses in the valley than all of the other developers put together.

The price of land was lucrative. The price per acre averaged $3,200 in contrast to San Fernando property, which could cost four to five times as much. Even within Simi Valley, the price could range considerably. Land without adequate water could be had for as little as $1,000 to $1,500 per acre. Land planted with walnut trees could command $1,500 to $2,500, while the prime citrus land could cost up to $3,500 per acre.

Although it was often a trying time for the local landowners who really did not want to sell, they very often held their own against the sophisticated businessmen they encountered.

Paul Griffin reminisced about one such meeting with Robert Harrington when he was negotiating to buy his property on Royal near the arroyo, adjacent to the Runkle ranch:

I remember going to visit him and sitting at the kitchen table. It's a delightful house. I remember the kitchen table with the oilcloth table cover. We sat there and had coffee and talked about his property. I was patiently trying to explain the flood problems on his property and he just looked at me like I didn't know what I was talking about. Couldn't understand that there were flood problems.

After I bought his property, I read his book in which he explained how the flood used to come across his property and he got washed away with the wagon and his horse . . . so he knew about the flood all the time I was explaining. He had been there first. But he wouldn't volunteer any information.

Griffin bought most of the Harrington property and built the Stonegate homes. Larwin bought the last piece around his house and developed it. The house still stands, looking down upon a cluster of tract homes.

Formerly, when a tract was opened, the purchaser bought the land and then built his own home according to the local zoning requirements. With the advent of the developers, subdivision homes became an assembly line operation.

In order to fill this surplus of homes, Larwin paved the way for very affordable housing, offering easy VA/FHA terms often requiring little or no money down. Such easy qualifications opened the door for many to purchase a home who were not really financially ready to do so. Thus, by the middle of the 1960s, the valley was overrun with abandoned homes ripe for foreclosures and easy buy outs. The quick turnover of homeowners gave the valley a very flighty image that demanded conscientious steps and time to overcome.

In 1960, as the available housing became more abundant, the population of the valley was 8,110, an increase of 5,000 since 1950. By 1970 the population would skyrocket to 61,150, representing a 1,930 percent increase in 20 years.

Until now the emotional climate of the valley had been one of giving—giving to the neighbors, giving to the soil, giving produce to the world. But now the focus became one of getting—of getting one's piece of the pie. It seemed the new Simi was created just to supply homes. Sixty-five percent of the developed land was given to single-family homes, a strong departure from the normal 40 percent of a typical U.S. city.

The influx of new people meant culture shock for many of the longtime residents. Land that they had so long tended and nourished was now being suffocated under cement slabs. Trees they had planted and nurtured were being cut down. Not everyone they met on the street had a familiar face.

These homes from the "Alpine" tract on Rowland Street were among many such structures that were built during the housing boom that began in the mid-1950s. Photo by Phil Parker

Homeowners flocked to Simi during the 1960s because of the availability of affordable housing with proximity to Los Angeles. Photo by Phil Parker

Often they were the faces of distraught women with small children who were discovering all was not well in paradise. The family life they eagerly sought was being drained by the long hours their husbands' jobs now required with lengthened travel time to and from work. Simi was rapidly becoming a community of young new families who had no extended family nearby, and initially, probably few friends. The sturdy community of the 1950s was being displaced by a population not yet steady on its feet.

As more homes were built, the plots of land began to be divided into even smaller plots of land. Soon newcomers had only enough property for token vegetable gardens. The size of home lots became a vocal issue right from the beginning.

Leonard Kline, president of the Simi Valley Chamber of Commerce, wrote in 1959 to the Ventura County Board of Supervisors challenging the one-fifth-acre lots that were becoming prevalent. It was the contention of the chamber directors that, not only was one-fifth of an acre insufficient space for a family to function well, but, also, the increased population that resulted put a strain on fire service, water supply, sewer systems, and educational facilities. On behalf of the chamber, Kline called for one-quarter-acre lots. A public meeting followed in which the county supervisors held that one-fifth-acre lots did not strain public services since permission to build was only granted based upon the reports of the public service departments. They further argued that one-fifth-acre zoning, in fact, would mean only 3.6 homes per acre once easements and streets were considered.

Local residents, on the other hand, made a loud pitch for one-third-acre lots, charging that overcrowding was the very reason they had left the San Fernando Valley and sought the openness of Simi Valley. In the meantime, Griffin had placed his "Cavalier" homes on the market.

Reinforcing the homeowners' position, these one-third-acre lots were selling like hotcakes at $14,750. Thus began a debate that continues today.

Supporting the one-fifth-acre lots was County Supervisor Alan Robertson, who hailed from Simi Valley. His father, Tom Robertson, had been one of the owners of the Hacienda Sinaloa Company, a loan and investment company whose holdings included the 500-acre sweep of land at Sinaloa Road south of Royal. At one time this property was the site of the local cemetery. In 1895, however, when the adobe road leading to the hill upon which it sat had become too muddy and slippery, Miss Clementine Paranteau moved the cemetery to its present location. Upon the recommendation of the Ventura County Cultural Heritage Board, application has been made to gain historical landmark status for the nearly 100-year-old Pioneer Cemetery at the northwestern edge of Erringer Park.

Married in 1919, Tom and his wife, Dorothy Utt, had lived in Los Mochis, Sinaloa, Mexico, for six years before coming to Simi Valley with his father, Louis Robertson, or "Dad." The Hacienda Sinaloa, named in honor of the Mexican state of Sinaloa, became a major producer of tomatoes for the local canneries. This led to the wholesale production of tomato seeds, which were marketed across the country. As Hacienda Sinaloa flourished, more and more relatives arrived, including Robertson's cousin, Jack Bunker, who with his wife, Jackie, had a house for many years up Sinaloa Road. There they grew acres of oranges. The acres were carefully irrigated, Jackie Bunker explained shortly before her death in 1990. They were first plotted out on paper to determine where the water would run down for maximum efficiency. Since it took nearly five years for an orange tree to produce a crop, there was not much time for error.

With the arrival of North American Aviation Company in 1955, Tom Robertson accurately predicted major population growth. Wanting no part of it, he returned to his beloved Sinaloa, Mexico.

Thereupon, Alan Robertson became one of the first minor subdividers, creating 27 lots among the orange trees overlooking Sinaloa Reservoir. The Robertsons had built the reservoir in 1929,

Mt. McCoy rises above the Sinaloa Ranch at the western end of Simi Valley. Courtesy, Simi Valley Historical Society and Musuem, Strathearn Historical Park

erecting a dam to hold back the water that gathered in a large, natural depression. If there was not enough rain in the winter, water could be run off from the "lake" at cheaper rates than those offered by the Metropolitan Water Company. If there was too much water, it would spill over and run into the ditch along Madera (formerly Kujawski) Road. Cattails were a common sight.

The existence of cattails, however, did not represent a surplus of water throughout the valley. In fact, county officials and local residents were becoming quite concerned about the local water levels. The water that had been so promiscuously promised to the original colonists was rapidly disappearing. There was no longer any denying that the water level was limited. The entire economic structure of the valley was undergoing major change as a result. Farmers were having to sell their homesteads. An influx of new homeowners was beginning to make unforeseen demands on the water supply.

As early as 1953, efforts were begun to import water to the valley basin and beyond. The Calleguas Water District was formed to serve the southern half of Ventura County from the Arroyo Simi to the Santa Clarita Valley.

Six years later the voters in the Calleguas district passed a $30-million bond to import water from the Colorado River through the Metropolitan Water District system, which, at the time, only extended as far as Burbank.

Until this time water sources in the valley had been very fragmented. Mutuals like Kadota Fig, Tapo, and La Placentia were fully owned by the homeowners they served. Wright Ranch Mutual was still owned by the developers; ownership would pass to the homeowners after 30 years. A few very small water companies were owned by families. Once Metropolitan water came to town, the state would no longer allow well water, the quality of which had been steadily decreasing since 1951. It was obviously time to coordinate the elements into a cohesive, workable entity.

Thus, a meeting was held in the La Placentia area with representatives from 15 of the 16 companies. The meeting was led by Harry Shetrone, a director for both the Calleguas Water District and the La Placentia Mutual. The only company not represented at the meeting was Kadota Fig. Trouble was beginning to brew. Glen Costin had arrived from Texas to manage J. Paul Getty's assets and to acquire land and utilities on his behalf. He, therefore, had made a purchase offer to both La Placentia and Kadota Fig. La Placentia turned him down; Kadota Fig was still considering the offer. Thus, they stayed away from the meeting. However, at the prompting of Gordon Lindeen, Duane Leonhardt did attend the meeting as an unofficial representative, unwittingly beginning a long-term involvement with civic affairs.

Once Calleguas brought Metropolitan to the valley, it would be incumbent upon each mutual company to hook up to the transmission lines. For then, water could only be retailed through the Calleguas district. Metropolitan would not deal with small independent companies. For some of the mutuals it would mean building a one-mile pipe; for most, the pipe would need to be considerably longer. Through the course of the meeting, it became painfully obvious that the companies were not going to be able to raise the capital to hook up with the main pipeline.

In the meantime, Kadota Fig Mutual had opted to sell to Glen Costin. However, some members of the mutual were strongly against the idea. They were determined that Kadota Fig would remain public. A lawsuit ensued to stop the pending sale.

Seeking a more amicable solution, Shetrone and Leonhardt established a committee to create a county waterworks district. In 1961 County Waterworks District #9 was formed. This included La Placentia, Wright Ranch, and Kadota Fig. Now the water resources would be unified under county sponsorship and administration. Now bonds could be issued to raise funds to hook up with the Calleguas Water District. The mutuals did not have that power to raise money.

Two other districts already existed at the time. District #3 served the Simi Colony and was steadily growing. District #8 had been formed in the Santa Susana Knolls area two years before.

The idea of county water districts was well received. Soon other mutuals were considering the benefits. Another waterworks district was formed when the Texas tract was developed. The property had belonged to Glen Costin, who sold it to Belwood and Alpine. Tapo Mutual, which had not joined District #9, began having financial problems. Initially, District #9 piped water to it from its own lines. Soon, however, Tapo Mutual formed its own county waterworks district. Eventually all the local districts would be joined as one entity, Waterworks District #8, to be operated by the City of Simi Valley.

County Supervisor Robert LeFevre, in 1962, formed an advisory board with representatives from each district. Duane Leonhardt, member-at-large, was named chairman, beginning a 20-year association with the Ventura County Waterworks Advisory Commission.

Success came in 1963. On November 15, a gala ceremony was held at the Ranch Club Roller Rink, formerly a walnut packing shed, to commemorate the arrival of Colorado River water to the Calleguas Water District. The water was piped along a 26-mile line from Burbank through the Santa Susana Mountains. It had only taken 10 years!

Honorary Mayor Lou Wright served as master of ceremonies of the event, which was cosponsored by Joe Appleton, president of the chamber of commerce and original director of the Calleguas Water District, and by Frank Schroeder, publisher of the *Simi Valley News and Advertiser.*

The pipeline, which had been tunneled through the Santa Susana Mountains, would eventually continue to Oxnard. Officials predicted the new water supply would stimulate economic development throughout the entire county. California Assistant Attorney General Charles Coker called the supply of water a miracle that would "bring life and happiness to Ventura County. The water will come but will not recede, flow but will not ebb. Long may the water flow." The newly created County Waterworks District #9 was the first to receive the "imported" water.

In 1965 Bard Reservoir was dedicated with Joe Appleton, now a county supervisor, presiding. The reservoir, located on Olsen Road, was named after Richard Bard, first president of the Calleguas Municipal Water District, which proudly built the reservoir without federal funds or loans. With the reservoir, excess water from winter could be stored to provide relief during the hot summer months or serve as an emergency supply if there were ever any problems receiving water through the pipeline during normal operation.

Perhaps now the abundance of water promised to new residents nearly 100 years ago would finally exist. Bard Reservoir certainly looked more capable of supporting a paddleboat than did the Arroyo Simi, falsely depicted as it was on the treatises distributed by the first developers in the

Fourteen of the Simi Valley Woman's Club's past presidents gather on the occasion of the group's 50th anniversary in October 1964. Photo by Maxine Rees, courtesy, The Simi Valley Woman's Club

valley all those many years ago. Residents now could trust that the water they needed was available.

When officials first initiated the process to bring water to the valley, the population was approximately 4,000. When it arrived in 1963, the population had climbed to 24,719. By 1970 it would be 61,150.

With the ever-burgeoning population, visions of cityhood danced in the eyes of several forward-looking citizens. Since it was a major step, however, it would require some time to raise the consciousness of the electorate.

The initial attempt for cityhood started in February 1964. However, it never really got off the ground as proponents of incorporation were unable to garner the required signatures to put the issue on the ballot. The major hitch was the lack of cooperation from the developers and major landowners. Not only did the measure require signatures of 51 percent of the registered voters, but approval from the owners of at least 51 percent of the open land also was necessary. Without cooperation from the developers, cityhood was a moot issue. That first group wisely put the idea on the back burner for the required two years. When the time had passed, a new group with new energy was ready and raring to tackle the idea of cityhood.

Prominent in the second bid for cityhood were Harry Shetrone and Duane Leonhardt with a full engine of civic steam, having recently come through the water and sanitation issues. John Montgomery, the young son of Wayne Montgomery, was now, at the age of 21, a county supervisor. In that capacity he sent an invitation to every organization in the valley requesting that a representative attend a meeting to discuss the idea of cityhood. This was one of the most roundly attended meetings in the community, with spokespeople from the Chamber of Commerce to the Busy Hands Garden Club.

Harry Shetrone, nominated by Frank Schroeder, was chosen chairman of the newly formed committee to study the feasibility of cityhood. When studies concluded that the quest for cityhood should be pursued, the committee officially became the City Formation Committee with Shetrone at the helm. Leonhardt served as chairman of the petition drive; his job was to canvass every neighborhood. Mary Speilman was secretary.

The signatures from the voters were gathered. But, like the committee before them, the signatures of the landowners were harder to come by.

Shetrone met with Larry Wineberg of the Larwin Company, a major landowner. Putting a little pressure on him, Shetrone reminded Wineberg that Larwin was not entirely in the community's good graces. Its rapid development of the area and seeming unwillingness to help develop roads had not endeared the company to the valley. Shetrone offered that signing the petition was a golden opportunity to redeem the company's standing. Apparently Wineberg recognized the wisdom in this thinking. The petition was signed. The committee took it to the county board of supervisors, who authorized the election for cityhood.

The work had just begun for the committee. Anticipating a budget of $4,000 to promote the

Officially opened on August 15, 1965, Simi Valley Community Hospital began as a 50-bed facility with 28 physicians on staff. In 1967 the hospital's name was changed to Simi Valley Adventist Hospital. As the hospital celebrated its 25th anniversary in 1990, the staff comprised 235 physicians and boasted 215 beds. Photo by Fred Bauermeister Photography

idea of cityhood, they established the "404 Club," signifying, among other things, that the valley was expected to be the 404th city in California if the election was successful. With this thought in mind, 404 buttons were sold at $10 each to raise the needed $4,000 revenue.

The ballot was to be twofold: to determine cityhood and to select a city council. Enthusiasm for the council was overwhelming, with 55 candidates. Shetrone, too, became a candidate, stepping down from his chairmanship. Leonhardt then became head of the incorporation committee.

Days before the election, the committee delegated their final $400 to a four-page ad in the *Enterprise.* The ad ran, but apparently the *Enterprise* never billed the committee.

Despite the advertisement and the campaign efforts, the measure for cityhood was narrowly defeated by fewer than 400 votes. Consequently, the selection of the council became a moot point. However, David Strathearn, Jr., earned the most votes and would have served as the city's first mayor had the valley become a city.

As it was, another two years had to pass before the next attempt at cityhood could be made. In 1968 a group was ready to try again. This effort was led by Glenn Schmidt. The $400 that the *Enterprise* did not collect for the previous committee's ad became the start-up funds for this bid for cityhood.

The pump was sufficiently primed this time. Voting took place September 30, 1969, with 59 percent of the 17,701 registered voters participating. The measure passed 6,454 to 3,365. The field of council candidates had shrunk to a mere 37 this time around. Lester Cleveland, the candidate with the most votes, was designated mayor. Second vote-getter James Dougherty became mayor pro tem. Other members of that first council were David Sigmon, Richard Ostler, and Howard Rogo. In that same election the residents were directed to choose a city name. Although there was much debate, votes ran nearly 2 to 1 favoring Simi Valley over Santa Susana. The city of Simi Valley became incorporated October 10, 1969, as the second-largest city in Ventura County, with a population of 56,000.

The first city council meeting was held in the multipurpose room of Royal High School before an audience of several hundred. They quickly moved through a 30-item agenda. Their first order of business was to declare a 90-day zoning freeze on the city to all but residential development. That was perhaps bravado.

In a 1983 interview Dougherty recalled: "We walked into a room and had absolutely no idea what to do. We didn't even know enough to get on a plane to Sacramento to file the incorporation papers." Later, as a Ventura County supervisor, he was able to offer valuable assistance to neighboring Moorpark when it attained cityhood.

They soon learned how quickly decisions could backfire. The freeze on zoning meant that two prospective companies, Shasta Trailer Company and Oberg Construction, could not set up operation in the new city. That meant a loss of jobs for local residents, who were rapidly becoming travel-weary commuting to jobs out of the area. At the urging of the Simi Valley Chamber of Commerce and the Ventura County Economic Development Association, the council enacted emergency industrial zoning on 120 acres, making it possible for those businesses to proceed as long as detailed development plans were approved before construction. The nine-member planning commission, which was authorized at the first council meeting, would oversee this.

While the valley was trying to attain self-destiny through cityhood, efforts were also under way to provide easier access to the realms beyond the valley. In 1964, following years of negotiation, the California Highway Commission determined the route of the Simi Valley Freeway. Three paths had been considered, rejected, and reconsidered. (One proposed route would have passed right through the Strathearn adobe!)

It was not until 1966 that construction actually began. It was none too soon. A Los Angeles Regional Traffic Study (LARTS) in 1964 indicated that during early morning rush hours (6 to 8 a.m.), more than 2,200 cars traveled along the two-lane road through the Santa Susana Pass. Although the traffic jam occurred leaving the valley, those who were staying behind did not escape the consequences. In 1966, in an effort to alleviate the increasing traffic problem, the Simi Valley Unified School District changed the opening hours for the local schools. High school would begin at 8:30 rather than 9:00; elementary at 9:00 instead of 8:30. It was hoped that the staggered hours would help relieve some of the congestion at the east end.

The community was jubilant when freeway construction was to begin. Festivities began a week in advance of the long-awaited event. The local board of realtors and the Moose Lodge sponsored a Simi Valley Freeway A Go-Go dance. Flyers and banners abounded. Then on April 23, 1966, the momentous time arrived. Thousands attended that ground-breaking ceremony, including County Supervisor John Montgomery and several state officials. Miss Simi Valley Freeway, Susan Welch, helped press the detonator that blasted the first chunk of rock from the mountain.

Construction continued for the next 26 months. Residents were warned by four short whistles when an explosion was to come. One long whistle meant all was clear. Through the course of construction nearly 30,000 pounds of explosive powder were detonated per day. Soon, however, it was time for the citizens to make the noise. The first lap of the freeway, stretching from Topanga Canyon Boulevard through the mountainside to Kuehner, was complete. A giant breakthrough celebration was staged on July 8, 1968. County Supervisor Joe Appleton was master of ceremonies. As part of the proceedings, a cavalcade was formed with one group on the Simi Valley side and one on the Chatsworth side. At a given signal, each group began the virgin 3.8-mile trek "through" the mountain. The Simi Valley cluster of cars then made the return trip to participate further in the festivities.

The six-lane freeway would eventually be 26 miles long, stretching from Moorpark to the Foothill Freeway in Sylmar. It was a monstrous undertaking. Only the thrill of the convenience it provided could compensate for the disruption it must have caused. From the first segment alone, 8.5 million cubic yards of soil were removed. In Simi Valley, meanwhile, soil was being added to the freeway construction. Soil from the Crinklaw property north of Erringer was removed to create pads for new homes. The soil was sold by the ton and moved by land movers across the Havens property, breaking water pipes daily. It became the 22-by-300-foot base for the Tapo Canyon-to-Sycamore stretch of the freeway.

The second segment of the freeway was completed on October 28; another cavalcade was held. By 1976 the freeway stretched to Moorpark. The final link was a five-mile stretch from De Soto Avenue in Chatsworth to Balboa Boulevard in Granada Hills, which was completed in December 1982. Future plans call for the freeway to connect with Highway 23. On May 12, 1970, the road to the world was officially named State Route 118, Simi Valley-San Fernando Valley Freeway. Although it was a route to the world, initially it was a very exclusive freeway. One could often find oneself the sole traveler on the freeway in the late evening hours after all the commuter traffic had reached its destination. It was a mixed blessing when the final segment of the freeway was complete, however, for now the valley was unquestionably connected with the outside world. And it was a two-way street. Residents could exit. Strangers could enter.

As the city scurried to keep up with the future, it became painfully clear that the rich past would have to be preserved or lost. The Simi Valley Historical Society was established in 1964 with Eleanor Taylor as the first president. The city was very fortunate when the Strathearn family donated six and one-half acres that became the Strathearn Historical Museum. The bequest included the Strathearn home, with its legacy from the Spanish and Chumash periods, and has since grown to include one of the original Colony homes, the original library, and the barn from the Adrian Wood ranch. The historical park operates under the auspices of the Rancho Simi Park and Recreation District and is conscientiously maintained as a preserve of the city's rich heritage

The Simi Valley Board of Realtors broke ground on a new home in 1990, the same year it celebrated its 25th birthday. Photo by Fred Bauermeister Photography

by city historian Pat Havens. The entire project is supported by a very active historical society that sponsors an old-fashioned, good-time barn dance annually.

The Strathearns donated the land when they began breaking up their holdings. Taxes were getting so high it became very costly to hold on to property. Thus, Bob Strathearn and Dave Strathearn, Jr., in conjunction with Union Oil, formed Moreland Investment Company with the intention of developing their vast holdings on the western end of town, extending into Moorpark. Union Oil was an outgrowth of Simi Land and Water Company, which originally owned all mineral rights on the property which they had sold to Union Oil for $10 and other considerations. If property owners did not have mineral rights, they could not develop the property. Therefore, the Strathearn brothers joined forces with Union Oil to regain mineral rights to their grandfather's property.

The county had approved zoning for the little villages they planned to develop. The master plan had been drawn. However, a real estate recession caused Union Oil to bow out of the deal, and the development was never realized.

They were able, however, to develop another project that had a more unique, long-term effect on the valley. They built Simi Bowl in 1963. For many, many years it offered one of the main sources of entertainment in the area. For the young housewives moving to Simi it was a godsend, offering them the chance to meet other young women in the valley and to make friends. It was the sole bowling facility until the mid-1980s when Brunswick Bowl moved into the eastern end of town.

In 1965 Metropolitan Theatres built a drive-in on Tierra Rejada Road, still the only drive-in in the immediate area and home of the immensely popular Sunday Swap Meet.

The valley was growing up, going through the gangly stage of puberty. It was trying to be sophisticated but lacking the experience and expertise to pull it off at this time. But it was moving in the right direction. Yes, Los Angeles Avenue was an eyesore with its glut of business signs. And yes, crops of homes were towering above the soil faster and thicker than weeds. But a new consciousness was developing, instilling in the new families the value of civic pride that the longtime residents so clearly felt. With the influx of new people came new energy and new ideas. Growth was inevitable.

When Bob Ain created his Ford Agency on First Street, it was incumbent upon him to name the new side street he would share in developing. He named it Easy Street—a very apropos name for the time. It reflected the attitude and intention of the community. There was a sense that if they worked together with innovation and foresight, everyone in town could be living on Easy Street. While the country was falling apart over the Vietnam War, Simi Valley was coming together.

VI

Threshold of the Future

T he valley's surge for newness and innovation was most obvious in the configuration of the new city with its city council-manager format. From the beginning, the philosophy was people-oriented, a willingness to take a chance on new approaches to standard city problems. The community was young, the movers and shakers were young, and they moved at a fast and idealistic pace.

Following a heated city council meeting in April 1971, 18 months after incorporation, the city decided to break with the Ventura County Sheriff's Department and form its own police force. Thus the Community Safety Agency was born, falling under the auspices of the Human Resources Department. Breaking away from the traditional authoritarian concept of a police officer, the city council and the first city manager, Bruce Altman, developed a "humanized law enforcement" team, 30 members strong. Simi Valley was the first city to use this concept. The agency, with its crisis intervention thrust, was headed by a civilian director, or community safety administrator. The military concept of rank—sergeants, lieutenants, chiefs—was gone. The emphasis of their work was on prevention, working with the community shoulder to shoulder.

Perhaps the most striking aspect of this "force" was the uniform. It included charcoal gray slacks, white or green shirts, and kelly green blazers with the Community Safety Agency emblem on the pocket. The city council selected the color from among four possible choices suggested by the Simi Valley Art Association. All officers traveled in standard civilian cars marked only with the city emblem. Although the city received nationwide attention for its innovative concept, for some officers it was a difficult adjustment. They felt they were not taken seriously. The force became a traditional police department in 1979 with Don Rush as the first chief of police. The Simi Valley Police Department now has more than 100 sworn officers. Despite a few years of internal friction, the Simi Valley Police Department was given a thumbs-up by the 1985 Ventura County Grand Jury. The department continues to enjoy a fine reputation, having recently participated in major drug busts. On the prevention level one of the department's main thrusts is the Drug Awareness and Resistance Education (DARE) program, which is conducted in the local schools. So impressive is their program that Nancy Reagan paid a personal visit to Sycamore Elementary School to

Al and Mary Salo dance to the tunes of the 1950s during the Simi Valley Days Parade in 1987. Courtesy, The Enterprise

Two officers of the Simi Valley Police Department pose proudly with their vehicle. Originally established as the Community Safety Agency in 1971, the police force now has more than 100 sworn officers. Photo by Fred Bauermeister Photography

acknowledge the participation of the students and officers.

From the beginning Simi Valley was a city on the move, facing challenges squarely as they encountered them. Almost immediately the city council and city officials had to grapple with the issues of land use and growth. Now that they had autonomy, they wanted to make more pertinent decisions than they felt the county had done. As early as November 1973 the council approved the planning commission's general plan for controlled growth. The city's open space plan was lauded by state officials as one of the earliest and best programs in the state. Although early projected growth figures predicted 125,000 in 1985, the fact is, in 1990 there were just over 102,000 residents.

In 1972 came one of the biggest challenges to the moral fiber of the community. Gambling reared its greedy head and kicked up quite a storm of controversy. Open debates and meetings were held in homes throughout the valley. Proponents for the pastime waged a heavy campaign. However, the city made its claim about the quality of life in Simi Valley. The initiative was defeated 2 to 1.

Having rejected the possible revenues from gambling operations, the immediate concern, now that enough of the city's operating agencies were in place, was a tax base to generate money to maintain the agencies and provide further programs. In the mid-1970s a campaign was launched to attract clean, nonpolluting industry into the valley to offset the "bedroom community" stigma. As it was, 90 percent of the valley's work force commuted outside of the valley. They also shopped out of the valley, leaving valuable sales tax revenues in other communities. Besides the convenience of shopping where they worked, many residents felt Simi Valley offered very little in the way of reliable businesses and product selection. It became the intent of the city council and the Chamber of Commerce to entice them to shop at home. "Shop Simi Valley" bumper stickers soon became a common sight. Theirs was a twofold attempt. First, they wanted to bring more jobs into the valley to keep the residents at home, and second, they wished to build a consciousness and pride in the business community that did exist in the valley.

Time was one of the best defenses. As young families left town once they found that a dream and a dollar were not enough to maintain a home, they were replaced with more financially secure young couples who were able to stay and intended to stay. Likewise, businesses were adjusting to the demands of dealing with a more sophisticated, stable clientele. They began to understand the needs and wants of their customers, thus providing better service and products. In the meantime the city and chamber made an all-out effort to bring compatible light industry businesses to the community. Whereas in 1972 there were no more than 3,000 jobs available (with the Simi Valley Unified School District as the largest employer), by 1990 the city offered well over 10,000 jobs. Outside of the school district the largest employers are Farmers Insurance, housed in the city's first and only "high rise," a five-story building, and First Interstate Bancard, the regional headquarters for the company.

The business community has continued to thrive under the direction of Nancy Bender, executive director of the Chamber of Commerce. With the assistance of a very strong chamber board, membership has grown to more than 1,000 businesses. Bender, a former member of the city council, was named director of the chamber in 1982 when she applied at the urging of Councilwoman Vicky Howard. Many innovative programs have been initiated under Bender's direction, including the Leadership Simi Valley program, begun in 1988, wherein young businesspeople participate in an extensive eight-month leadership training course, learning all the ins and outs of the functions of the city. (The chamber had originated in 1915 but had never gained momentum. It resurfaced in 1953, tottering along on shaky legs until it became a leader among chambers.) In June 1990 the National Association of Membership Directors of Chambers of Commerce named the Simi Valley chamber one of the 10 best chambers in U.S. cities with less than 200,000 population.

That first decade of cityhood was a time of trial and error. Sometimes it took a while for the weaknesses in the system to emerge. Before the influx of people, the valley was very cohesive. While each resident was independent enough to speak his own piece, there are few accounts of disharmony among the residents, a remarkable quality in and of itself. But there was something about cityhood. Maybe it was because they had not sweated shoulder to shoulder bringing in a crop. Maybe it was simply that now each citizen had official permission to speak on a level that could generate immediate response, as opposed to talking to county officials. Because they could express opposing ideas, citizens very often did. And they made no bones about council decisions they didn't like.

One such vocal group was the Simi Valley Businessmen's Council, which gained strength before the chamber became the solid organization it is today. In the wake of Proposition 13, at the instigation of this group, Mayor Ginger Gherardi and Councilman Bill Carpenter were recalled in

United States Congressman Elton Gallegly (R-Simi Valley) meets with constituents in an open house in the 21st district. Courtesy, The Enterprise

May 1979. Gherardi and Carpenter, who served as head of the Sanitation District, had raised the sewer rate from $5 to $10. The Businessmen's Council apparently believed this was not in keeping with the spirit of Proposition 13. The sewer rates were lowered, but not before careers were damaged. However, as two new openings were then created on the board, the Businessmen's Council sponsored two candidates. Elton Gallegly and Gregory Stratton also ran and won the positions. Both continue to serve in government today.

Gallegly held his position on the council until the 1982 election, when the first separate vote for mayor was on the ballot. Previously, whichever elected councilmember received the most votes routinely was selected by the other council members to serve as mayor, strictly a figurehead position for city functions. Gallegly became the first elected mayor. In 1986 Gallegly expanded his horizons, running for and winning the seat for the 21st U.S. Congressional District, the first person from the area to attain that level. He serves on the House Foreign Affairs Committee and was one of only two Republicans to travel to Brussels to participate in the negotiations with the Soviets in 1989.

From his national perspective, Gallegly contends, "There are few communities in this nation, if any, that have more people who epitomize President Bush's 'thousand points of light.'"

His position gives Simi Valley constant national recognition. As he has stated:

They know where I'm from. I always say I have not been to or heard of any district that I would trade anyone for. I appreciate that I have the good fortune of being able to have the job I have and go back to my home and go out and pick oranges off my tree.

The recognition has spilled over into the local citizenry. The Reverend Frank Witman, minister since 1969 of the United Methodist Church, was invited upon Gallegly's recommendation to give the opening prayer at the House of Representatives in May 1990.

Simi Valley has sent representatives to the state level of government as well. Republican Cathie Wright was first elected to the California State Assembly in 1980, representing assembly district number 37. Wright had her first successful bid for city council in 1978. One year later she was chosen to serve as mayor. She then moved on to the state level, where she has authored many bills including several on child care.

Stratton, who was elected to the council along with Gallegly, served as mayor pro tem from 1980 to 1986. When Gallegly ran for congressional office, Stratton waged his campaign for mayor, winning the 1986 election. He was reelected in 1988.

Stratton, whose tenure in local politics is the longest running in the city's short history, is a product of one of the most innovative and effective programs instituted by that first city council—the Neighborhood Council program. The city was divided into five geographical areas

Assemblywoman Cathie Wright, a former mayor of Simi Valley, addresses the audience at the 20th anniversary celebration of cityhood. City Hall is behind her. Courtesy, The Enterprise

(now four) with a maximum of 13 representatives from each area who meet on a regular basis. Although anyone is welcome to apply, the candidates are screened by the council before being selected for appointment.

It is the function of the neighborhood council to hear issues that affect their portion of the city. Often representatives from major developments will first enlist the ear of the neighborhood council members for it is known that their approval or disapproval could carry significant weight when passed along to the voting city council members. Occasionally input at the neighborhood level can alert the council that an issue is brewing where none had been anticipated, as when the Mormon church sought permission in 1988 to build a major facility on Sinaloa Road. The proposal met with great resistance from the neighborhood. However, before a packed, vocal gathering of church members and neighborhood residents, the city planning commission approved the project.

The Neighborhood Council program was begun in 1972, and has spawned many civic leaders who have gone on to hold significant elected and appointed positions in the city. In 1989, unfortunately, apathy threatened to shut down the program. With nurturing, urging, and cajoling from the

Nine-year-old Kirsten Nicholas participates in the 100-yard freestyle event in the 11th annual Labor Day swim meet at the Rancho Simi Community Park swimming pool. Courtesy, The Enterprise

city council, however, the program has regained its momentum.

It was also in 1972 that the city began its bus program, initially using minibuses. The small buses have now given way to standard buses that run the full length of the valley, with connections to the Southern California Rapid Transit District. Or, if they prefer, travelers can once again take the commuter train, catching it at the outdoor platform just west of the proposed Tapo Canyon Road extension south of the railroad tracks.

That same year the city began to look for a permanent location for its administrative offices. Although in 1969 the council had immediately decided to meet in the old courthouse, it was quickly outgrowing the facility. So it chose a locale rich in historical significance—42 prime acres at Tapo Canyon and Alamo roads. The land was purchased from four landowners, including Ernie Volz. The 860-square-foot home he had lived in his entire life became temporary offices for the developers of the new Civic Center. The land was the center of much activity during the valley's agricultural heyday. The city hall itself now sits where the apricot pitting shed used to be. The Department of Motor Vehicles, which opened in May 1989, sits on the ground of the labor camp.

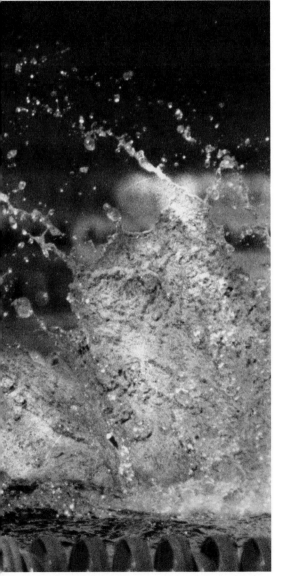

Just to the left of the employment office and about 200 feet back stood the Tapo Citrus Packing Association House. The land that Volz had purchased for $7,000 per acre was sold to the city for $36,500 per half-acre. Following the sale of his home and land to the city, Volz moved just down the street. Through the back windows of his home, he has been able to watch the construction of the new courthouse.

Aside from a few fruit trees Volz attends to on his own property, the only remains of his agricultural days are a cluster of orange trees on the southeast corner of the city Civic Center complex. Volz planted them in 1952. They were threatened in February 1990, but the Simi Valley Planning Commission gave them a reprieve. The commission approved a city application for a Civic Center office building on the condition that the trees remain standing until ground is broken for a 8,150-square-foot restaurant on that spot, scheduled for 1992.

Although a prosperous community requires much of its land be given to revenue-producing businesses and product-purchasing homeowners, lands must be left open to keep the community balanced. Play space is as vital as work space.

Simi Valley is a family community, a city of young people. The median age is 25.9. The city has taken great pains, through the park district, to establish facilities for the entire family to enjoy.

The Rancho Simi Recreation and Park District was formed by a vote of the citizens in October 1961. The independent organization received its charter on October 25, 1961, eight years before cityhood. The five-member elected board makes policy regarding all the parkland that falls within its 113-square-mile jurisdiction, which encompasses areas of Agoura. David Strathearn, Jr., served as the district's first chairman. The majority of the district's funding comes from property taxes. Parkland is generally acquired through developers who are required to dedicate a portion of their development to the good of the community.

Currently Rancho Simi oversees 53 park sites, 32 of which are partially or fully developed, as well as the nine-hole Sinaloa Public Golf Course on the west end and the 18-hole Simi Hills course on the east end of the valley. A variety of classes, from crafts to dance to self-defense, is offered for all ages. The district is often host to invitational swim meets at its 50-meter Rancho Simi pool. The most popular of the parks is Rancho Simi Community Park, dedicated December 21, 1974. The 33.5-acre park is the busiest, with a 2.5-acre lake that is home to more than 400 ducks and geese. The lake is also regularly stocked with fish and, since no license is required, any child can be Huck Finn for a day. On July 3, 1976, the Bicentennial Arbor and Amphitheater was erected, financed—in true community spirit—solely through cash donations from residents, business groups, and social clubs. The annual Fourth of July fireworks show, cosponsored by the Rotary Club of Simi Valley, draws thousands annually for a lavish display of community involvement and dramatic sky art.

One of the enduring charms of Simi Valley is its rural atmosphere. Although the population has expanded significantly from the horse-and-buggy days, the horse is still alive and well in this city. The southwestern rim of the valley is dedicated to equestrian zoning as is a coveted area in the center of town along Adam Road. The Bridle Path Homes snaking up the southern hillside are a magnet for horse people, who are drawn to the open trails throughout the development and the 1,700-acre open park, accessible only to residents.

A longtime dream of the equestrian segment of the community came true in April 1990, when the Arroyo Simi Equestrian Center had its grand opening ceremony. The nine-acre center proudly offers a 300-by-150-foot equestrian arena with 8,100 square feet of corral space. The idea for the center, located off Royal Avenue between Sycamore and Sequoia, first began in 1974. In 1986 it verged on reality when the Santa Monica Conservancy helped to secure a $356,000 grant. The trailhead will connect the Rim of the Valley Trail corridor to the Arroyo Simi Backbone Trail. When the trailhead is complete, riders will be able to travel from Simi to the sea, experiencing the area much as it was when people first began arriving in the valley. The local horse enthusiasts are all saddled, ready, and waiting.

Equestrian riders annually have an opportunity to strut their stuff during the Simi Valley Days Parade, one of the high points of the weeklong celebration commemorating the city's heritage.The first official Pioneer Day celebration as we know it was held in 1962. It was a one-day affair featuring a rodeo and a parade that started at Center Junior High School. For many years the event was coordinated by the Simi Valley Jaycees. When that organization encountered membership difficulties, the Simi Valley Chamber of Commerce took over the function. The very first "pioneer day" celebration, however, took place in 1932, involving many of the pioneer families. Like its modern-day counterpart, the celebration began with a parade. Ball games and a street dance were also the order of the day. Rose Printz, who had been postmistress since 1904, organized the event. Learning that it was the year of the Bicentennial Postal Celebration, she felt such an event would be a good way to put Simi on the map. As president of the Simi Pioneer Society, she was very conscious of the valley's place in the scheme of history. As it was, this was probably the only community in the state to celebrate the event. All in all, the day's activities were very well received. An anticipated crowd of 1,000 soon burgeoned to 2,500. Irene Gates, sister of Jim Runkle, was honored as the first Miss Simi Valley.

Over the years since incorporation, Simi Valley has enjoyed increased visibility, self-destiny, and size. By far the largest annexation to the city has been that of Wood Ranch, the property last owned by the Adrian Wood family, who had purchased it from the McCoy children. Upon Adrian Wood's death in 1971, the ranch was left to Ailene Wood Claeyssens. In June 1978 Nu-West Development Corporation of Arizona was granted title to 3,600 acres of the ranch property. It is believed that once the only route from Simi Valley south to the Conejo Valley ran through the western portion of this ranch.

When Nu-West had developed the specific plan and received approval from the city, it sold the property to the Olympia/Roberts Company, a partnership of Canada-based Olympia York and The Roberts Group, owned by Bob Levenstein. The development consists of four villages, the first of which was marketed in October 1985. The third village, Sycamore, was constructed in 1990. The master plan calls for an elementary school, gifted by the Olympia/Roberts Company, and for which the Simi Valley Unified School District invited bids in late 1989. The final village will be in Long Canyon at the end of First Street, which is scheduled to connect with Wood Ranch Parkway. The overall master plan calls for 4,026 dwelling units to be built by several different builders. The Wood Ranch development boasts a first-class, 18-hole golf course, which hosted the GTE Classic Senior PGA Tour in 1987.

Appreciating the historical significance of the Wood Ranch property, Levenstein invited the Simi Valley Historical Society to hold its first authentic barn dance in the barns. The event was a tremendous success, drawing nearly 1,000 participants. Levenstein then donated the barns to the historical museum, where they have continued to be the focal point of future barn dances.

While ranches on the valley floor were being sold to developers because lack of water and increased taxes were putting undue strain on the owners, ranchers on the hillsides were able to endure. Accustomed as they were to the limited water supply, hillside farmers had long ago converted to dry farming, harvesting crops that required a minimum of water. Such was the case with Carl Vanniman, who began farming when most others were leaving the business. It was 1955 when he stepped in to temporarily take care of the farming operation at the Big Sky Ranch while his father-in-law, Theodore Beesmeyer, recovered from a heart attack. At the time he was a teacher in La Cañada. Farming quickly got into his blood.

"I woke up one night from a nightmare," he says. "I dreamed I had to go back to teaching."

He started with 750 acres subleased from Newhall Land and Farming, which leased the land from Getty. By 1975 he was farming 2,500 acres. Primarily Vanniman farmed safflower and barley—that is, until the 1980 Soviet grain embargo. "Prices went sky high," he recalled, "so everyone jumped on the bandwagon. Prices plummeted when the competition saturated the market and knocked the price all to heck."

Dry farming could be a very risky business. As the name implies, no irrigation system was used. Instead the farmer relied upon the annual rainfall. In dry times he would strategically plant half of his field while letting the other half lay fallow. Thus, a good crop was more assured.

In 1986 Vanniman was finally calling it a day, the last big farmer in the valley. Times had changed. "Farming and people don't mix too well," he mused. As people move into the valley and to the outer rims, encroaching upon the natural beauty and expanse, farming becomes more difficult. The property is still being farmed by Dick Giesler and Ernie Gomez, his longtime assistant.

Even though the growing population seems to be encroaching on all available land, the hills have legislative protection. In 1986 the issue of growth on the hillsides became very heated. Following much public debate and sometimes public ridicule, two sets of ordinances were placed on the ballot. Measures D and E were favored by those wishing a moratorium on growth. The spirit of these measures was very restrictive. To counter them, opposing factions developed Measures A and B, which were intended to provide controlled, balanced growth. Proponents of each side of the issue were very vocal. In defense of Measures A and B, CUBS (Citizens United for a Better Simi) was formed. The apparent result of the vote was the passage of A and B and the defeat of D and E. It is debatable whether either side won. The compromise restrictions have contributed to the limited affordable housing currently available. The debate, however, did bring the need for reasonable and balanced growth clearly into the public mind.

All hell nearly broke loose in March 1983 when the 50-foot, earthen Robertson Dam, which retained the 24-acre Sinaloa Lake, threatened to crumble following heavy rains. Local, county, and state officials rushed to the scene to try to stave off a disastrous flood. Fourteen hundred residents were evacuated from their homes at 10 p.m. to spend the night at the local junior and senior high schools. The dreaded flood did not happen. Engineers were able to siphon the water sufficiently to take the pressure off the wall. However, state officials, who had been requesting the Sinaloa Lake Homeowners Association to test the dam for stability, apparently saw a golden opportunity to alleviate their concern. The lake was drained. Homeowners contend excessive weed cutback contributed to the freak threat. The issue has been in the courts since then in a lengthy legal battle that has steadily moved through the courts. Resolution of the matter is imminent, however.

The valley's people and resources have changed dramatically over the past 20 years. Whereas in 1972 there were 11,800 first- through sixth-graders, by 1990 there were only 9,423 students in kindergarten through sixth, a trend that had forced the school district to close down four elementary schools a few years earlier. In 1972 there existed two hospitals providing 150 beds. In 1990 only one hospital, the Simi Valley Adventist, remains, but its overall bed capacity is 215. Eight urgent care facilities now exist, demonstrating a trend toward neighborhood health care. Where two newspapers had once existed, the *Enterprise* remains, although Los Angeles papers have made major thrusts into its distribution area. In 1972 the valley was proud to have its first modern-day motel. Now it boasts three stylish hotels. Residents once could connect with the sewer services for $325. Today's installation fee is $2,270.

In 1990 the median disposable household income was $48,700, making Simi Valley the wealthiest city in the county. In 1972 a nice home could be purchased for $35,000. Today's minimum hovers around $200,000, while some homes on the west end have skyrocketed to million-dollar price tags. In March 1990 the Simi Valley-Moorpark Board of Realtors celebrated 25 years. The organization, begun in 1965 by Bonnie Dingman of Mark IV Real Estate Company, had 19 members at the time. Today there are more than 900 members who farm neighborhoods for culling sales. In those early years it was easy to get into a home and difficult to keep it. Today's challenge is affordable housing for the first-time buyer and innovative financing just to get in the door. Record home sales in 1977 reached 2,634. In 1989 the board of realtors put out a call to determine the resident who had lived the longest time in his or her home. The winner was Rebecca Currier, who had resided in her home on Royal Avenue since she and her husband, Doss, had begun apricot ranching in 1929. They had continued to do so until 1979, when Doss retired, the last apricot rancher to do so.

The fourth new post office to be constructed in the valley was the Galena main office, built in 1982. The third office, which had opened in 1963 with Neil Havens, now houses a dental business. Havens also served as postmaster of the Galena facility until his retirement in 1989, ending a long line of Havens family service to the post office. Neil was the third generation to serve the postal system in Simi Valley, having garnered his postmaster position in 1958. His commission was signed by President Eisenhower in 1959. When Simi Valley became incorporated, those residents in Santa Susana would receive their mail a day late because it would first have to be processed through the Simi Valley Post Office.

On October 10, 1989, the City of Simi Valley celebrated its 20th birthday. The city has made remarkable strides in its short history. It has gone from a community that often felt orphaned by the county to one that is a leader, setting the standards for conscientious, planned communities that offer a balance of work, home, and play facilities.

But, "now that we are out of our teens," cautions Mayor Stratton, "in the next 20 years, we'll reach the real peak of being a city. But we can't let it decay . . . that will be our biggest challenge."

City officials plan to continue to expand the economic base. A major regional shopping center is scheduled to be built on the Lucille Estes Baker property at First Street north of the freeway. Bugle Boy Industries has moved its major operation to the valley. A comprehensive update of the general plan was adopted in 1988, providing very efficient guidelines for conscientious growth in the city. This, coupled with the sign ordinance originally adopted in 1971 and followed by several revisions, will keep the city growing in an aesthetically pleasing and economically productive way.

As Simi Valley leads the nation in automobiles per household, traffic is of major concern in the forthcoming years. However, Mayor Stratton, in his 1990 State of the City address, named air quality to be the issue of primary concern: "The easy and obvious things have already been done. Unlike transportation problems which are solvable with money, the solution for air quality requires change in life-style—change in the way we do business."

In the near future we may see more people working at home and shopping at home. In an effort to decrease driving and pollution, there may be a rise in alternative transportation—bus, bicycle, and foot—perhaps bringing us in alignment with the good old days.

Even so, the return to yesteryear would be very limited. There is too much future at hand.

The valley began to reach toward the future in 1955 with the arrival of the North American Aviation Company, otherwise known as Rockwell International. The Santa Susana Field Laboratory has actually conducted research and testing in the Simi Hills since 1948. Much of the area was given to rocket testing and development for NASA and the U.S. Air Force. The facility reached its zenith in the 1960s and 1970s. Janet Scott Cameron, in *Simi Grows Up,* wrote in the early 1960s: "Perhaps it is a bit noisy at times but we feel that the noise means something—protection, security, and a trip to the moon. It is mysterious and therefore intriguing."

Residents of Santa Susana Knolls and Chatsworth in 1990 found the facility mysterious also. But the educated public did not think it was so intriguing when a Los Angeles County newspaper ran a story warning of possible nuclear leaks. The Rocketdyne Testing facility, which has helped send astronauts to the moon, underwent an accelerated cleanup program to allay the fears of the local residents, although authorities had determined there

Bob Tuttle, Rocketdyne manager of radiation and nuclear safety, demonstrates the level of radioactivity with a Geiger counter at the sodium burn pit in the Santa Susana field laboratory in 1989. Courtesy, The Enterprise

Built on 100 acres off Olsen Road, the Ronald Reagan Presidential Library and Museum is expected to attract numerous visitors to Simi and to generate substantial revenue. Photo by Phil Parker

Ronald and Nancy Reagan touch a piece of the Berlin Wall during the groundbreaking ceremony at the site of the Ronald Reagan Presidential Library, west of Simi Valley. Courtesy, The Enterprise

was in fact no imminent threat to the public.

Simi Valley has garnered much national recognition in and of itself. In 1978 *Ladies Home Journal* named the city one of the 15 best suburbs in the United States. *U.S. News and World Report* named it "one of the top ten cities in the nation where rich and promising development will occur." However, one development that very few saw occurring was the selection of Simi Valley as the home of the Ronald Reagan Presidential Library and Museum. In fact, from a field of 30 locations, the selection was narrowed to four. It seemed destined at one point that the library would be built at Stanford.

Until, that is, President Reagan took an auspicious flight over Simi Valley with Representative Elton Gallegly on board Air Force One. When Gallegly pointed out the land, the President became very excited. Friends of the President agreed that this would be an ideal location. Since the library is being built by private funds, the donation of 100 acres of land by Blakely Swartz no doubt added to the appeal. The $40-million, 153,000-square-foot, nonpartisan library is being constructed to resemble an old Spanish mission. Nestled in a bluff, the library is reached by entering Presidential Drive in Simi Valley, which winds its way back a mile out of sight off Olsen Road. The massive structure, built by Peck/Jones Construction Company, which bid the job at no profit, is expected to stand up without major problems for 300 years. The layout includes 20,000 square feet of exhibits, a 300-seat auditorium, and a 120-seat theater as well as meeting rooms and expansive storage for archives. This, the largest presidential

*Royal High School star soc-
cer player Cam Rast takes
the ball away from Culver
City's Ron Chandra on the
way to a 3-0 victory in the
first round of the CIF southern section 4A play-offs.
Rast is on the right.
Courtesy, The Enterprise*

library built, will undoubtedly generate impressive revenue for the area. Estimates of daily visitors range from 300 to 700, many of whom may be fortunate enough to espy Ronald or Nancy as they visit their respective offices at what has been called the "Crown Jewel" of presidential libraries.

Two thousand area residents had their first taste of the historical importance of the library when they attended the invitation-only ceremony on the site April 12, 1990, wherein former president Reagan was presented with a large piece of the Berlin Wall. A representative of the Berlin Wall Committee Group, upon unveiling the piece of the wall, quoted from the 1987 speech President Reagan had made at the wall: "This wall will fall for it cannot withstand faith. This wall cannot withstand freedom. It must come down." The slab of concrete—drab gray from the Eastern side, emblazoned with bright graffiti on the Western side—will remain on permanent display at the library.

The future of the city does not lie only in rockets and libraries. It lies also in its young people, many of whom are making inroads nationally, particularly in the sports arena. Basketball star Don Maclean impresses college sport enthusiasts with his remarkable basketball style and expertise as a member of the UCLA Bruins. Eric King is a member of the Chicago White Sox, with Scott Radinsky following closely behind in the White Sox minor leagues. Dave Milstein moves up the minor-league ladder of the Boston Red Sox. Cam Rast stuns soccer fans with his speed and finesse

*Right: Simi Valley High
School basketball player
Don Maclean goes up for a
shot over Warren High
School's Ray Winick during
the Pioneers' 74-54 victory
in the second round of the
CIF southern section 4A
play-offs in 1988. Courtesy,*
The Enterprise

*Facing page: Taken from
Box Canyon Road at the
east end of the Valley, this
vantage point along Pioneer
Pass offers a spectacular
view west over Simi. Photo
by Patty Salkeld*

on the field as a member of the U.S. Olympic team. And bringing the valley full circle, 1988 Royal High School graduates Stacy Duncan and Jose Pascual were admitted to Harvard University, 115 years after the valley's first farmer, Charles Hoar, arrived from Harvard.

As Simi Valley approaches the twenty-first century, it is balanced on the threshold of promise. No longer is it the orphan community of the county. The city has grown into a well-adjusted, balanced city, certain of itself and where it is going. As pride in the community strengthens, it reflects in the members of the community. This rediscovered pride that was temporarily lost in the days of haphazard growth has raised a consciousness in its citizenship that is reflected in the levels of accomplishment. Whether it be a national political office, a famed physicist like Jack Woods, an athlete perfecting his craft, national recognition for the superintendent of schools, John Duncan (elected to the six-member governing board of the American Association of School Administrators), or the unsung heroes—teachers who cultivate the students who go to Harvard, coaches who propel their team to moments of glory—Simi Valley is rich in the resources that make a community a place of pride, a place to raise a family and an issue or two. The blending of the longtime members of the community with the spurts of energy and excitement brought by young, idealistic newcomers has created a balanced community where experience and enthusiasm work side by side.

The future of Simi Valley will be woven into the tapestry of the rich past, creating a work of art for generations to come. It is a city on the move, headed straight to the future, but always with an eye to the past, reminding one of the legacy the valley has given, to be nurtured just as it has nurtured all those along the way.

Above: A brisk jog around the path affords exercise for two on a spring afternoon in Rancho Tapo Community Park. Photo by Eric Draper

Left: Cacti in bloom adorn this mailbox in the hills of the southeastern end of the valley. Photo by Patty Salkeld

Far left: Wood Ranch, located at the western end of the valley, was once the home of the McCoy family and is now a housing development consisting of four villages, which feature a regionally famous golf course. Photo by Phil Parker

Right: The Strathearn home, shown here, is the centerpiece of the Strathearn Historical Park and Museum. Established in 1969 with a donation of land from the Strathearn family, the park incorporates three periods of Simi history—Chumash Indian, Spanish Rancho, and American—and includes an original Colony house, Simi Library, and barns from Wood Ranch, among other historical buildings. Photo by Phil Parker

Above: Seen here during construction in 1990, the Ronald Reagan Presidential library is nestled against a hill overlooking the valley, and now includes a 300-seat auditorium as well as a 120-seat conference room. Photo by Phil Parker

Above: Horse enthusiasts abound in Simi. The southwestern rim of the valley is dedicated to equestrian zoning and the area has one of the largest equestrian trail systems in the country. Photo by Bo Richards

Left: Blooming prickly pear cacti, seen against the backdrop of the Simi Hills, form a dramatic desert landscape. Photo by Bo Richards

Facing page: A cowboy rides a wild one at the rodeo, part of the Simi Valley Days celebration, a week-long event commemorating the city's heritage. Photo by Ed Skowronski

Right: An aerial view of the Chamber of Commerce Trade Fair, held at Sycamore Drive Community Center, reveals a host of brightly colored tents set up to house attending businesses. More than 25,000 people participated in the two-day event in 1989. Photo by Ed Skowronski

Good times are had by all at the Spring Arts and Crafts Show at Rancho Tapo Community Park. Participants exhibit fine handmade arts and crafts items, and food and musical entertainment are all part of the day's offerings. Photo by Ed Skowronski

Facing page: Skydivers descend to the valley floor while fireworks explode overhead. The show is part of Simi High School's 1990 July Fourth celebration. Photo by Ed Skowronski

Golfers take advantage of the sumptuous greens of Wood Ranch's first-class, 18-hole golf course. The facility hosted the GTE Classic Senior PGA Tour in 1987. Photo by Phil Parker

Above: The first full service hotel opened in Simi, the Clarion Hotel offers guests a swimming pool, spa, full dining room, and catering facilities in its impressive ranch style structure on Madera Road. The hotel, which opened in 1986 and until recently was known as the Posada Royal, also boasts the largest suite in Ventura County, its five-room presidential accomodations. Photo by Phil Parker

Left: With more than 32 partially or fully developed parks, Simi Valley is an ideal place to raise a family. Photo by Eric Draper

*Above: Two young girls
share a joyful swing ride at
Rancho Simi Community
Park. Photo by Eric Draper*

*Facing page: A fisher enjoys
the early morning solitude
of the lake at Rancho Simi
Community Park. Photo by
Eric Draper*

126

Left: Bugle Boy Industries, whose corporate headquarters are shown here, is one of the valley's largest employers in the manufacturing industry. Photo by Bo Richards

Facing page: Community parks host a number of sports-related events, from invitational swim meets to self-defense classes. Softball remains a traditional favorite with many of Simi's young people. Photo by Patty Salkeld

Buster CRABBE

KING OF THE WILD WEST

with
AL (Fuzzy) ST. JOHN

MADY LAURENCE
HENRY HALL
STEVE DARRELL
STANFORD JOLLEY
KARL HACKETT
ROY BRENT

Produced by SIGMUND NEUFELD

Original Story & Screenplay
by ELMER CLIFTON

Directed by SAM NEWFIELD

IN "LIGHTNING RAIDERS"

VII

Partners in Progress

Although Simi Valley has transformed from a sleepy agricultural town into a modern city, it never lost that special family atmosphere it had from the beginning. Nowadays Simi combines those small-town values and friendliness with high-technology and modern progress.

Simi Valley began as a ranching and orchard farming community in the mid-1880s. By the end of that century, a small urbanizing movement had started, which progressed with improvements in transportation, especially the railway system. In 1888 John Sawtelle opened Simi's first store in an old railroad boxcar.

Simi Valley continued to be an agricultural community until the late 1950s—known for its sheep, cattle, and citrus. When ranching declined, developers looked to the pastoral land for homes and businesses. Tired of smog and traffic, people from the congested Los Angeles area welcomed the chance to move to scenic Simi Valley, and the population has grown steadily ever since. The growth was further boosted by the western movement of industry into Ventura County and the opening of new freeway links to the major Southern California regions.

Since then Simi Valley has blossomed not only as a "bedroom community" for commuters, but as a thriving city in its own right, attracting many major industries. In recent years several large corporations relocated to the area, and some smaller ones developed there. Currently the majority of commerce in the area is comprised of service-oriented corporations, light industry, computer and high-technology development, and aerospace and defense-related companies.

Over the years the rest of the world has seen Simi Valley's majestic landscape, thanks to its use as a popular filming location for movies and television, as well as its choice for the location of the Ronald Reagan Presidential Library. The Corrigan Movie Ranch (now preserved as Corriganville Park) was the site of thousands of westerns, including "The Lone Ranger." The popular television series, "Little House on the Prairie," was filmed near the Gillibrand family land. The entertainment industry still uses Simi Valley's panoramic views for location shots, and the Reagan Library will undoubtedly make Simi a prominent spot on the international map.

In light of the controlled growth and planned progress, Simi Valley has been rated one of the nation's top 10 employment growth areas. By the late 1980s it had the highest median family income in Ventura County, and the future looks bright, with more companies looking at Simi Valley and a major regional shopping center due to open by 1993.

The organizations and individuals that are profiled on the following pages have chosen to support this important literary and civic project. They illustrate the variety of ways in which individuals and their businesses have contributed to the growth and development of Simi Valley.

Buster Crabbe was among the hundreds of cowboys who rode the "Wild West" of Simi Valley. More than 3,000 westerns were shot there during the 1940s and 1950s. Courtesy, Corriganville Preservation Committee.

129

SIMI VALLEY CHAMBER OF COMMERCE

Although the Simi Valley Chamber of Commerce was not incorporated until January 25, 1962, its origins date back several decades to when ranching was the mainstay of the area. As houses replaced ranches in the 1960s and commerce replaced ranching, the chamber grew with the local business community. What had started with a handful of ranchers in the early days had grown to more than 1,000 members by 1990.

With a professional staff and numerous volunteers interested in governmental affairs, the chamber serves as a watchdog for the business community by monitoring proposed legislation on the local, state, and national levels.

"We're very involved in legislative matters affecting all businesses, large and small," says Executive Director Nancy Bender, who represents the chamber locally and at meetings throughout the state.

Bender, who has been with the chamber since 1982, has helped bring more business to the Simi Valley area. "We used to be a bedroom community with 80 percent of our residents leaving the area to go to work," says Bender. "Now only 60 percent leave, and I'd like to see that drop to 50 percent."

The Simi Valley Chamber of Commerce has pioneered several innovative programs, including Leadership Simi Valley, which was designed to identify and develop effective community leaders. In the intensive nine-month program, community leaders share their knowledge and skills with potential future leaders.

To serve the local business community, the chamber has four divisions—membership, government relations, communications, and finance. Chamber committees also tackle a range of vital social and environmental issues, such as transportation, child care, and disposal of hazardous materials. "The biggest challenge of the 1990s will be to match good, solid economic strength with environmental concerns," says Bender.

The Simi Valley Chamber of Commerce promotes local economic growth by offering area businesspeople numerous opportunities to meet the community and each other. The chamber sponsors several monthly meetings and hosts a yearly trade fair at which more than 140 businesses showcase their products to 30,000 attendees each May.

RIGHT: Chamber offices moved to 40 West Cochran in summer 1990. The chamber occupies 2,000 square feet of space in the new building, part of the Simi Valley Business Center.

BELOW: Chamber board and members on parade during Simi Valley Days, an annual event sponsored by the chamber.

A leader in community service, the chamber has become well known for its widespread volunteer participation. It also sponsors the Simi Valley Days festivities each September. The chamber also provides members the opportunity to receive free management assistance and specialized counseling through its Small Business Resource Center.

Throughout the years, the Simi Valley Chamber of Commerce has grown in size and numbers to meet Simi's business needs. In 1981 it tripled its size when it moved from a 400-square-foot room in the Bank of A. Levy to offices at 250 Easy Street. It increased in size again in the summer of 1990, when it moved to a 2,000-square-foot office near the Simi Valley Freeway at 40 West Cochran Street.

PETER QUINN, D.D.S.

Gentle, quality dental care is the theme that Dr. Peter James Quinn demands of himself and his staff.

"We will go out of our way to make your dental experience as pleasant as possible," says Dr. Quinn, whose family dental practice strives to meet a family's dental needs—from grandparents to grandchildren. His office is located at 2925 North Sycamore Drive, Suite 107, next to the Simi Valley Adventist Hospital.

Knowing that most people are nervous at the dentist's office, Dr. Quinn makes an extra effort to relax his patients.

"I get a great deal of satisfaction from easing people's anxieties. This also helps me gain their confidence, which is a very important step toward successful treatment."

With his goal of successful treatment of each and every patient, Dr. Quinn runs his Simi Valley dental practice on four major premises—being gentle in his touch, demanding excellence in his work, explaining

procedures thoroughly, and listening to each person's treatment needs.

"Your smile is my business, and I take great pride in creating and maintaining your smile," says Dr. Quinn to his patients. Dr. Quinn provides all the usual services to keep teeth and gums healthy, including teeth cleaning, gum maintenance, fillings, root canals, crowns, and bridges.

In addition to the routine services, Dr. Quinn also specializes in cosmetic dentistry, which can create a stunning smile by one or a combination of procedures. "There are many techniques for improving a smile, which could be as simple as adjusting the edge of a front tooth, or as elaborate as a combination of bleaching, orthodontic movement of teeth, porcelain crowns, and bonded porcelain veneer techniques." Dr. Quinn stays abreast of this rapidly evolving area of dentistry by attending frequent seminars.

A graduate of the University of Southern California Dental School, Dr. Quinn began

practicing dentistry in Simi Valley in 1985, after working two years in Santa Monica. Having grown up in the San Fernando Valley and having lived in Simi while in college, Dr. Quinn was glad to return to the area. He worked with another local dentist for three years before branching out on his own, assuming the practice of Dr. Leland Nixon, a longtime Simi dentist and community leader who chose Dr. Quinn as his successor before he died in 1988.

Upon taking over the practice in May 1988, Dr. Quinn modernized the office with computers and is constantly upgrading the facility with the most modern equipment for diagnosis, sterilization, and treatment.

Dr. Quinn is a member of the American Dental Association and the California Dental Association, including a local Ventura County chapter. He also belongs to the Simi Valley Rotary and Chamber of Commerce and intends to continue his supportive community activity.

ABOVE: Peter J. Quinn, D.D.S.

RIGHT: Dr. Quinn's office is located at 2925 North Sycamore Drive, next to Simi Valley Adventist Hospital.

BLAKELEY WESTERN

Blakely Western, formally Blakeley Swartz, acquired the majestic 640-acre ranch on Madera Road in the Tierra Rejada Valley in June 1985. With an emphasis on environmentally sensitive planning and cooperation with public, private, and nonprofit sectors, the present and long range goals for the ranch have evolved into a variety of land uses.

In 1987 Blakeley Western helped bring worldwide recognition to Simi Valley with the donation of 100 acres of land for the Ronald Reagan Presidential Library. With an opening scheduled for 1991, the library will serve as the official archives of American History during the two terms of the Reagan presidency, from 1980 to 1988.

Set on top of one of the most beautiful and prominent parts of Simi Valley, the site will also be the home of the Public Affairs Center. The center will provide a facility for advanced study and research in the areas of world peace, economic prosperity, and protection of individual liberties. Adjacent to the library will be the International Meeting Place, which will serve as a location for conferences among local and world leaders as

RIGHT: Ronald and Nancy Reagan take part in the ground breaking for the Reagan Library, scheduled to open in 1991.

BELOW: Vicinity map.

well as scholars and historians.

The master plan for the remainder of the ranch includes a seniors' community. Named Rancho Madera, the gated community will feature individual homes for those over 55. Also included will be a continuing care center with area-wide outreach programs, a neighborhood shopping center, a service station, and many support and recreational facilities.

Country Hills, a single-family neighborhood of 35 custom homes and 18 estate lots, will be developed at Country Club Drive East and Madera Road. A Catholic church and parish school will be constructed on the westerly side of the intersection of Presidential Drive and Madera Road. The Uplands area of the ranch is envisioned to include estate homes.

Blakeley Western is coordinating with the Rancho Simi Recreation and Parks District to design and include equestrian trails across the entire ranch in each phase of its development. Blakeley Western will also donate land for a park site around Mt. McCoy, a historic landmark dating back to the early days of settlement in the Simi Valley.

Blakeley Western is very excited to be a participant in the growth and progress of Simi Valley. Gerald W. Blakeley, Jr., has long been considered a leader in the real estate industry. As chairman, president and principal stockholder of Cabot, Cabot & Forbes for more than 25 years, Blakeley was instrumental in developing the Boston-based firm into one of the largest real estate companies in the country.

Blakeley was responsible for introducing many innovative ideas into both the real estate and finance industries. His desire to integrate development with the natural environment led to the concept of the landscaped industrial park. Throughout his career, Blakeley has worked with community groups in the planning and development of his projects.

He is credited with the planning and initial development of Laguna Niguel, California, in 1959. He also participated in the rejuvenation of a half-dozen of the nation's city centers, and built landmark buildings in Boston, Buffalo, Chicago, Washington, Los Angeles, St. Louis, Philadelphia, and Baton Rouge.

Active in civic, philanthropic, and educa-

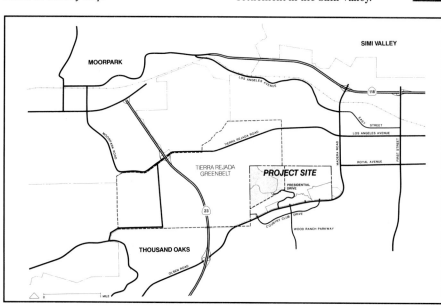

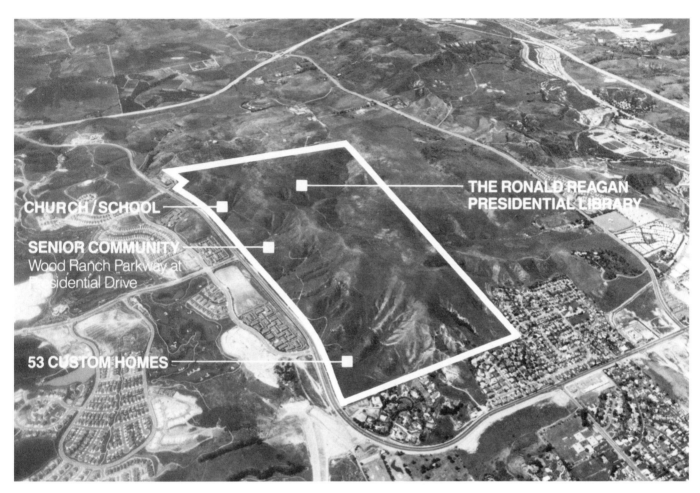

Project components.

tional endeavors, Gerald Blakeley has served on the boards of many national corporations and financial institutions as well as charitable organizations. He and his wife, Olympic gold medalist and practicing physician Tenley E. Albright, reside in Boston.

Donald E. Swartz was the West Coast partner in Blakeley Swartz. He first became involved in real estate development when he joined Cabot, Cabot & Forbes in 1970. In 1977 he formed his own real estate brokerage and consulting firm. In 1981 he joined Hillman Properties.

A California native, Swartz is a 1968 graduate of Stanford University, where he captained the football team in his senior year. He received his MBA from the Stanford Graduate School of Business in 1970.

William Beck, a graduate of the Wharton School at the University of Pennsylvania, has recently joined Blakeley Western. Beck is chief executive officer of Western Resources, doing business as Blakeley Western, and will be the West Coast director. He was executive vice president and chief executive officer of Laguna Niguel Corporation

from 1960 to 1970, and has developed more than 400 houses in the Benedict Canyon section of Beverly Hills as well as projects from Idaho to Acapulco. He was also a vice president of Cabot, Cabot & Forbes.

Rancho Madera, a seniors' community.

DANTONA AND ASSOCIATES

James Rocco Dantona was born in Chicago, Illinois, on August 5, 1948. A sickly child who suffered from asthma and bronchial problems, his health was the reason his family relocated to California in 1953. His condition slowly improved, largely the result of the warm, dry climate, his parents' concern and care, and his active participation in sports—particularly baseball.

Educated in Catholic elementary schools and high schools in the San Fernando Valley, Jim Dantona distinguished himself as an athlete. He excelled in Little League, Babe Ruth League, and Colt League (from 1958 through 1963) as an all-star hitter and solid fielder at several positions in the infield, outfield, and as a catcher. At Bishop Alemany High School in Mission Hills, he set a varsity record for batting average that stood for many years. His achievements there (from 1962 through 1966) were largely the result of his love for the game that he desired to make his career.

After two years on the Pierce College baseball team (1966-1968), Dantona was invited to try out with the Chicago Cubs as a free agent in the spring of 1969. Alongside his idols—Hall of Fame stars Ernie Banks, Billy Williams, and Ron Santo—he experienced his long-held boyhood dream of playing with the Chicago Cubs, although it was only for part of that spring.

Over the years Dantona never lost his love for baseball, even when married and raising a family, completing his education with a degree in political science at California State University at Northridge, and working several jobs to make ends meet.

Dantona taught at St. Ferdinand School in San Fernando, where he also coached football, basketball, and baseball. Later he would do the same at his alma mater, Bishop Alemany. He spent a good deal of his time outside of the classroom and off the playing field counseling youngsters, including some who needed help avoiding drugs. He felt that sports was a principal means to achieving that end.

During this time Dantona was constantly active in state and local political campaigns, coordinating field operations and orchestrating "get out the vote" drives. In 1977 he decided to make politics his career when California State Senator and President pro tem David Roberti offered him a staff position.

Dantona worked as a field deputy for Roberti for six months, before becoming his chief deputy. As such he handled all aspects of operation for Roberti, who was

TOP: Jim Dantona, president of Dantona and Associates, a government and public affairs consulting firm now headquartered in Simi Valley.

LEFT: Jim and Karen Dantona on the happy occasion of their wedding day.

Jim Dantona with his oldest son, Jim (back left), daughter Jennifer, and son Robert.

majority leader. Working for Roberti gave him insight into governmental operations as well as valuable contacts at the state capitol. Additionally, he took leaves from the senator's office to work on statewide political campaigns and several ballot measures.

Remaining active in athletics, Dantona also managed teams in Simi Valley's Santa Susana Boys Baseball League for several consecutive seasons.

In 1985 Dantona began his own business. Dantona and Associates is a consulting firm that serves other businesses in governmental and public relations; organizes and conducts nonprofit fund-raising; and provides local, state, and national political campaign advice. Knowing how to open doors and initiate action, Dantona's goal was to be a liaison between the public and the private sector. In February 1990 Dantona and Associates moved to Simi Valley, where Dantona has lived since 1982.

Additionally, Ventura County Supervisor Jim Dougherty noted Dantona's expertise in state government procedures and the legislative process, and appointed him as a member of the Ventura County Transportation Commission, where he uses his knowledge in community service.

Over the years Dantona has worked on many national political campaigns, including Congressman Joseph P. Kennedy (D-Mass), eldest son of the late Robert F. Kennedy. Kennedy summoned Dantona to Boston to help him run his campaign for the congressional seat once held by his uncle, the late John F. Kennedy. Dantona obliged, and while commuting from California to the East Coast, as well as running some operations by telephone, a successful campaign was waged.

Despite Dantona's chaotic schedule of work, politics, and community activities (including volunteer time to youth, athletics, and anti-drug programs), his children have always come first. His oldest son, James Angelo, takes after his father and plays baseball at Simi Valley High School. Son Robert Francis (named after the late Senator Kennedy) enjoys acting, and recently appeared in a Neil Diamond music video. His daughter, Jennifer Annette, is an honor student and also an athlete. Stepsons

Terry and Andrew love attending baseball games with the family. Dantona's wife, Karen, is his support in all his demanding roles as political expert, community activist, and devoted parent, as well as in his commitment to baseball and youth.

On October 13, 1989, after two years of planning and investment of his own money, he founded Baseballers Against Drugs (B.A.D.), a nonprofit organization established for the purpose of capturing the attention of today's young people and helping them focus their energies into positive thinking and action.

Enlisting the assistance of major league owners, general managers, field management, and players, as well as the business/corporate community and concerned individuals, the organization has the goal of delivering a persuasive anti-drug message. Through education, program funding, scholarships, event coordination, and sponsorship events, Dantona hopes to provide young people with positive role models, straight talk, and an alternative to drug addiction.

B.A.D. represents the successful merging of Dantona's political savvy, activist spirit, passion for baseball, and love for children.

Ernie Banks (left), Baseballers Against Drugs (B.A.D.) national chairman and Chicago Cubs Hall of Famer, and Jim Dantona, president and founder of B.A.D., team up to educate children in the fight against drugs.

WANGTEK

Wangtek Model 5525, 525-million-byte capacity Quarter Inch Cartridge tape drive.

Wangtek was formed in 1982 to help meet the growing need for computer data storage products. The Simi Valley company designs and manufactures memory-storage tape drives and associated controller boards and software, which it sells to computer manufacturers and systems integrators.

Leading the market in technological developments, Wangtek has an advanced marketing and technology group that studies and creates products for the future, keeping pace with the needs of its customers. Soon after its formation Wangtek was the first company to manufacture and ship half-height, five-and-one-quarter-inch form factor cartridge tape drives. The products are used as backup devices for Winchester disks in micro- and minicomputers and local area networks. Wangtek's backup devices are used to store information, ensuring computer users that their data will not be lost if their disk drives malfunction.

In the late 1980s Wangtek was the first company to provide a digital audio tape (DAT) storage solution for its customers, again leading the way of cutting-edge technology. DAT has condensed data storage

to the size of a business card, making it an economical and efficient method of storing information. Future advancements will use magneto optical recording devices, says Jim Kaufmann, vice president of sales and marketing.

"Our goal is to be the leading supplier of backup products in the industry," says Kaufmann.

Already a top company, Wangtek sells its products to such computer manufacturers as AT&T, Compaq, Toshiba, Xerox, and NCR. Wangtek offers a wider range of products than most other companies of its kind, says Kaufmann. Its products can accommodate anything from small personal computers to large, complex systems.

Wangtek employs 250 people at its 65,000-square-foot plant at 41 Moreland Road in Simi Valley. The Simi facilities serve as the corporate headquarters where prototypes are designed and products are launched, marketed, and

manufactured. Wangtek also has a manufacturing plant in Ponce, Puerto Rico.

Wangtek experienced a pivotal year in 1989. Building on its reputation for delivering high-quality products on time, the company rebuilt its engineering and research and development organization to finalize the design and development of higher capacity products to meet the changing demands of the marketplace. This dedication to meeting the needs of its customers, along with its commitment to quality, technology, and on-time delivery, should allow Wangtek to continue its leadership in the secondary storage market.

Wangtek is a subsidiary of Rexon Incorporated. Rexon also holds the Tecmar subsidiary, an Ohio company that produces tape drives and related products for the end-use market and manufactures personal-computer enhancement products. The Sytron subsidiary develops and markets software for file backup for personal computers through operations in Westboro, Massachusetts. All of the subsidiaries work together and complement each other in the computer industry.

Wangtek Model 6130, HS 1,300-million-byte capacity tape drive using Digital Audio Tape (DAT).

WHITTAKER ELECTRONIC SYSTEMS

Whittaker Electronic Systems (WES) is an operating division of the Whittaker Corporation, dedicated to design, development, production, and field emplacement of electronic systems with tactical, strategic, and test/training applications.

The division evolved from the merger and acquisition of numerous electronic technology product lines and businesses over the past 40 years. In 1984 the company built its modern facility in the Peppertree Industrial Park, located in Simi Valley, and has continued to grow and expand ever since. There are now more than 400 employees at the Simi Valley facility, 100 in Carlsbad, and another 100 at various military installations worldwide.

Robert Whittaker started the Wm. R. Whittaker Co., Ltd., in 1942 to provide replacement aircraft valves that were machined from aluminum die castings. After World War II the demand for aircraft valves diminished, and the company turned its precision die casting and machinery capability to the manufacture of miniature cameras. The company continued to expand its growing line of fuel valves and acquired an aircraft hydraulic valve company just prior to the beginning of the Korean conflict.

A second acquisition added aircraft guidance controls, and by 1955 the company's

Sophisticated test equipment, such as this radar tower, is used at Whittaker.

Whittaker Electronic Systems is located in the Peppertree Industrial Park.

annual sales reached $22 million. The following year Whittaker became a public company by merging with Telecomputing Corporation. During the next seven years many product lines were developed and acquired, including magnetic amplifiers, ceramic capacitors and relays, electromechanical counters, air traffic control beacons, and high-temperature adhesives.

In 1968 Tasker Industries was acquired by Whittaker, and the existing technology businesses were consolidated with the Tasker capabilities. This acquisition provided the critical technology base for the expansion of the Simi Valley division. The combined Tasker-Whittaker organization represented a significant electronics capability in the field of primary and secondary

radar, high-speed information systems, and air traffic control systems.

The Tasker Division changed its name to Whittaker Electronic Systems (WES) in 1987 and expanded its capability to include the following product lines: electronic warfare; radar systems; and command, control, and communications. Along with these three primary business thrusts, the division has an integrated logistics support capability for each of the product lines.

WES offers a wide variety of command, control, communications, and intelligence products and services worldwide, including cryptographic, TEMPEST, and interoperability requirements. The electronic warfare product line has evolved over many years of product development.

WES is a major supplier of electronic countermeasures hardware and radar-threat simulation and ground-based training and simulation systems. Whittaker pioneered the development of Digital RF Memories and remains the world's technology leader. Whittaker Electronic Systems has a leadership position for design, development, fabrication, installation, integration, and tests of sophisticated radar systems for a wide spectrum of United States and foreign military testing and training purposes.

HIROSE ELECTRIC (USA) INC.

Hirose Electric Co. Ltd. is a major worldwide manufacturer of electronic connectors whose United States subsidiary, Hirose Electric (USA) Inc., is headquartered in Simi Valley.

Hirose started in 1937 as a small shop in Tokyo, Japan, making screw machine connectors. At that time its products were delivered by bicycle and pull carts, recalls Toshi Doi, corporate secretary.

The company grew in the 1950s—an era of the development of more advanced electronic applications and the increased use of computers. In the late 1960s Hirose began exporting its products and established itself on the international market. During the 1980s the company began to create manufacturing and sales facilities worldwide, including in California.

Hirose established its United States subsidiary in 1980. Originally located in an 8,000-square-foot Chatsworth plant, the company moved to a new 18,000-square-foot building at 2685-C Park Center Drive in Simi Valley in 1988. Although most of its manu-

facturing currently takes place at plants in Japan, the company has purchased property in Simi Valley on which to build U.S. manufacturing plants, says Peter Stevens, general manager of operations.

Hirose Electric specializes in manufacturing high-quality connectors for the electronics industry. It serves customers internationally, in mainly the industrial product field, with a growing array of connector products. The main family of products consists of multi-pin connectors, including circular, rectangular, ribbon cable, printed circuit board, and nylon connectors. Next in importance is the line of high-performance coaxial and optical connectors used in microwave and other high-frequency signal applications. These products, together with a variety of specialized devices, are shipped to major manufacturers of computers, computer terminals, word processors, telecommunications devices, measuring systems, and broadcasting systems, as well as manufacturers of

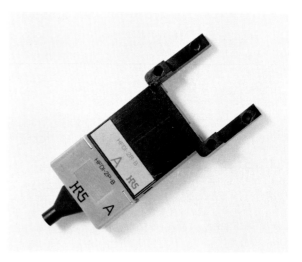

Hirose's new FDDI connector for fiber optics (model HFDI) provides a foolproof locking system and meets ANSI interface standards. Four different keying positions are available.

such consumer products as videocassette recorders (camcorders) and audio/video equipment.

Hirose's client roster is impressive, and includes major corporations such as Hewlett Packard, IBM, MCI, Rockwell, Apple Computers, NEC, and Mitsubishi. Those and other manufacturers use Hirose's connectors in personal computers and peripheral equipment, analytical instrumentation, and communications devices, such as modems that link telephones to computers. The connectors are also used in medical instruments such as blood analyzers, heart monitors, and TENS machines (used to help patients relieve their pain).

Currently Hirose Electric (in combination with its subsidiaries) is the eighth-largest company of its kind in the world. Hirose Japan is the second-largest company of its type in Japan.

"We have one of the broadest and most complete range of product lines," says Jim Erickson, marketing and sales manager. "Our image is one of innovation, new product development, state-of-the-art manufacturing technologies, and as close to perfect a quality record as any company has."

Indeed, its goal of having a perfect record has been recognized and rewarded by Rockwell International, which has given

A wide assortment of Hirose electronic connectors.

An assortment of high-density connectors.

Hirose its Quality Excellence Award for several consecutive years.

Quality control is important to Hideki Sakai, a Hirose employee since 1952 and the company's president and CEO since 1971. Sakai's goals are to put Hirose USA in the top 10 in the U.S. marketplace by the year 2000 and to increase its status as a major player worldwide.

"Our next goal is to become a truly unique electronics manufacturer capable of making greater contributions to industry the world over. By having paid close attention to efficient management, high-quality technology, and high value-added products, we have already achieved impressive results," states Sakai in a recent company report.

"At all times, we have tried to achieve the maximum benefits from having a small organization in which new ideas and knowledge can be immediately applied on a practical level, and in which each person can be aware of his or her role and effectiveness. These ideas, in fact, form the basis of Hirose's slogan, 'Creative Links to World Electronics,'" he adds.

Since 1968 Hirose has expanded and improved its network of overseas agencies to keep pace with the growing world market. Presently it has 22 agencies in 20 countries. In 1987 the company opened an office in Taiwan. To start full-scale business activities in Europe, Hirose established subsidiaries in West Germany and the United Kingdom in 1988.

"With plans for a United Europe by 1992, we will be on an accelerated course for manufacturing as soon as possible to reduce imports there," says Erickson.

Hirose USA now has more than 60 employees in Simi Valley, and that number could grow to more than 250 when manufacturing is increased. Currently the Simi facilities are used predominantly for import, assembly, sales, and distribution of products manufactured in Japan and at the company's overseas plants. In 1988 Hirose USA expanded from its base in Simi Valley and opened new regional sales offices in Boston and Dallas to meet increasing demands in the United States.

Employee development and education are key to the company's management philosophy. The Simi Valley facilities contain classroom-style conference rooms for continual training. The offices have an open styling, so that employees can conference together and learn from one another. In Simi Valley Hirose USA sponsors recreational teams and activities for its employees and is a member of the Simi Valley Chamber of Commerce.

In the future Hirose Electric may manufacture more connectors for automotive electronic use. As more and more cars use sophisticated electronics, more connective devices are needed, and Hirose Electric (USA) Inc. hopes to fill that need.

Surface-mount technology (SMT) memory card connectors.

MICOM COMMUNICATIONS CORP.

Headquartered in Simi Valley, MICOM Communications is a global supplier of a broad range of local and wide-area communications networking equipment.

The company was founded in Chatsworth in 1973 to design, manufacture, sell, and service data communications products, focusing on the application of microcomputer chips in solving various data communication problems. One of the country's largest independent manufacturers of communications equipment, MICOM specializes in the production of economical yet high-performance networking equipment, which is acquired by its users to connect computer systems manufactured by other vendors.

MICOM's corporate offices, sales and marketing departments, and product development areas are housed in this 220,000-square-foot Simi Valley facility.

Since its foundation, the company has flourished and showed healthy profits after the early years of research and development. Rapid growth came between 1978 and 1984 and continued to increase annually.

MICOM moved to 4100 Los Angeles Avenue in Simi Valley in December 1984 to consolidate its growing needs. Sprawling over 10 acres, the custom-designed Simi facilities cover 220,000 square feet. In the mid-1980s the company also had manufacturing facilities in nearby Northridge and Moorpark which have since been consolidated to Simi. MICOM also has a manufacturing plant in Caribe, Puerto Rico, which employs about 300 people.

Nearly 350 people work at the Simi Valley headquarters. A people-oriented company, MICOM refers to its employees as "team members" and holds them in high esteem.

"Besides being one of California's most beautiful communities to work in, Simi Valley provides MICOM with an excellent talent pool of motivated and well-educated workers," says Gil Cabral, MICOM's president and chief executive officer. "MICOM echoes the cultural mix of Southern California's communities. Touring our facility is like touring various parts of the world. We thrive on the diversity of our backgrounds and benefit from the variety of experiences."

Many of the employees feel the same way about MICOM. Bill Weber, an engineer with MICOM for more than 10 years, has positive reflections on his affiliation with the company.

"Ten years is a long time for an engineer to stay at one company, especially a smaller company," says Weber, a Simi Valley resident who started working for the company when it had less than 80 employees. "For me to stay here 10 years is a sure indication that it's tough to find a better or more rewarding place to work. I am looking forward to the next 10 years."

In addition to placing value on its employees, the company revolves around a philosophy of quality, with a constant goal of having defect-free products. All employees go through an extensive Quality Education System designed to help them meet that goal.

"Not many companies put so much money into such programs," says Rich Borden, company spokesman. MICOM's Quality Education training recently paid off in a big way when the company's Caribe facility was awarded the Beacon Award for Quality, becoming the first Puerto Rico-based operation to be so honored.

MICOM's products are used worldwide, enabling businesses to send their data

Since the founding of the company in 1973, MICOM has developed communications products that offer customers a winning solution: saving them money on computer communications costs. MICOM communications equipment is known around the world for high performance and durability.

and voice traffic more economically from office to office.

"The magic that gets information from Des Moines to New York and back are MICOM products," says Borden.

It all began in 1977 with MICOM's Micro800 Data Concentrator. MICOM created a major industry breakthrough by applying microcomputer technology to solve the minicomputer user's data communications problems. The Data Concentrator not only reduced line costs by allowing more than 32 terminals to share a single telephone line, but also ensured more efficient transport of data and corrected errors previously caused by noisy telephone lines.

Today MICOM is the low-end market leader in installed statistical multiplexors, with more than 220,000 units shipped worldwide. The statistical multiplexor is the convenient device that permits several computer products to share a single leased phone line to a remote host computer. This "multiplexing" saves its users lots of money in monthly transmission costs.

Now MICOM is making similar breakthroughs in compressing voice transmissions to save companies thousands of dollars in toll-call costs. Through MICOM's exclusive voice digitization process, the company's new products compress the human voice without losing voice quality. This allows customers to fit more conversations or data transmissions onto one leased phone line. MICOM expects its new voice products to do extremely well, since reducing phone costs is important to virtually every business operating today.

MICOM has also emerged as a local-area network solutions leader with products that support industry standards and comply with federal government mandates. MICOM products have always maintained an outstanding reputation among local, state, and federal government agencies.

From the beginning, MICOM's objective has been to take the mystique out of communications by designing products that are less costly and far easier to use than anything previously conceived

by the data communications industry. MICOM not only creates products that are different from those being developed by the rest of the industry, but also uses a unique direct marketing approach designed to provide full service to its customers.

To meet that objective, MICOM Communications Corp. put together a four-pronged strategy that is still in effect today. First, it developed a product line that provides a single source for meeting the complete communications product needs of the customer. Second, it ensures that the products are simple to use, service, and install, and are user-friendly and compatible with other communications products. Third, MICOM prices and discounts its products to attract and motivate a widespread distribution organization capable of reaching many thousands of computer users and systems houses. Finally, the company provides informative seminars oriented toward the needs of the communications equipment user.

MICOM's Simi Valley "Team Members" celebrated the completion of their Crosby Quality Education System training by forming a human "Q" on a nearby lawn, emphasizing the company's commitment to quality products. All Simi Valley-based MICOM employees completed the company-funded training.

THE VOIT COMPANIES

Local job opportunities and area revenues continued to increase in the late 1980s, thanks in part to the Simi Valley Business Center, a major commercial development created by The Voit Companies.

The Voit Companies is a privately owned real estate development and management company. Its objectives are to develop and manage quality real estate holdings in the western United States. With its primary interest in creating long-term value, the company has established an enviable track record for developing office, industrial, and retail facilities that are noted for their design excellence, quality management, and successful operations.

To date, Voit's largest project is Warner Center, an impressive development in Woodland Hills that includes more than 2 million square feet of high-rise office space and the 475-room Warner Center Marriott Hotel. The Simi Valley Business Center is Voit's second-largest endeavor,

with 85 acres of land in Simi's west end industrial area, encompassing approximately 1.2 million square feet of multiuse facilities.

In 1986 Voit broke ground on the Simi Valley Business Center, located about 300 feet from the Simi Valley Freeway at Madera Road. Some buildings were in use by 1989, with total buildup planned by 1993.

Voit chose Simi Valley as a logical place to expand from the San Fernando Valley, says project manager John Gebhardt. What particularly drew them to Simi, he added, was the fact that the area is master planned for controlled growth.

The Simi Valley Business Center is a multiuse facility, accommodating commercial, industrial, and retail tenants. Some of the major companies include CardKey Corporation, Control Data, Hirose Electronics, and Dream Quest, a special effects company.

A $3-million landscape plan enhances the campus-like setting of the Simi Valley

Business Center. The main entry is lined with a grove of mature oak trees, some more than 100 years old, providing tenants and visitors with a dramatic and visually pleasing introduction to the project. Broad thoroughfares bordered by eucalyptus and acacia trees provide easy access to the buildings. Tenants can also enjoy a centrally located park that features a waterfall cascading over a sculpted rock outcrop.

The entire Simi Valley project was conceived with the needs of its users in mind. To comfortably accommodate employees, Voit has provided for three parking spaces for each 1,000 square feet of space leased. When completed, the Simi Valley Business Center will house up to 3,000 employees, some of whom may have previously had to leave the Simi area to commute to work. Voit hopes that the project will increase area jobs, so that more Simi residents can work closer to home.

Indeed, Voit always runs its operations

around the needs of the people that will use the developments.

"We're flexibly responsive to businesses and our communities—the public, government, and businesses. We have a lot of people to answer to," says Gebhardt.

In each of its major projects, The Voit Companies creates programs to accommodate such crucial needs as child care and transportation, and even some extra goodies such as arts programming. The company also leases space to restaurants and drugstores in its projects so that employees will not have to leave the office complex for meals or errands.

"We promote quality. It doesn't cost much more, and it pays off in the long run," says Gebhardt.

The Voit Companies was founded in 1971 by Robert D. Voit (grandson of the founder of the Voit Rubber Co.), who continues to be the company's owner and president. As such, Voit is involved in virtually every as-

pect of company operations, with particular emphasis on long-range planning, project development, and client relations. Prior to forming The Voit Companies in 1971, Voit was an office leasing specialist with Coldwell Banker. A graduate of the University of California, Berkeley, Voit holds a master's degree in American Studies.

Since its inception the company has developed or has in advanced stages of planning more than 5 million square feet of office, industrial, and retail facilities in California, Arizona, and Nevada. A major milestone contributing to the company's success occurred in 1974, when The New England/Copley provided capital funding and became a joint venture partner in The Voit Companies' projects in Warner Center. That relationship, which assures long-term staying power, has continued with The New England/Copley being a financial partner in several major projects in addition to Warner Center.

Valley Construction Company, formed in 1978, is affiliated with The Voit Companies and provides construction services for some of the projects developed by the company. It also delivers timely and efficient tenant improvements in buildings managed by Voit and undertakes projects for other clients.

In addition to Valley Construction, The Voit Companies has other corporations, including the Scher-Voit Brokerage Company in Orange and San Diego counties and The Firm, a businessperson's health club developed by Voit for prestigious locations such as Warner Center.

The history of The Voit Companies is still being written. Armed with a young, dynamic, and highly competent management team, the company is continuing to aggressively seek new real estate development and management opportunities. In the future The Voit Companies may branch into multifamily residential housing.

SCRIBNER'S ELECTRONICS

Not every Tom, Dick, and Harry can run a successful company, but in the case of Simi Valley's Scribner brothers, they run two: Scribner's Electronics and the Scribner Brothers Racing Team.

The close-knit family began their electronics business in Northridge in 1964, when the brothers started making printed circuit boards with their parents, Tom and Tootie, who were experienced in the field. The company started small, with family members working 20-hour days, holding second jobs, and sharing household expenses to make ends meet. Unfortunately,

Apollo 11 flight to the moon. Currently, its circuit boards are used in various electronic equipment, including home and car stereos, computers, pacemakers, and medical monitoring devices.

The company has 25 employees, many of whom are part of the family. Most of the brothers' children work or have worked for the shop, including Harry's children, Harry Jr. ("Nibbie") and Cindy; Tom's children, Ray, Elvy, and Debbie; and Dick's children, Shane, Dottie, and Sheila. Harry and his wife, Renee, also have a younger daughter, Jamie. All of the brothers live in Simi Valley.

The company has a family atmosphere; most of the other employees average 15 to 20 years with the firm. The Scribner brothers base their operations on quality production and knowledgeable workers. In addition, they use only American-made products.

In addition to their electronics company, the brothers professionally race cars, turning a hobby into a business with the Scribner Brothers Racing Team. The Scribners have been involved in championship drag racing since 1957 and have many trophies to show for their efforts. They race in NHRA and IHRA competitions all over the United States and Canada and won the World Nationals in 1988. Also in 1988, they were the first to win the California Nationals competition. Dick Scribner promotes the racing business on a full-time basis, while Tom and Harry run the electronics company.

Each year the Scribners participate with other drag racers in Christmas for Children, a charity function that raises money for the area's needy children. The brothers also play in several annual local golf and bowling tournaments for various area charities.

LEFT: The Scribner family (from left): Phyeria "Tootie" Scribner; Thomas Scribner, Jr.; Richard S. Scribner; and Harry S. Scribner, with portrait of Thomas Scribner, Sr.

BELOW: Scribner's Electronics has been located at 4568 Industrial Street since 1971.

Tom Sr. died in a car accident in 1969, just as the company was beginning to flourish. The company grew and moved to its current location at 4568 Industrial Street in Simi Valley in 1971.

At that time business was just beginning in the Simi Valley, and the city council was eagerly wooing companies to the area. When the Scribners built their building, the industrial area of Simi Valley was not much more than vacant lots, and the brothers remember quail hunting on land across the street.

Scribner's Electronics manufactures printed circuit boards for many uses. Its products were used extensively for the

ROBERT O. HUBER

Concerned with the welfare of Simi Valley, Robert O. Huber has been an active participant in the community since he arrived in 1969. Over the years he has worked extensively with the chamber of commerce, served on the city council, and initiated several milestone programs.

Career wise, he has traveled two distinct paths—first as a mortician and then as a lawyer. In 1969 he founded Huber Chapel/ Funeral Directors at the old Methodist Church property on Los Angeles Avenue. He chose the profession because he wanted to help people, just as his grandfather, a minister, had done. After several years of helping people through the grief of funerals, Huber decided he wanted to counsel them in another way—through the law. He attended the University of LaVerne College of Law part time for four years, graduating as

ABOVE: *This building, located on Los Angeles Avenue, served as Huber Chapel from 1969 to 1978.*

LEFT: *Attorney Robert O. Huber at his office.*

a member of the Law Review in early 1976.

Huber was a deputy district attorney for one year before joining a private Oxnard firm. In 1982 he opened his own office at 1791 Erringer Road. Huber specializes in corporate and business law, estates, and personal injury. He also serves as a judge pro tempore for Ventura County, volunteering his services to help ease the overloaded system.

In 1978, after becoming a lawyer, Huber sold the mortuary. The land has since been used for a temple and a church.

Despite the intense demands faced in both of his professions, Huber has consistently found time to volunteer for the community. In 1969 he chaired the community campaign that saved the historical Colony House for future generations to enjoy.

When Simi Valley became a city in 1970, Huber became president of the chamber of commerce, a position he held for two years. During his terms Huber founded the chamber's retail promotion division and conceived the city's official slogan, "Simi

Valley—Gateway to Ventura County."

Huber has also served as president of the local YMCA, Boy Scouts, and United Methodist Church Administrative Board.

In 1972 Huber rallied businesspeople together to keep gambling clubs out of Simi Valley. The Businessmen Against Card Club Ordinance was instrumental in keeping gambling out of the area.

As a member of the city council from 1980 to 1984, Huber supported economic development and commercial growth. Among his accomplishments, he initiated the city's tree-preservation ordinance and founded the city's affordable-housing committee.

Even after leaving the council, Huber remained active in community affairs. In 1989 he chaired the committee that successfully passed the $35-million school-rehabilitation bond.

Huber has received service awards from many organizations including the Jaycees, Rotary Club, and Simi Valley Chamber of Commerce.

LLOYD BOLAND, D.C.

After injuring his back and recovering with the help of chiropractic care, Lloyd Boland decided to return the favor to others by becoming a chiropractor himself. Since then he has established a successful practice, with several specialties, in Simi Valley.

Boland grew up in the San Fernando Valley. He was an honors student at California State University, Northridge, where he earned his undergraduate degree in biology and did graduate work in that field. In 1980 he graduated with honors from the Los Angeles College of Chiropractic and has since taken several postgraduate specialty courses from various institutions.

Boland began practicing in Simi Valley in 1983 after working in Glendale and Chatsworth. He opened up his current office at 2139 Tapo Street in 1986.

As a chiropractor, Boland provides drug-free relief for all types of neuromuscular-skeletal disorders, ranging from back and neck strains to joint pains, sports injuries, and muscle spasms. He uses the latest techniques in diagnosis and treatment, including gentle manipulations and therapeutic modalities.

"Chiropractic should be the first choice of treatment for spinal-related injuries. It's a noninvasive conservative method," he says. "It's important that anyone who seeks chiropractic care seeks a person who is up to date. That's why I continue my studies."

In 1984 Boland received three special certifications, after a year of graduate courses. As a certified Independent Medical Examiner and Disability Evaluator, Boland serves as an independent examiner in court cases and disability reviews. As a Certified Industrial Consultant, he conducts seminars on injury prevention and employee health at many local businesses. He also inspects and reviews work sites, offering suggestions to reduce the risk of injury.

Boland is also involved in an intense three-year program that will also make him a diplomate of the American Board of Chiropractic Orthopedics in 1991.

Although his specialties sometimes draw him away from the office, Boland always makes time for those who need him, sometimes working 16-hour days.

"I enjoy working with patients and keeping them well," he says.

In addition to his busy practice, Boland is extremely involved with the Simi Valley community. He is the 1990 president of the Simi Valley

Chamber of Commerce and previously served as vice president. An original planner of Simi Valley Days, he works on the event annually, and was the chairman in 1989.

He also sponsors and chairs the Senior Citizens' Easter Breakfast and has served on the board of directors of Rotary Club of Rancho Simi.

Boland has received several commendations for his contributions to the community. In 1988 Rotary International named him a Paul Harris Fellow. Also that year he received the Norka Image Award, an honor bestowed by a local corporation for outstanding community involvement. In 1989 Boland was selected to appear in the 19th edition of *Who's Who in California* for his "outstanding professional achievement, superior leadership, and exceptional service."

LEFT: Dr. Lloyd Boland has been practicing in Simi Valley since 1983.

BELOW: Boland keeps abreast of the latest developments in chiropractic care by pursuing postgraduate studies.

GREEN ACRES MARKET

Although Green Acres Market has evolved into a meat and produce specialty store, it still maintains the same family feeling it had when it was a general store in the 1920s.

"I don't think we'll ever lose that small-town atmosphere," says store owner Dick Rhoads, who enjoys chatting with customers on a regular basis. Some of today's shoppers are the grown children of long-time customers.

Originally called Alvarez Market, the grocery store was one of the first in the Simi Valley area, built and operated by Manuel Alvarez in the late 1920s. In the early 1930s Alvarez sold the store to his brother-in-law, Bill Luna, who ran the market until the early 1960s. When Luna retired he sold the store to Russ Burris, who changed the name to RR Market.

Burris had RR Market until 1968, when Rhoads came into the scene with partners Bob Shaver and Ken Hoshida. At that point Rhoads was a partial owner, leasing the meat section as the butcher. In 1972 he took full ownership, which he currently maintains and will pass on to his children.

Located at 2918 Los Angeles Avenue, the market has undergone more than just

RIGHT: In the late 1920s Manuel Alvarez built and operated Alvarez Market, one of the first grocery stores in the Simi Valley area.

BELOW: Today Green Acres continues to offer the freshest produce and meats available, along with old-fashioned quality and service.

name changes over the decades. For many years it served a multitude of needs as the community general store, complete with gasoline pumps in the front lot. The gas pumps, along with a house that was on the property, were moved off for expansion in the 1950s.

When Rhoads and his partners bought the store in 1968, it carried a little of everything, from cosmetics to toys to food. Because the larger chain stores could more effectively merchandise a wide range of products, Rhoads decided to reorganize the market to specialize in meats and pro-

duce—items he could provide fresh, on a high-quality basis.

Since then, he has continued to provide that quality to his customers by stocking fresh meat and produce as well as some groceries, dairy products, and beer and wine. He also has a full delicatessen and catering service.

Although the store has grown to 28 employees, it is still very much a family operation. Rhoads' wife, Brenda, has worked with him from the start. Their son, Randy, now manages the store; and their daughter, Julie Dobin, runs the catering business. Their

son-in-law, Brad Dobin, supervises the back-room operation of the meat department.

In addition to making sure the community has fresh meat and produce, Dick Rhoads has been very involved in local service organizations, so much so that he was named Businessperson of the Year in 1986 by the Simi Valley Chamber of Commerce. Rhoads has served on the board of directors for the chamber and the Rotary Club. He was the honorary chairman for the Boys and Girls Club, a charter member of the Elks Club, and a member of the Simi Valley Masonic Lodge. He was also one of the local businesspeople who founded the Simi Valley Bank.

P.W. GILLIBRAND COMPANY

Phil Gillibrand provided the foundation for much of the growth of Simi Valley. Through his rock, sand, and gravel company, he literally helped pave the way for many local projects.

"I was fortunate to be in a community that was starting to grow. My timing was right," says Gillibrand, who founded P.W. Gillibrand Company on January 1, 1957.

A true local, Gillibrand grew up in the area and played on the football team when he was a student at Simi Valley High School. His grandfather, Edward Clayton Gillibrand, was one of the area's founders, owning 1,003 acres of cattle ranch land in Tapo Canyon in 1888.

Currently, Phil Gillibrand owns nine acres of that same land and has purchased an additional 1,100 acres in Tapo Canyon, on which he runs a mining operation. He also mines industrial minerals in Soledad Canyon, where he is developing a large titanium deposit.

Gillibrand grew up around the mining and construction materials industry. His father, John Clayton Gillibrand, ran the old oyster shell mine in Simi Valley, and worked for S.W. Paving during the Depression. Phil Gillibrand started working when he was 11 years old, and at 19 he was the youngest person in California to obtain a general engineering contractor's license.

As a young man supporting a new family, Gillibrand began his company during his daytime off-hours while holding down a full-time night job at Rocketdyne. He started small, with a few pieces of machinery, paving driveways and selling gravel to local farmers for roads. In 1959 he was able to quit his night job and devote his full attention to his growing company.

Since then, P.W. Gillibrand Company has grown to more than 100 employees and extensive equipment and on-site processing

plants, much of which Gillibrand designed and built himself. Originally mining and producing materials off the old Mine Road, he moved his Simi Valley operations to its current location at the end of Bennett Road in 1967. Over the years the company has outgrown its office space, which is planned for additional expansion in 1990.

Gillibrand's Simi Valley mining area spans 1,100 acres near the Big Sky Ranch in Simi's rolling hills, adjacent to the land used in filming television's "Little House on the

ABOVE: The old oyster shell mine in 1940.

LEFT: Workers at the oyster shell mine in 1950.

Prairie." The beautiful panoramic view is buffered from the mining operation, thanks to Gillibrand's careful ridgeline planning. In addition to preserving the view, Gillibrand conserves the land by replacing the topsoil and using everything that is mined.

Because of its rich mineral deposits, Gillibrand's Simi Valley property has been designated by the State of California as a significant natural resource, to be protected from urban encroachment. One of the canyons in the Tapo Canyon area was named Gillibrand Canyon by the United States Geological Survey.

will lower that figure, as more domestic titanium feedstock is produced. The Soledad Canyon mine also yields apatite, zircon, magnetite, and rare earths.

A hard worker and dedicated family man, Gillibrand believes in perseverance, even when the going gets tough. A machinery accident in 1966 took one of his legs but none of his spirit.

"There's nothing I can't handle. It may be extremely difficult, but it can be done," he says.

Gillibrand gives partial credit for his success to the lessons he learned from his father.

LEFT: The current P.W. Gillibrand Company facilities in Simi Valley.

At the Simi Valley location, Gillibrand mines two different natural resources: an ocean formation and a fresh-water formation. The processing plants on the property convert the raw materials into several commodities, including a full line of both wet and dry construction aggregates used in concrete, asphalt, paving materials, and industrial sands. The asphalt goes into highways and roads while concrete is used in building construction. The use of industrial sands ranges from golf courses to glass bottles.

The Simi Valley plant produces 600 tons of materials per hour. Gillibrand sells about one million tons yearly and estimates that to triple in the coming years.

Much of the paving materials produced in Simi Valley are used in the area, says Gillibrand, who, as a contractor, paved the roads in many Simi subdivisions. He also supplied materials for several major highways and airports.

One of his first major projects was the widening of Topanga Canyon in the San Fernando Valley from two to four lanes in 1962. In 1967 he supplied concrete aggregates and base materials for the white paving on the first phase of the Simi Valley Freeway.

In addition to his Simi Valley operations, Gillibrand also mines industrial minerals in Soledad Canyon, where he has the largest known deposit of titanium in the continental United States. Titanium has many uses,

ABOVE: The company is developing a large titanium deposit at its Soledad Canyon facilities.

including medical implants—it is a metal that the body does not reject. The versatile mineral is also used for cosmetic pigments and for aerospace machinery for the Space Shuttle.

Currently, more than 78 percent of the titanium feedstock used in the United States is imported. Gillibrand hopes his new mines

"From the time I was a small boy, he taught me to be respectful, not to be lazy, and not to ask of others what you wouldn't do yourself."

Gillibrand and his wife, Celine (known as "Billie"), live near the P.W. Gillibrand Company in Simi Valley. Both are active in the community—Phil supports various youth groups and Billie serves on the Simi Valley Historical Society. They have two grown daughters, Madeleine and Theresa.

GI INDUSTRIES

Manny Sr. The company offices and 10-acre collection facility are headquartered at 195 West Los Angeles Avenue in Simi Valley.

Over the years most of the members of the large, close clan have worked with the family business. Manny Sr.'s wife, Gloria, drove the trash trucks when they were newlyweds. GI Industries has always maintained a friendly, family atmosphere, even when it grew into a public corporation.

Ever since they came to the Simi/ Moorpark area in the mid-1970s, the Asadurians have been very involved with

LEFT: GI Rubbish collects refuse within a greater than 60-mile radius of Simi Valley.

BELOW: GI Rubbish Co.'s offices are located at 195 West Los Angeles Avenue.

When Sam Asadurian emigrated to Los Angeles from Armenia in 1924, he had no idea he would start a business that would grow and prosper for decades to come. Although he spoke little English, he started a small trash-hauling company that grew over the years into a multimillion-dollar family empire, extending to Simi Valley and beyond.

Originating in the Venice Beach area, Sam started Venice Rubbish around 1925. During the next five years, his wife gave birth to two sons, Sam Jr., and Manuel, who eventually took over the business and worked with their sons, Carl and Manuel Jr.

The Asadurians changed the company name to GI Rubbish after World War II, honoring the popularity of America's returning veterans. In the 1970s the Asadurians extended their trash collection into the San Fernando Valley and later into Ventura County. The company had become one of the largest privately held trash haulers in the area when it diversified and went public in 1987, becoming GI Industries.

Since then the company and its subsidiaries have continued to grow, collecting much of the trash in more than a 60-mile radius of Simi Valley, including Thousand Oaks and Moorpark, where some of the family lives on a sprawling ranch. In addition to the trash business, the Asadurians also raise thoroughbred horses.

Today GI Industries has more than 100 employees and 50 trucks, serving more than 20,000 customers in the area. The company also extends into Los Angeles and other areas of Southern California, where it runs additional vehicles.

GI Industries picks up every form of refuse, including commercial, industrial, and residential trash. For years they actively participated in recycling programs, even before it was the popular thing to do, says

the community, participating in Simi Valley Days with the chamber of commerce, and helping charitable organizations such as Care and Share, Boys and Girls Club, and local sports teams. The Asadurians are always willing to help whenever needed, especially when children are involved, says Carl.

"The bottom line is the Asadurians are the kind of people that if you call them up, they'll be over to help," he says. "We're proud to grow with the community."

JACK'S SHOES

As Jack Spotts puts his best foot forward in Simi Valley, he helps others do the same, with the large selection and friendly service he offers at his shoe stores.

A longtime Simi resident, Spotts opened Jack's Shoes at 4364 Valley Fair Avenue in January 1974. Since then he has nearly tripled his shop from its original 1,300 square feet and has expanded to include an outlet store across the street and a satellite shop in Westlake Village.

Spotts grew up in Pottsville, Pennsylvania, where his father was an executive with Kinney's Shoes. As a young man he was a musician who did not want to follow his father in the shoe business, but later he changed his mind. He began by working as an assistant manager, later managing Kinney Shoes stores throughout the East Coast.

In 1952 Spotts met his future wife, Marietta, who was working her way through college as an employee in a Kinney's store he managed in Pennsylvania. The couple married in 1955, when she graduated from college. They have five children: four daughters and a son.

Spotts came to California in 1969, when Kinney's transferred him to North Hollywood as a manager of the chain's Pacific division. During that time he moved to Simi Valley, which he found to be the only community

around with affordable housing large enough for his brood. Spotts liked Simi so much that he did not want to transfer back to the East Coast (as Kinney's had required), so he quit his job in December 1973 and opened up his own store the following month.

At first Jack and Marietta ran Jack's Shoes as a small "mom-and-pop" store that sold only men's and boys' shoes. They added women's and girls' footwear in 1982 and now carry shoes for the entire family. They have also become one of the largest athletic-shoe suppliers in Southern California and serve as the shoe source for many local sports teams.

With more than 60 brands of shoes, employees at Jack's Shoes and outlet store cheerfully offer full service to all customers. "Self-service is against our belief," says Spotts.

Except for two of the children—Peggy Jern, a gymnastics coach, and Caroline

Jack's Shoes is a full-service shoe store offering more than 60 brands of shoes for men, women, and children.

Corralejo, a nurse—most of the family still works at the shoe stores. Lisa, John, and Kathy Spotts are part of the management team at their father's stores. Marietta Spotts returned to her profession of teaching at the Simi Valley Adult School.

In addition to Jack's Shoes, Spotts has been extremely active in the community. He served a term on the Youth Employment Board, has been a board member and past president of the Simi Valley Chamber of Commerce, and was named 1985 Businessman of the Year. He was on the Planning Commission for four years and chaired the 1988 Planning Commission, whose task it was to update Simi Valley's general plan. In addition, Spotts served a term as president of the Simi Valley Cultural Association.

Jack's Shoes has tripled in size since its opening in 1974. This photo shows construction at the rear of the store that helped to expand its original 1,300 square feet.

ROBERT N. BROWN, JR., M.D.

Orthopedic surgeon Robert N. Brown, Jr., was the second in his family to practice medicine in Simi Valley. His father, Dr. Robert Brown, was a general surgeon who brought his practice to Simi when the hospital opened in 1965 and retired 10 years later.

Following in his father's footsteps, Dr. Robert N. Brown, Jr., established his Simi practice in 1973, after doing his residency at White Memorial Medical Center. Because he was interested in sports medicine, his residency program included a three-month fellowship with Drs. Robert Kerlan and Frank Jobe, team physicians for the Los Angeles Rams, Lakers, Dodgers, and Kings. He completed his undergraduate and medical studies at Loma Linda University.

In his practice as a "body and fender man," Dr. Brown treats a range of problems, from limbs to joints to necks and backs. More than half of his practice is devoted to sports medicine.

Dr. Brown has cared for most of the local athletic teams since he began his practice. He and his associates, Drs. William Frank and Todd Anderson, attend all of the home football games at Simi Valley and Royal high schools to treat injuries. They also have a free Saturday morning sports clinic to care for Friday night football injuries.

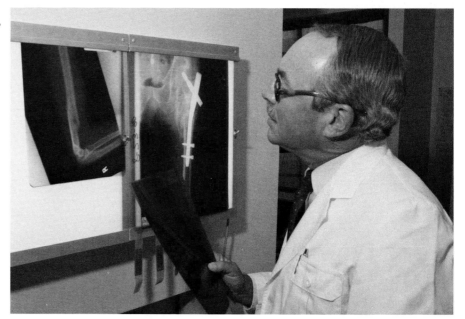

Dr. Robert N. Brown, Jr., has practiced in Simi Valley since 1973, specializing in sports medicine and treating most of the local sports teams.

"My goal as a physician is to return each young person to their hobby or sport as soon as possible, without allowing any further injury to themselves," says Dr. Brown.

Constantly involved with young athletes in the community, Dr. Brown gives preseason physical exams to all of the area teams. He was also instrumental in the organization and backing of the Simi Valley Institute of Sports Medicine, which provides funds and medical coverage for local athletics and educates coaches, parents, and athletes on injury prevention.

Throughout the years, Dr. Brown has donated thousands of dollars for sports equipment to local schools. He also helped to start a voluntary drug-testing program at the high schools—a program that was commended by former First Lady Nancy Reagan.

Dr. Brown is certified by the American Board of Orthopaedic Surgery and a fellow of the American Academy of Orthopaedic Surgery. He is on the staff at Simi Valley Adventist Hospital and was chief of staff in 1976 and chief of surgery in 1975. Nowadays more than half of his operations are done by arthroscopy—entering the knee, shoulder, or any joint with a camera that allows him to see and repair the joint. For his patients' convenience, he also employs a registered physical therapist, Richard Homokay.

Active in the community, Dr. Brown is a member of the Rotary Club and was president of that organization in 1978. Through the Rotary Club he founded the Sparky Anderson (then the Ron Perranoski) Celebrity Golf Tournament to raise money for youth charities in Simi Valley. He was also president of the board of directors of the Simi Valley Boys and Girls Club in 1976.

"I love this valley, and have and will do everything I can to make it a better and safer place to live and for young people to grow up," he says.

Early in 1990 Dr. Brown moved to a new office at 3695 Alamo Street.

Dr. Brown in his physical therapy gym.

DAVE'S CLUB SERVICE

Dave McCormick has helped the motoring public for many years, first as a reserve deputy sheriff and later as the operator of a towing company. He brought his services to Simi Valley in 1975, when he started Dave's Club Service by purchasing a towing company from Harper-Collins.

Dedicated to the welfare and safety of the motoring public, the company's primary function is to provide road services at reasonable prices. Motorists with car problems can call Dave's Club Service to troubleshoot the problems and tow their vehicles to places where repair work is done. Dave's Club Service also handles minor roadside emergencies such as changing flat tires, jump starting dead batteries, or helping motorists who are locked out of their cars.

In addition to helping stranded motorists, Dave's Club Service is an official police tow, towing cars from accident scenes and righting overturned trucks. The company also works with the police to provide security for impounded vehicles.

Although Dave's Club Service mainly covers the Simi Valley and Moorpark areas, it has helped customers as far away as Sacramento and San Diego. The company is headquartered at 890 West Los Angeles Avenue in Simi Valley.

Since Dave's Club Service began in 1975, the number of employees has tripled, from four to 12. McCormick constantly upgrades his equipment to keep up with the ever-changing models of vehicles.

"We've had the opportunity to grow with the community. We like putting something back," says McCormick, who is also active in several service organizations.

McCormick is a charter member of the local chapter of the International Footprint Association, a service club dedicated to improving communication between law

Dave McCormick, owner.

enforcement officials and community businesses. As a former reserve deputy sheriff in Santa Barbara and current Simi businessperson, McCormick understands the concerns of both entities.

McCormick was also instrumental in reviving Simi Valley Days in 1985 and bringing professional rodeo back to the valley for that event. He served as the chairman of the 1988 Simi Valley Days and works on the project annually. He also served as president of the Simi Valley Chamber of Commerce in 1988-89 and is a charter member of the Rotary Club of Simi Sunrise.

In addition to community service organizations, McCormick also belongs to several trade organizations. He has served on the board of the California Tow Truck Association. In 1980 he founded a Tri-County Chapter of that organization, covering Ventura, Santa Barbara, and San Luis Obispo counties. He also served as the first president of that group.

McCormick and his family live in the community. His wife, Beverly, and daughter, Janice, also work in the office at Dave's Club Service. The McCormicks also have a younger daughter, Jessica, and a married daughter, Joyce Cordone, who lives in Texas.

Dave's Club Service assists stranded motorists by providing towing services and performing minor roadside repairs.

CHARLES NEAULT, D.C.—SOUTHERN CALIFORNIA BACK CENTERS

For patients considering back surgery, Dr. Charles Neault provides a last hope, often saving them from the operating table and allowing them to live a normal life.

Neault, a chiropractor and executive director of Southern California Back Centers, specializes in a nonsurgical technique for cervical and lumbar disc herniations and ruptures, a condition commonly treated by surgery. Neault studied the technique, known as "closed-reduction distraction," with its creator, Dr. James Cox. Neault was one of the first California doctors to use the technique and now teaches it in the United States and Canada.

Most of Neault's patients sought his help after being told their conditions required surgery. His nonsurgical procedure stretches the disc fibers, creating a natural vacuum that gently moves the nucleus back where it belongs. Several area back surgeons consult with Neault, who is on staff at a Canoga Park hospital.

"One fascinating aspect of the technique is that, when done properly, there is no way that it will harm a patient. If a patient is not 50 percent improved within three to four weeks after initiation of treatment, they are referred for surgical options," he says.

For other back-related problems, Neault and his staff at Southern California Back Centers use standard chiropractic manipulations, therapeutic modalities, and nutritional counseling.

A graduate of the Cleveland Chiropractic College in Los Angeles, Neault holds a master's degree in biology and a certificate in clinical nutrition from Bridgeport University. He began in Simi Valley in 1978, working for another chiropractor, and opened his own practice in March 1978. In 1986 he formed Southern California Back Centers, and he opened a smaller satellite office in Westlake Village in 1988. Eventually he hopes to have several offices throughout Southern California that offer the special technique.

Due to his hectic schedule, Neault sees mainly the most difficult cases, but all of the chiropractors in his offices are certified in the Cox procedure. Neault also acts as an independent medical examiner for injury and disability claims and consults with area businesses on health and safety matters.

Because many back injuries are preventable, Neault offers free "back schools" for the community twice a month at his offices at 2345 Erringer Road in Simi Valley.

Neault is a past president of the Ventura County Chiropractic Society. In addition to his busy work schedule, he has served on the board of the Boys and Girls Club, the Simi Valley Chamber of Commerce, and the Rotary Club. He is a lay minister and member of the Bishop's Committee of St. Francis Church. In 1981 the Jaycees named him one of the Outstanding Young Men in America. Neault is an associate professor at Cleveland Chiropractic College and is on the postgraduate faculty of National College of Chiropractic and Life Chiropractic College West.

Dr. Charles C. Neault, executive director of Southern California Back Centers.

LEDERER DEVELOPMENT GROUP

The Lederer Development Group was formed in 1979 by the husband-and-wife team of Gene and Jeanie Lederer and their associate, Chuck Morgan. Each has a different area of expertise—Chuck is an architect; Gene is a real estate attorney; and Jeanie is a leasing agent.

Impressed with the city's standards for land development and zoning, Chuck Morgan encouraged the Lederers to explore Simi Valley. Touring the area in 1979, Gene chose a parcel of land at 2585 Cochran for a commercial project. The land had been slated for condominiums, but Gene felt his plan would be better for the area, so he acquired the property and went to great lengths to have it rezoned.

His insightful vision became the Landmark Center, an award-winning 30,000-square-foot commercial building, which opened in 1985 with restaurants and shops. Morgan designed the structure with split levels to use the natural slope, while maximizing street visibility and aesthetics. The center received its name after an area newspaper awarded its design as a landmark building in 1986.

Lederer's second major Simi Valley project was a 50,000-square-foot shopping center at the corner of Madera and Royal, completed in 1988. With a drugstore, a grocery store, restaurants, specialty shops, and offices, the Madera Royale Plaza contains a well-balanced tenant mix. As the leasing

agent, Jeanie strove to create a perfect balance of retailers. The center is very well located, with approximately 50,000 cars passing it daily.

"We spent a lot of time in research, finding out what the neighborhood wanted," says Gene Lederer. They promised to give the residents what they requested, even when it meant losing money by keeping a liquor store out of the development.

"The goal of Lederer Development has always been to develop quality environment with emphasis on the public good," says Morgan, a member of the American Institute of Architects.

In 1991 the company will begin construction of a 25,000-square-foot office building located on 1.6 acres behind the Landmark Center. Lederer has also developed several Los Angeles structures, including an office building near the Beverly Center.

A 1961 graduate of UCLA Law School, Gene Lederer started his career with a law firm that represented the Building Contractors Association. He later founded his own firm, eventually specializing in real estate tax law. In 1989 he gave up his practice to focus on real estate development. Gene Lederer is also a member of the International Council of Shopping Centers, the Rotary Club of Century City, the Arizona State Board of CPAs, and the California Bar Association.

The Lederer children, who enthusiastically attended city council and planning meetings with their parents when they were younger, have grown up to follow in their parents' footsteps. Son Mike began developing houses shortly after he graduated from USC, and daughter Deanna, a marketing major at the University of Arizona, works with her brother.

ABOVE: The award-winning Landmark Center was the first Simi project for Lederer Development Group.

BELOW: Chuck Morgan (left), Jeanie Lederer (center), and Gene Lederer (right) at the Madera Royale Plaza.

C.A. RASMUSSEN, INC.

a helicopter pad at its Simi Valley headquarters to provide efficient transportation to distant work sites.

The Rasmussen brothers' early years of fieldwork and personally operating the equipment have given them insight into the needs of their workers and have caused them to be concerned about the welfare of the people in the field.

C.A. Rasmussen, Inc., is one of the few companies in Southern California to offer a complete general engineering construction service. To provide better service for a variety of customers, the company is divided

LEFT: Company founder Carl A. Rasmussen, seen here in 1972, envisioned a promising future through innovation.

BELOW: C.A. Rasmussen, Inc., purchased the first Caterpillar D10 tractor in Southern California in 1979. Its debut marked a milestone in local construction history. Vicki Rasmussen, Dean's wife, inaugurates the new Cat D10.

As California real estate boomed in the early 1960s, Carl A. Rasmussen formed a construction company to meet a portion of the expansion. In 1964 he began grading the way for the transition of Simi Valley from an agricultural area into an attractive suburban community. By the time of his death in 1989, his business had become the largest earthmoving company in Southern California.

The company began in 1964 when Rasmussen left the L.M. Wilson Company of Simi to found his own company. Although he started with limited resources, Rasmussen participated closely in local development, providing excavation and grading services to many builders and developers who were creating numerous new subdivisions. As the area population and economy expanded, C.A. Rasmussen grew with it. One of the company's major early projects was the access road to the Magic Mountain amusement park.

Over the years the business grew under the joint management and leadership of Carl and his sons, Dean, Larry, and Charlie. In 1978 Carl sold the business to his sons, who continue to run the successful com-

pany. All three are working managers who go to great lengths to maintain good relations with each other, with their customers, and with their employees. The company employs a union work force of more than 500 people and has been signatory to the Operating Engineers Agreement since its inception. The company also is signatory to the Teamsters, Cement Masons, and Laborers agreements.

Family life is important to the Rasmussens, who try to see that their employees have the time they need to spend with their families.

"The philosophy of the company, historically, is not to operate more than one hour from the office, so that employees work eight hours per day, five days per week," says Dean Rasmussen, who likes to see each employee go home every night without a long, tiring drive and without having to live at the work site. To meet that end the company hires local workers and has

into three divisions: earthmoving, fine grade, and public works.

"We reshape the earth to better suit God's intended plan. In areas prone to erosion, we reinforce the ground," says Dean, who holds a degree in construction engineering from Arizona State University.

Between Dean and the rest of the staff, the company has the in-house ability to provide a variety of services, including grading highways and roads, flood control channels, asphalt and concrete paving, site developments, storm drains and pipelines, demolition and clearing, curbs, gutters, sidewalks, bridges and foundations, and dams and reservoirs.

C.A. Rasmussen, Inc., offers a turnkey approach that provides a service to private developers by assuming responsibility for all of their site development needs. Because of this the company has become a dependable source of diversified construction packages that include work normally requiring several contractors, or large-scale subcontracting by contractors whose separate talents might not equal that of C.A. Rasmussen, Inc.

The company motto encompasses three key objectives: "Safety, Quality, and Service." Safety is the first order of work on all Rasmussen projects. The company's safety program is a model for the industry, exceeding all federal and state requirements. To ensure quality the company developed standards of performance that exceed normal specifications in public works. Service is never more than a quick phone call away. A 24-hour emergency telephone service and comprehensive radio communication system enable them to respond to emergency situations and natural disasters on short notice.

"We are highly innovative and on the cutting edge of high technology," says Dean. "We feel we have an edge over our competition because we assess new products and incorporate them into our system far earlier than other companies."

C.A. Rasmussen is so innovative, in fact,

ABOVE: The corporate helicopter provides Rasmussen managers immediate access to all job sites.

RIGHT: Rasmussen takes pride in its position as an industry innovator. All equipment and methods used by the company are state of the art.

that the Caterpillar tractor company uses the firm to demonstrate and test its latest equipment. Rasmussen's engineers also collaborate with Caterpillar on new designs. In 1979 Rasmussen was the first company to use Caterpillar's revolutionary D10 tractors, which allow the moving of stubborn ground without traditional blasting.

C.A. Rasmussen, Inc., has worked on dozens of local developments, including Wood Ranch, Indian Hills, and huge projects for Larwin, JBR, and Griffin Homes.

"Some years have been extremely busy, while others have been slow," says Dean.

The company also donates its time and equipment to the community and has helped build many soccer and little league sports fields in the communities it serves.

"We want to keep roots in Simi Valley," says Dean, who has served as treasurer of the Southern California Contractors Association and on the board of the Viewpoint School. The other brothers also are active in community activities—Charlie has been active with the Boy Scouts of America, and Larry has served on the boards of the Henry Mayo Hospital, the Boys and Girls Club in Newhall, and the City of Santa Clarita General Plan Advisory Committee. C.A. Rasmussen, Inc., also belongs to the Building Industry Association and the Association of General Contractors of California.

C.A. Rasmussen, Inc.'s corporate office, located at 2360 Shasta Way in Simi Valley.

SIMI VALLEY BANK

As Simi Valley experienced burgeoning growth in the 1970s, it became apparent that the community needed its own hometown bank to provide local financial services for residents and retailers. In 1978 a group of area businesspeople came together to meet that need and formed the Simi Valley Bank.

That year Robert Pegg, then manager of the Simi Valley Chamber of Commerce, got the ball rolling by setting up a meeting between County Supervisor Ted Grandsen, former mayor Jim Smith, attorney James Basile, and Harry Fein, a Beverly Hills bank manager who advised the businesspeople. The group then conferred with a state banking official who told them that they would need about $45,000 for an initial prospectus and licensing fees.

The seed money was then collected from 21 area businesses, each of whom invested $2,000. The community was enthusiastic about the endeavor, says Pegg, who acted as bank secretary until Susan Deese joined the staff when the bank opened in 1981.

"When the word got out, people were coming up to me with $2,000 checks. We got more than we needed and had to return some," he recalls.

During the next three years bank organizers obtained the necessary state and federal licenses, sold stock, and scouted out locations. With an initial capitalization of $1.5 million, Simi Valley Bank opened its doors on March 16, 1981. Of the 21 founders, several served on the board of directors, including Mike Schweitzer, James Basile, Harry L. Fein, Robert Landegger, James Smith, Robert Pegg, Riley Spencer, Jr., Richard Rhoads, Elvin Gaines, M.D., and Bruce Strathearn. Other bank founders were Sander Bass, James Dollar, Gregor Hartung, Jerome Kimmel, Jerome Label, Douglas Leming, William Nelson, Robert Shaver, David Strathearn, Jr., Thomas Vujovich, Velma Warne, and James Waters.

The bank opened with 10 employees in a small temporary mobile unit at what is now the rear lot of the main office at 1475 East Los Angeles Avenue. Richard Shaffer was the bank's first president; E. Wayne Cottle was vice president; and Susan Deese (still with the bank) was their assistant. In 1985

ABOVE: This trailer was transformed into the original office of Simi Valley Bank, opening for business with 10 employees on March 16, 1981.

LEFT: The Moorpark branch, located at 95 East High Street, was opened in 1986.

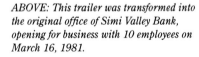

the bank opened its permanent two-story main office building. Also that year, R.F. "Dick" Riggs became president and chief executive officer and began serving on the board of directors.

"Our philosophy has been, is, and always will be to service the needs of the community, retail, and consumer business better than other banks," says Riggs.

One way it has met those needs is by placing several branch offices at strategic locations throughout the area, says Riggs. The bank added a branch in Sycamore Plaza in 1984; Stonegate Square in 1985; and on High Street in Moorpark in 1986. Additional branches may be added in the future.

Standing, from left: Riley J. Spencer, Jr.; James N. Smith; Elvin C. Gaines, M.D.; and Bruce Strathearn. Seated, from left: Michael Schweitzer, Richard Rhoads, R.F. Riggs, and Robert E. Pegg.

"We want to service eastern Ventura County. We're not particularly interested in going outside of that area. We still address that primary region," says Bruce Strathearn, chairman of the board. "Most of our loans are made to local residents, so the money stays in the community," he adds.

Indeed, all loan decisions are made in Simi Valley. Once the Simi Valley Bank opened, local borrowers did not have to leave the area to seek a loan for their home, car, or business. Because they are familiar with the area and its residents, Simi Valley Bank officers can analyze loan requests at the local level and give their decisions in a relatively short amount of time.

Simi Valley Bank offers a full range of banking services, including checking and savings accounts, competitive interest rates, all kinds of loans, nationally accessible automatic teller machines, and international credit cards. What makes the bank unique is the hometown spirit and personal attention it gives each client. Simi Valley Bank

is the only one in the area that has sit-down banking—customers sit at individual stations while interacting with the tellers.

"I think there's a real warmth in this bank that people really like. People know they can get ahold of the president or the chairman of the board. You can't do that at big banks," says Barbara Williamson, vice president and branch manager.

"At larger banks, customers become statistics," says Strathearn. "Here, bank personnel know their customers."

With the growth of the bank and the addition of branch offices, the number of bank employees grew from the original 10 to more than 80 by 1990. Most of the staff live in Simi Valley and are involved in community activities, including the Simi Valley Chamber of Commerce, the Boys and Girls Club, and other organizations. The bank participates in Simi Valley Days and other community events.

Over the years Simi Valley Bank has grown with the community while continuing

to meet its customers' needs. While it offers major credit cards, it records its customers' accounts on in-bank computers (not at a faraway location), giving direct and easy access should problems arise.

Simi Valley Bank stock is sold over the counter, and stockholders have done well with their faith in the local bank. Historically the directors have given cash and stock dividends almost every year. By 1989 the bank's assets had grown to more than $79 million.

Although Simi Valley Bank has grown up with the community, it has not outgrown its trademark one-to-one service and friendly, hometown style.

"We'll continue to beat the big banks at their own game," says Strathearn. "Service—being recognized when you walk in—that's our creed."

CENTURY 21 TABOR REALTORS

A former automobile mechanic, Fred Tabor entered real estate in 1971 because he enjoys helping people through the challenging maze of buying and selling houses and property. Today he owns Century 21 Tabor Realtors, one of the most successful real estate companies in Simi Valley.

Tabor started in Simi Valley real estate in 1971, after moving to the area from Canoga Park. Tabor came to California in 1961 from Missouri. In 1973 he purchased Dynamic Realty, Inc. By 1976 he had created a company of 650 employees with 13 Southern California offices. He merged with Seb Serpa in 1981, forming Serpa-Tabor Gallery of Homes. In 1985 they sold the company to Merrill Lynch; Tabor, however, retained the Simi Valley office.

When Tabor reopened Tabor Realtors in 1986, it was practically like starting from scratch, with only six people working in the office, but the business grew quickly. By 1989 Tabor had more than 100 staffers in four area offices: two in Simi Valley, one in Camarillo, and one in Oxnard. He plans to add a Moorpark office in the early 1990s.

In 1988 Tabor joined Century 21, one of the largest international real estate networks, with 7,000 offices in the United States and 1,000 internationally. Tabor was so successful that he grossed $1.6 million his first year, making his the first Simi office to earn Century 21's prestigious Centurion status.

Century 21 Tabor Realtors offers a full range of real estate services, including residential and commercial sales, property management, and relocation planning. The company also has escrow and mortgage divisions. In his business, Tabor works closely with his sales agents and his clients.

"To sell a property once, you really have to sell it twice—once to the sales force and then to the buyers," he says. "My goal is to get the most money in the shortest period of time with the fewest inconveniences to the seller."

Tabor advertises his listings on cable television, with local weekly shows televised throughout Ventura County and the western San Fernando Valley.

Century 21 Tabor Realtors is headquartered in the Executive Center in Simi Valley. The company specializes in residential and office buildings and offers services in planning, processing, sales, escrow, and mortgages.

Active in many professional organizations, Tabor was the president of the Simi Valley Board of Realtors three times—in 1977, 1978, and 1986. He currently maintains memberships on six area boards. In addition, he has been a regional vice president of the California Association of Realtors.

Tabor lives on a Moorpark ranch with his wife, June. They have two grown children, Jamie and Christina. In his spare time, Tabor raises and shows horses.

Fred Tabor, owner of Century 21 Tabor Realtors.

OAKRIDGE ATHLETIC CLUB

As Americans became more conscious of health and fitness in the late 1970s, it became apparent that Simi Valley needed exercise facilities. To meet that need, a group of five local businessmen bankrolled the Oakridge Athletic Club, which opened as a racquet club in June 1980.

The endeavor was such a success that three years later the club expanded its facilities to include a full range of popular exercise options, including aerobic classes, swimming, and weight training. A large heated outdoor pool was added for lap swimming and water aerobics. To date, it is still the only club to offer so many facilities at one location.

Situated on three scenic acres directly off the Simi Valley Freeway at 2655 Erringer Road, the club has five lighted outdoor tennis courts and seven indoor racquetball courts. Oakridge Athletic Club offers tennis and racquetball lessons and actively promotes league participation. Additionally, a full range of other social events in both sports is ongoing.

Although the club began with its primary

focus on racquet sports, it evolved into a full-service health club with exercise classes and equipment for people of all ages and fitness levels. Friendly employees offer personal instruction on the various modes of exercise, which include stair climbing, treadmills, and rowing machines; Lifecycles (electronic exercise bicycles); a 12-station Nautilus circuit; and 4,000 square feet of free weights. More than 50 employees help to deliver a high degree of service to Oakridge members.

Certified instructors teach 11 aerobics classes daily, including water aerobics, which range in intensity and impact levels. The classes are given in a 2,500-square-foot room that has state-of-the-art flooring and stereo sound equipment for maximum

Aerobics classes taught by certified instructors are conducted in a 2,500-square-foot, carpeted room featuring a stereo sound system.

enjoyment and health benefits.

The spacious athletic club also has a pro shop, snack bar, coed whirlpool area, and separate saunas, showers, and locker rooms for men and women. Future expansion plans include an indoor basketball court, indoor swimming pool, cardiovascular center, and expanded weight facility. A supervised nursery is available for children during most of the club's operating hours.

Paramount to the club's success is its philosophy of superior service to its 5,000 members.

"We are a no-contract club. When you join, you pay a one-time initiation fee and monthly dues, but you're not obligated to remain—you can walk away anytime without owing the club future dues. That puts the onus of performance on us," says managing general partner Ron Meek.

In addition to keeping Simi Valley residents in shape, the Oakridge Athletic Club also helps the community with donations and participation in a wide range of local charities and special fund raisers.

In the future, the club plans to expand its offerings in the area of health education, such as community classes on such topics as quitting smoking. The club also will develop more programs for senior citizens. Oakridge Athletic Club will continue to change to meet the growing needs of Simi Valley.

LEFT: Oakridge is a full-service health club for people of all ages and fitness levels.

BELOW: Oakridge members have access to the club's heated outdoor pool.

THE CALLAHAN FAMILY

Longtime Simi Valley resident Roger Callahan remembers the cold mornings at his grandparents' walnut farm.

"Early in the morning, I could hear my grandfather in the kitchen. By the time you smelled the coffee, it was usually warm enough to get up," reminisces Callahan, grandson of pioneer walnut farmer James H. Callahan.

In 1918 James and his wife, Ann, set out with their three sons—Robert, Eldon, and Frank—to farm walnuts in Simi Valley. The pioneering family had already owned a livery stable near Garden Grove and had homesteaded land in Arizona. They then chose Simi Valley, where members of Ann's family (the Houghtons) had begun farming.

When they arrived in Simi, they settled on 20 acres on Walnut Street in the Tapo area of what was then Santa Susana. James planted walnut trees and raised beans and vegetables on the fertile soil while waiting for the trees to mature.

In 1938 Robert and his father purchased an additional 145-acre ranch in Santa Susana, bounded by Cochran, Tapo, and railroad tracks. What later became commercial land then had only walnut and apricot trees on it.

In 1937 Robert married Theda Williams of Ventura. They had three children: Roger, Joyce, and Lyndel. James Callahan died in 1945, but Robert carried on the walnut business.

In 1947 Robert completed construction on a house on the corner of the ranch, where a Texaco station now stands at Cochran and Tapo. In the year following, he built a large dehydrator building to process the walnuts, which were dried, bagged, and sold. Roger grew up around both ranches, working as a ranch hand in the family operation. During the autumn Harvest Crews joined the Callahans to harvest the crop.

By the late 1950s farming had declined in Simi Valley due to a decreasing water table and increasing urbanization. In 1960 the Callahans harvested their last crop of walnuts. They then sold part of the ranch to JBR Developments for housing projects, but the Callahans kept the land along Tapo for commercial development. In 1961

A truckload of dried walnuts, ready for shipping.

INSET: James Callahan (center) holds grandson Roger, with son Robert on the right, at the ranch on Walnut Street.

Robert Callahan founded the Tapo Village Shopping Center (between Alpine and Industrial streets).

Roger Callahan took over the property management when his father, Robert, had a stroke in 1963 and then died in 1975. Roger has three children—Debra, Tracy, and Robert. He lives in the house his father built, which was moved to Avenida Simi in the early 1960s.

Active in the community, Roger Callahan was named the 1988 Citizen of the Year by

the Simi Valley Chamber of Commerce. He also has been chamber president, a member of the first City Planning Commission, and past president of the noontime Rotary Club. He and his wife, Lee, also are active in the Simi Valley Historical Society.

GARY D. CHAFFEE, D.D.S.

Dr. Gary Chaffee has enjoyed providing general dentistry and orthodontics in his Simi Valley practice since 1979. Located at 2720 Cochran Street, his second-story office offers a view of beautiful Simi Valley from every chair. In fact, some of the most breathtaking sunsets in all of the southland

premedical courses at Pacific Union College in Northern California. He earned his dental degree in 1975 from Loma Linda University Dental School in San Bernardino County. Upon receiving his Doctor of Dental Surgery degree, he and his wife, Tricia, served the next three years at a missionary hospital in

Trinidad, West Indies. They helped provide dental services and health education in urban and rural areas, and returned to California in 1979.

In addition to his regular practice, Dr. Chaffee often visits local elementary schools and preschools where he teaches students about nutrition and oral hygiene. He also gives office tours to help children feel more comfortable with their surroundings prior to regular office visits.

Dr. Gary Chaffee is a member of the Santa Barbara-Ventura County Dental Society, the California Dental Association, and the American Dental Association, as well as being active with youth groups in the Seventh–day Adventist Church and supporting community projects.

Dr. Chaffee would like to see all of his patients maintain a healthy smile. After all, he says, "Your smile is one of my best assets!"

ABOVE: (From left) Dr. Gary D. Chaffee, Melody Harris, Teri Ash, and Terri Lynn Crook.

RIGHT: (From left) Donna Flores, Ann Marie Allen, Tricia Chaffee, Mary Beth Lev, and Jill Hadden

have been viewed from the westerly facing windows of his dental operatories.

Patients often comment that "his office has such a warm and friendly atmosphere." Dr. Chaffee modestly attributes this to his caring, well trained staff.

Dr. Chaffee and his dental team provide a wide range of services, including preventative dental care, endodontics, orthodontics, and teeth whitening. Dr. Chaffee offered dental care for patients of all ages, and seeing a patient's smile improve is what he enjoys most about his practice.

A Granada Hills native, Dr. Chaffee took

CITY OF SIMI VALLEY

When Simi Valley incorporated on October 10, 1969, the goal of the City's leaders was to create a balanced community that could grow in a well-planned manner while meeting the needs of its residents. Simi Valley has managed to meet that goal, blossoming from a bedroom community of less than 50,000 people to a thriving city with more than 100,000 residents and many major corporations.

When ranching declined in the late 1950s, developers arrived on the scene in search of inexpensive land near the San Fernando Valley and Los Angeles. What they found was cleaner air, less traffic, majestic views, and wide open spaces. Since then, people have flocked to Simi Valley as a refuge from more congested areas, and the population has grown an average of 3 percent annually since 1970.

Major companies have been attracted to Simi Valley for the same reasons and a few more—leasing or constructing a facility in Simi Valley costs considerably less than in the Los Angeles or San Fernando Valley areas. Simi Valley's highly skilled and educated work force provides corporations with quality employees who prefer to work close to home. Chase Econometric Associates,

Inc., identified Simi Valley as part of the fifth-highest job growth area in the nation during the 1980s.

New businesses sprang up in the 1970s and 1980s as commercial developers became aware of Simi Valley's comparatively inexpensive land, and corporations learned of all the desirable aspects of Simi Valley. In 1982 Farmers Insurance Group was the first major company to locate in Simi Valley. Development continued to soar when interest rates dropped in 1984, the year in which two other major companies—First Interstate Bancard and Whittaker/Tasker—came to town. Gibraltar Savings came in 1987 and Bugle Boy Industries relocated its fashion and distribution headquarters to Simi Valley in 1989. A large regional mall is planned to open in the early 1990s.

Because of the managed growth and planned progress, Simi Valley has been

rated one of the nation's top 10 employment growth areas and has the highest median family income in Ventura County. The City has actively promoted the development of clean industry, drawing successful and respected industrial and commercial enterprises to the area.

The City government is committed to maintaining the high quality of life in Simi Valley. Throughout the years the City Council has achieved a rare balance of acknowledging progress and maintaining a superior environment.

"The goal of the City has always been aimed at protecting the quality of life," says Mayor Greg Stratton. "Our goal is to acquire commercial development, but not give up our semi-rural life-style.

"When it comes to important issues, Simi Valley's City Council has been proactive, rather than reactive," states Stratton.

RIGHT: The Santa Susana Pass Road was the only eastern entry to Simi Valley prior to the construction of the 118 Freeway.

BELOW: Simi Valley has something for everyone: wide open spaces, as well as a residential and commercial sector.

"This is a city government that really wants participation. Our City Council doesn't stand on being aloof or being afraid to do something different," he adds, noting that Simi Valley has been a leader in no-tax cities (the City levies no ad valorem property taxes, subsisting mainly on subventions from retail sales taxes collected by the state).

The City Council is the City's legislative and policy-making body. The four Council Members are elected at large on a nonpartisan basis for four-year terms, staggered so that only two seats are up for reelection every two years. The mayor, elected biannu-

Transportation is convenient and abundant in Simi Valley. Train service and municipal bus transportation are available. Camarillo Airport and Burbank Airport are within a half-hour drive.

ally on a nonpartisan basis, is a member of the City Council and is the ceremonial head of the City who presides at all Council meetings. The City Council and its members also preside as the Board of Directors of the Simi Valley County Sanitation District, Ventura County Waterworks District No. 8, the Community Development Agency, and the Simi Valley Industrial Development Authority.

Much of Simi Valley's success as a balanced community is attributable to the active role of its residents. Residents have several opportunities to become involved in local decisions. Many address the City Council with their concerns. Other are active in their individual Neighborhood Councils, to which every resident, age 18 and above, belongs. Simi Valley is divided into four Neighborhood Councils, who are advisory to the City Council. The City also has an active Youth Council and individual members sit with and report to the Council at regular intervals.

The City Council also appoints citizens to advisory boards, such as the Planning Commission and the Council on Aging.

The City's staff has grown considerably since the first City Council meeting in 1969, when the Council appointed five employees; by 1990 there were 487 City employees. The 35,000-square-foot city hall complex at 2929 Tapo Canyon Road was completed in 1984, with a 10,000-square-foot addition in 1988.

"People are proud they live in Simi Valley. The City is well maintained," says Mayor Stratton.

Throughout the years the City of Simi Valley has provided a plethora of top-notch community services, with programs geared toward residents of all ages. The City has its own transit maintenance facility for its buses, which connect all industrial areas with residential tracts and commercial facilities on an hourly basis. The City also sponsors a variety of housing programs. City youth services include employment, job training, and delinquency prevention programs. Simi Valley's low income senior citizens can receive rental assistance and home-delivered "Meals on Wheels." In 1985

RIGHT: Simi Valley is a safe community. The city's K-9 Unit is one resource utilized to deter crime.

BELOW: The 45,000-square-foot City Hall blends in well with the environment.

the City completed its Senior Center, which offers employment assistance, van and volunteer escort services, recreational and educational classes, weekday lunches, health care, and social services.

A leader in environmental issues, Simi Valley was the first city in Ventura County to initiate a curbside recycling program.

Simi Valley is also a safe community that has experienced the lowest crime rate in the nation for a city of its size.

As the City of Simi Valley heads through the 1990s into the twenty-first century, its leaders will continue planning and maintaining a community that has a balanced and vibrant economy. Simi Valley will continually strive to remain a community that responds to the needs of its citizens and accommodates business relocation to the area.

SPECTRUM LAND PLANNING, INC.

Spectrum Land Planning, Inc., was founded in 1976 as a subdivision engineering firm dedicated to providing superior service to its clients.

Today Spectrum continues to provide that service in land planning and civil engineering, specializing in hillside development. Since 1982 the firm has also provided complete architectural design services on a wide variety of residential, commercial, and industrial projects within the Southern California area.

Spectrum Land Planning was founded by Dick Odle and Ken Boswell in 1976. The two, having previously worked for the same engineering firm, decided to start their own company based on their understanding of the importance of business relationships and priority of service in an engineering firm. Bill Fowler joined the firm in 1978 and is currently the president. Boswell left the company in 1984 and Odle in 1990.

Originally located in Canoga Park, Spectrum moved to Simi Valley in 1980 after a restaurant fire damaged part of their office building on Topanga Canyon Boulevard. At first, they moved into an incomplete 800-square-foot office, with only one telephone, and have since grown to an 8,500-square-foot suite in the same building at 5775 Los Angeles Avenue. Since the firm began, the number of employees has increased from six to 35.

Spectrum's staff includes licensed civil engineers and licensed architects who offer their longtime experience in a wide diversity of design solutions. The staff is supported by numerous consultants—dedicated to Spectrum's philosophy of service and design excellence—who provide structural, mechanical, electrical, and landscaping design.

In addition to land planning, Spectrum is one of only six companies nationwide that designs military family housing for the U.S. government. This began in 1979 with a project at Ford Ord, and to date the firm has provided more than 7,800 units of housing nationwide.

The firm's design experience includes 705 factory-built units within three projects constructed at Adak, Alaska, and Fort Irwin, California. The project at Adak was granted an Award of Merit by the Pacific Coast Builders Conference. Spectrum also completed several site-built projects ranging in size from 100 to 583 units in seven states.

In designing the military housing, Spectrum's team works with general contractors to develop proposals that fit the government's stringent cost/quality criteria. Together, they create housing designs that are cost efficient while meeting the government's technical standards and specifications.

Critical to Spectrum's success is a business and design philosophy that mandates teamwork.

The Spectrum Land Planning, Inc., team works extensively with the latest computer technology, using computer assisted design and high-quality laser graphics.

Call and let Spectrum's team work for you.

The Spectrum Land Planning team.

RANCHO SEQUOIA VETERINARY HOSPITAL

Dr. Douglas Aberle offers a full range of animal care services at his practice, Rancho Sequoia Veterinary Hospital.

Rancho Sequoia Veterinary Hospital offers a full range of pet care for dogs and cats, as well as other household pets. Services range from routine checkups and preventive vaccines to dentistry, nutritional counseling, radiology, cardiology, internal medicine, surgery, laboratory diagnostics, and intensive care. Emergency service is available around the clock.

The hospital is equipped with state-of-the-art operating room and X-ray and laboratory equipment. Because veterinary patients cannot verbalize their aches, pains, and discomforts, great emphasis is placed on the physical examinations, histories, and diagnostic tests.

"My goal is to offer the highest quality veterinary medicine possible and to keep the lines of communication between the doctor and the client [pet owner] open," says Aberle. "We also attempt to obtain the latest equipment and have the highest quality of staff available, from the doctors and animal health technicians to the receptionists, veterinary assistants, and the kennel-persons."

Rancho Sequoia Veterinary Hospital subscribes to the high standards of the American Animal Hospital Association (AAHA), an accrediting organization that inspects and evaluates veterinary hospitals regularly. The hospital is certified by AAHA.

In addition to their medical services, Aberle and his staff volunteer time in the community, teaching pet care at local schools and talking with teenagers at high school career days. They also work with Pet Assistance and other nonprofit groups that raise funds to assist people with the costs of spaying and neutering their pets. Aberle is also a member of the Simi Valley Kiwanis Club.

Rancho Sequoia Veterinary Hospital is located at 3380 Los Angeles Avenue. Aberle purchased the property once belonging to longtime Simi resident Frisbie Brown. The Brown family had owned the land since 1904. For many years Alice and Irving Brown (Frisbie's parents) operated a walnut grove on the site.

Douglas and Sandy Aberle live in Simi Valley with their daughters Shayna and Lindsey.

When Douglas Aberle was growing up on a farm in Kansas, he spent some long nights bringing young calves in from the cold to warm up in a bathtub. Today Aberle continues caring for animals as a veterinarian in Simi Valley at the Rancho Sequoia Veterinary Hospital.

Aberle came to Simi Valley in 1971, having received his doctor of veterinary medicine degree in 1971 from Kansas State University. He worked for other Ventura County veterinarians for several years. He opened his own practice, the Rancho Sequoia Veterinary Hospital, a 2,800-square-foot facility, on March 25, 1978.

At first Aberle was the sole veterinarian at his hospital, but over the years the practice grew to include several veterinarians, technicians, and assistants. To meet the needs of the growing practice, Aberle's wife, Sandy, a former educator, became the full-time office manager in 1982.

CERTIFIED AUTO GLASS

Certified Auto Glass owner Joseph Moradzadeh believes in giving his customers the best he can and then some. His attitude earned him the nickname "the generous one," which he uses proudly as his company's slogan.

"I like pleasing people and giving them what they like," he says. "I deliver what I promise for a fair price."

When Moradzadeh opened his shop in 1981, it was the first in Simi Valley to specialize in auto glass replacement. Working for insurance companies, car dealerships, and the general public, Certified Auto Glass replaces windows and windshields in all makes of cars and trucks. Prior to opening the shop, Moradzadeh worked for more than a decade in an upper management position for a similar company in the Los Angeles area.

Moradzadeh chose to locate his business in Simi Valley because he lived there and felt the need for such a shop in the area. He started his company as a one-man, one-

truck operation. Within eight years the business increased to six employees and five vehicles. His shop grew from its original 400 square feet at 4359 Shopping Lane to a larger shop at 2205 First Street to his current 2,000-square-foot facility at 2180 First Street. He has been at the current location in the Auto World Center since 1987.

Moradzadeh and his staff replace auto glass at their shop and at the customer's location, be it a car dealership, body shop, home, or office. They use state-of-the-art installation tools, high-quality sealants, and glass approved by the car companies for each specific model.

"The auto glass industry is changing so fast. Consumers should find out if the glass

Joseph Moradzadeh with one of several trucks used by Certified Auto Glass to provide service at the customer's location.

used is the same as the original." If not, they could have problems later on, he warns. Even with the wide array of cars on the road, Moradzadeh can usually procure the necessary replacement parts within two hours.

Certified Auto Glass also does some minor construction jobs as well as glass and mirror work in homes and offices.

Although he puts in long hours six days a week for his business, Moradzadeh also finds time to volunteer to the Boys and Girls Club. He has donated his glass-crafting skills and materials to make aquariums that the club auctioned to raise money for various projects. He enjoys the chance to support the community whenever possible.

Born in Persia, Moradzadeh came to the United States with his parents as a child. He has lived in Simi Valley with his wife, Lynne, since 1980. They have two children, Jolyn and Joshua.

Family ties are important to Joseph Moradzadeh, seen here with his wife, Lynne, and their two children, Jolyn and Joshua.

FARMERS INSURANCE GROUP

Driving through Simi Valley one cannot help but be impressed with the five-story, 240,000-square-foot Farmers Insurance Group building located on a 14-acre site at the northwest corner of Cochran Street and Galena Avenue.

Farmers opened its regional office in Simi Valley on April 29, 1982. The facilities house both the Los Angeles and Simi Valley regions, marking the first time two regions have operated from one facility.

Designed by Peter A. Lendrum Associates, the impressive building is modern in design and extremely energy efficient. Ribbons of reflective glass accent the exterior. An outdoor patio dining area adjoins the cafeteria on the first level.

The 1,500 employees at the Simi Valley offices handle Farmers' business from the Tehachapi Mountains on the north

The Farmers Insurance Group's Simi Valley/Los Angeles Regional Office is an area landmark. The energy-efficient, 240,000-square-foot structure sits on 14 acres at Cochran and Galena.

to the southern boundary of Los Angeles County. Each region has separate facilities. A drive-in claims office is in a separate building on the site.

Farmers Insurance Group was founded in Los Angeles in 1928 by Thomas E. Leavey and John C. Tyler. They formed the company on a concept that changed the insurance industry and made insurance more equitable for people who live in rural and suburban areas, such as Simi Valley. Tyler and Leavey reasoned that since rural areas did not have the same problems and associated costs as heavily congested urban areas, they could market insurance at lower costs in rural towns, particularly to farmers, hence the name Farmers Insurance Group.

Based on that simple concept, the company prospered throughout the years, growing from the west into the midwestern and northwestern parts of the country. Currently, it does business in 27 western states. The Farmers Insurance Group of Companies includes the third-largest U.S. home and auto insurers and is the seventh-largest property

and casualty group in the country, as well as major life insurers.

Farmers grew from a small office on Spring Street in downtown Los Angeles to headquarters on Wilshire Boulevard and regional offices throughout the area. The company put down roots in the San Fernando Valley when the Los Angeles region was established in Mission Hills in 1957. Continued growth made it necessary to divide that region into two—Los Angeles and Simi, prompting the relocation to the beautiful Simi Valley in 1982.

Nationally, Farmers Insurance Group has more than 15,000 employees and 15,000 agents and district managers. The company writes more than 40 percent of its business in California and is the largest California-based auto and home insurer. Farmers Insurance Group is also proud to be California's leading insurance company for hospital liability coverage, providing insurance to nearly half of the state's hospitals. The company also contributes funds to many California colleges and universities.

THE ROBERTS GROUP, INC.

During the years when ranching was the mainstay of the Simi area, the Woods family owned and operated an expansive ranch at the east end of the valley. In the 1980s the Roberts Group acquired the land with its partner, Olympia/Roberts Co., and began to develop the master-planned Wood Ranch community.

The Roberts Group, Inc., was formed in February 1980 by Robert Levenstein, formerly the president and director of Kaufman & Broad, Inc., of Los Angeles (the largest multinational home builder in the United States). The Roberts Group, together with Olympia & York Homes Corporation (a subsidiary of the largest commercial developer in North America) formed a California general partnership to develop Wood Ranch and other land in Chino, California.

The Roberts Group has two functions. In addition to being the managing partner of Olympia/Roberts, it also provides management services to each of the Roberts companies, which themselves build homes not only in Olympia/Roberts master-planned communities but also in other locations throughout California.

Even with the modern developments, the ranch's past is not forgotten. In keeping with tradition, the Roberts Group has its Wood Ranch offices in what was formerly the caretakers' quarters and smokehouse of the old Woods Ranch.

The master-planned Wood Ranch community consists of 4,026 acres, bounded on the north by Olsen Road and the 23 Freeway, extending south to Thousand Oaks, west near the old Sheriff's station on Madera Road, and east at First Street.

"The responsibility of the Olympia/ Roberts partnership is to provide overall land development of the master-planned community of Wood Ranch," says Hamilton Smith, vice president. "Our goal is to develop a planned community, unified in nature, and offering all types of amenities with the advantage of comfortable, country living."

In 1983 the Olympia/Roberts partnership entered into a development agreement with the city of Simi Valley. The partnership offered to provide many amenities (to be completed as the community was developed),

including park and school sites, equestrian trails, and day-care facilities. The partnership also provides the major infrastructures, such as storm drains, sewer and water systems, underground utilities, rough grading, main arterial highways, street paving, gutters, and major monuments.

After the land is prepared, the pads are sold to developers for homes, apartments, condominiums, and retail establishments. One of the Roberts companies, the Roberts Group III, was the first developer to initiate building in 1985, and the first to complete and sell homes in Wood Ranch. Since then the Roberts groups have built many houses throughout Wood Ranch in Mountain View, the Fairways, the Club, High Meadows, and Ridgemont.

The Wood Ranch area offers peaceful surroundings with spectacular views of natural ridge lines. Even after the project is completed in the mid-1990s, 80 percent of the entire acreage will remain in its natural state (including a 200-acre golf course).

"Living at Wood Ranch offers the best of both worlds. Families can enjoy the benefits of small-town living, combined with all the conveniences of city life," says Ida Moore, director of sales.

Wood Ranch is divided into four main villages: Country Club Village, Lake Park Village, Sycamore Village, and Long Canyon. Each has its own distinct character, with different building styles and color themes.

Bordering on the fairways of Wood Ranch Golf Club, Country Club Village has a variety of condominiums, townhomes, duplexes, patio homes, and single-family detached homes. The Lake Park Village provides vistas of Wood Ranch Lake, the golf club, and the mountains. Sycamore Canyon Village and Long Canyon Village are located deeper within the ranch, and feature a larger selection of spacious 40-acre estate homes.

Since its formation, the Olympia/Roberts partnership has developed more than 2,000 rough graded pads within two of the four

Robert Levenstein, founder of the Roberts Group, Inc.

villages at Wood Ranch. The third village of 1,200 pads is in the completion phases, and the fourth will be started in 1991. When developed completely, Wood Ranch will consist of 4,000 home sites, a commercial center, an equestrian facility for residents, a school site, and a fire station.

Olympia/Roberts also built and runs the Wood Ranch Golf Club, which has been in operation since 1985. The 18-hole championship golf course was designed by internationally famous golf architect Ted Robinson. The course was created to offer a stimulating test of point-to-point golf and is considered by many to be one of the most challenging in Southern California.

With five lakes totaling 13 acres of blue water, the course provides an opportunity for scratch golfers to test their wits against more than 7,000 yards of bent grass fairways, undulating greens, nine water hazards, specimen trees, and strategically placed sand traps. The Wood Ranch course offers four sets of tees: tournament, championship, regular, and ladies'.

The Wood Ranch Golf Club has been

the site of the GTE Classic (a major event on the Senior PGA Tour) and other professional and local tournaments. The golf course also is available to companies, clubs, and other organizations for tournaments and other events.

With majestic views from every angle, the North Ranch Country Club offers social membership as well as golf memberships. The 38,000-square-foot clubhouse sits high atop a hill overlooking the scenic golf course. The clubhouse (itself a showcase building) accommodates groups of up to 300 people and is often used for weddings and other functions. The staff includes experienced event planners and award-winning chefs.

In addition to the golf course and other amenities, the Roberts Group's Wood Ranch is within close proximity of the Ronald Reagan Presidential Library.

Aerial views of Wood Ranch, a master-planned community of 4,026 acres.

MELVIN SIMON & ASSOCIATES

Simi Valley residents no longer have to trek out of town to shop at an indoor mall, thanks to Melvin Simon & Associates, Inc., the development company responsible for bringing a major mall to Simi Valley.

Planning began in 1986 for the regional shopping center, which will have its first phase completed by 1993. The enclosed mall, to occupy a 120-acre site at First and Erringer streets north of the Simi Valley Freeway, will encompass nearly one million square feet. Included are five major department stores, 125 to 150 smaller shops, a food court, and movie theaters. Also involved in the project is Homart, the development arm of Sears, Roebuck and Co., which entered a joint venture with Simon.

The Simi Valley mall was designed to fill the unique needs of the area, as is each mall developed by Simon.

"We look at a site, a community, and see what the needs are. We tailor the project to complement the community. We're not a cookie-cutter developer. Everything has to fit the community in which the development takes place," says Kevin Kudlo, a West Coast

development manager. The Simi mall layout was designed to preserve the surrounding hillsides, he adds.

Melvin Simon & Associates was founded in 1960 by Brooklyn-born brothers Melvin and Herbert Simon in Indianapolis, Indiana. At first the brothers developed strip centers in the Midwest, later expanding to regional malls and eventually creating the mega-malls of the 1980s and 1990s. The company also helps to revitalize communities with urban redevelopment projects.

To date, the Simon company has developed many creative mixed-use centers around the country, including the Mall of America, a 4.2-million-square-foot complex to open in 1992 in Bloomington, Minnesota, as the nation's largest covered retail, lodging, and entertainment center. The facility will include stores, hotels, and a Knott's Berry Farm amusement park.

Closer to home is the Hollywood Promenade, a multimillion-dollar mixed-use project that embraces and preserves the legendary Mann's Chinese Theatre, replacing vacant land and parking lots with

An artist's rendering of the Simi Valley regional mall currently being developed by Melvin Simon & Associates. The first phase is scheduled to be completed by 1993.

new retail, hotel, cultural, entertainment, and office space and a museum dedicated to the entertainment industry.

Indianapolis-based Melvin Simon & Associates is one of the most well-known and respected names in the shopping center industry. It is currently ranked as the nation's largest shopping center manager and the second-largest shopping center developer. The company owns or manages more than 200 shopping facilities, encompassing 72 million square feet of space in 38 states. Over the years it has developed the respect that draws major retailers to its malls.

In 1984 Melvin Simon & Associates expanded its operations to the West Coast, opening up a Los Angeles office to oversee projects in the western United States. In addition to its Indianapolis headquarters, the company also has offices in Chicago, Dallas, and New York City.

WHITNEY AUTO AND RV CARE CENTER

Ralph Whitney has helped keep automobiles running on Simi Valley's roads—even before there were many streets on which to drive or residents to drive on them.

Whitney and his wife, Marty, came to Simi Valley in May 1961 and in September 1963 purchased Bob Finrock's Chevron station at 1269 Los Angeles Avenue, changing the name to Whitney's Chevron. The following year, Standard Oil built a new Chevron station at the corner of Los Angeles Avenue and First Street, where Whitney ran what became a community landmark for 21 years. The station closed down in 1985, after Standard Oil decided it could no longer meet the terms of the lease proposed by the owners of the land. Since then, Whitney and his eldest son have run Whitney Auto and RV Care Center.

For the more than two decades, Whitney's Chevron was practically a motorist's institution in Simi Valley. In 1963 only 12,000 people lived in Simi, and the Whitneys knew most of them. Throughout the years, Whitney helped hundreds of high school and college students meet expenses with part-time jobs. And the community helped Whitney in 1969, after fiery blazes burned the station down in a matter of minutes during a warm afternoon on September 29.

"That community spirit is part of Simi Valley. It continues to be that way," says Ralph, who with Marty has returned the favors with donations of money and service to many community organizations, including the Las Manitas Children's Home Society Auxiliary, United Methodist Church, Meals on Wheels, and the Rotary Paul Harris Fellowship Foundation.

Although the fire destroyed the shop and office, it spared some of the gas tanks, so Whitney continued to pump gas, working out of a little wooden shed—until a truck fell on it. It took one year to rebuild the service station because Simi Valley became a city two days after the fire, and

ABOVE: *Ralph Whitney and son Gary in March 1966.*

BELOW: *Today Ralph and Gary run Whitney Auto and RV Care Center together.*

Whitney had to wait for the city to appoint a planning commission to approve plans for his renovations.

Whitney was not happy when the station closed in 1985, but he would not abandon the motorists of Simi Valley, so he moved his automotive service and repair equipment to 920 Chambers Lane, where he continues to work with son Gary, who now is a partner in the business. The shop handles a wide range of automotive services, including state-required smog-check certifications.

Throughout their tenure in Simi Valley, the Whitneys have been very active in community organizations. Marty, a registered nurse, directed volunteer services at Simi Valley Adventist Hospital for more than 20 years. Ralph has been active in the Noontime Rotary Club, the International Footprinters Foundation, and the Simi Valley Chamber of Commerce. He also founded the Lee Nixon Memorial Golf Tournament to raise money for local high schools' student scholarships.

In addition to Gary, who continues the family tradition of auto care, the Whitneys have three other children—Kathy, Carrie, and Danny, accompanied by a son-in-law, Richard Scranton; daughters-in-law Trudy and Dena; and grandchildren Kristi, Ryan, and Joshua.

DATAQUIK CORPORATION

Mary Jo Nelson (seated), founder of Dataquik Corporation, and her four daughters (from left): Valerie Lee, data control manager; Toni Koontz, data entry manager; Carolyn Shearer, office manager; and Jackie Nelson, systems analyst and consultant.

Dataquik Corporation is the result of the aspirations of Mary Jo Nelson to form, manage, and develop her own company.

Nelson came from a large family in rural Nebraska where higher education was neither encouraged nor readily available. In the area where she lived, it was assumed that a woman's place was solely in the home. Not satisfied with those limitations, she moved with her husband and children to California in 1956.

The young mother of five soon began working full time in Los Angeles, developing expertise in data entry operations and management. It was during this time that she began to dream of the challenge and satisfaction of starting and making a success of her own business.

Although she possessed the knowledge, experience, and the business contacts to sustain her company, she needed capital to get started. Nelson interested some partners, including her brother, Dallas attorney James J. Hartnett, who adds to the general planning and investment policies but is not involved in the daily operation and management of the corporation. With Nelson as principal owner, director, president, and general manager, Dataquik Corporation was formed on November 6, 1978.

Dataquik offers a full range of data processing services. This is the data entry room, where the bulk of the company's work is done.

A resident of Simi Valley since 1964, Nelson wanted to locate her business there to offer other local people, especially women, opportunities for employment. Other factors were Simi's emergence as a dynamic city and its proximity to Los Angeles, Ventura, and Santa Barbara.

Dataquik offers a full range of data processing services, including data entry with transfer to tape or diskette, file maintenance, mailing labels, and computer consultation. Somewhat of a family operation, Nelson's four daughters all worked for the company and eventually became part of the management staff. Carolyn Shearer is the office

manager; Toni Koontz manages the data entry department; Jackie Nelson is the systems analyst and consultant; and Valerie Lee is the data control manager.

Initially Dataquik employed 18 people in a modest rented office at 4444 Cochran Street, but growth of the company soon required expanded quarters in the Investment Savings Bank Building. In 1986 it became apparent that Dataquik had to move again, and Nelson wanted the company to acquire a building of its own for future expanded operations. She found just the right location—an 18,000-square-foot building—at 780 Easy Street. The company currently uses 8,000 square feet that was tailored for its use and leases out the rest of the office building until it is ready for further expansion.

Dataquik has several hundred clients, covering a broad range of industry services in several states, with sales figures into seven digits and 60 employees.

Dataquik Corporation is a trailblazer, demonstrating effective women management and majority ownership in a competitive industry.

COMCAST CABLEVISION CORPORATION

The history of cable television in Simi Valley parallels its general development nationwide, says Don Granger, vice president/general manager of Comcast Cablevision. Cable TV began in the 1960s for the purpose of bringing rural viewers better television reception and has exploded into the 1990s with full entertainment services, from regular network programs to music, movies, and even home shopping.

Community antenna television (CATV) began in Simi Valley in 1964 with two separate franchises: Clarity TV, Inc., and Valley Community Cable. The two served Simi residents until 1967, when NBC purchased Valley County Cable. In 1970 Teleprompter purchased Clarity TV. By 1979 Teleprompter had acquired both companies through King Video. In 1981 Westinghouse Broadcasting (Group W Cable) acquired Teleprompter. Comcast then acquired the cable companies from Group W in 1986.

Comcast began in Tupelo, Mississippi, in the early 1960s. From its initial base of 1,800 subscribers served by its five-channel system in Tupelo in 1963, Comcast has grown to more than 2 million subscribers in its owned and affiliated systems and has become recognized as one of the nation's leading cable companies.

In Simi Valley Comcast brought quality service and a variety of programming, which continued to expand and improve through the 1970s. During the 1980s a myriad of programming was added, including movie channels, music-video networks, and satellite channels devoted entirely to business, news, or sports. By 1989 Comcast offered 37 services and planned for future expansion.

The company is currently renovating its transmission systems throughout the city, replacing older cables with the latest electronic equipment. The $6-million upgrade will be completed in the early 1990s.

ABOVE: Comcast's system headend/receive site.

LEFT: The Comcast local origination crew prepares for its coverage of the Simi Valley Days Parade.

BELOW LEFT: Tim Daggett (right), a U.S. Olympic gold medalist in gymnastics, presents Comcast's Youth Leadership Award scholarship.

In the future, Comcast plans to add more specialized cable channels and offer high-technology services such as pay-per-view, interactive television, and High Definition Television (HDTV).

"Comcast is committed to cable TV and the future, in both programming and entertainment and in putting service first," says Granger. At Comcast, the motto is "Serve our subscribers," and all employees are trained in top-notch customer-service procedures. Comcast's commitment to service excellence is exemplified by its consistent high satisfaction marks from customers.

In addition to national television broadcasts, Comcast serves as a venue for local programming in Simi Valley.

"We are a participant in the community," Granger adds. "We're not only here as a business, we also give back to the community."

Granger hosts a monthly interview show called "Your Community." Comcast Cablevision Corporation also televises continuous public information "bulletin boards" and covers city council meetings and special events, such as the Simi Valley Days Parade. The company also sponsors youth recognition programs and awards scholarships to area students.

SIMI VALLEY-MOORPARK BOARD OF REALTORS®

The 1990 officers and directors of the Simi Valley-Moorpark Board of REALTORS®. From left: Nelson Carrillo, second vice president; Shannon Rich-Wolf (in front); Karen Burke (in back); Bonnie Walters, first vice president; Carlyn Paterson; Sam Hare; Jody Hoover, 1990 president; Lodge Coatman; Tom Ford, 1989 president; and Harvey Gandel, treasurer. Not pictured: Edith Wells, secretary; Lou Hillenbrand; Helen Thompson; and Barbara Swink, executive vice president.

In 1989, the Simi Valley-Moorpark Board of REALTORS® celebrated 25 years of professionalism and community service.

What began in 1964 with a meeting of 19 area brokers at a local school has evolved into a flourishing organization with 1,000 members, a permanent headquarters, and a modern, computerized Multiple Listing Service.

More than 4,000 residents every year rely on REALTORS® and the MLS to market and sell property. Over the years, residents of Simi Valley and Moorpark have come to expect quality service and high standards from local REALTORS®. Residents now take for granted the board's marketing tools, professional support systems, community activism, and efficient service.

Residents know REALTORS® endorse and actively promote equal opportunity in housing. They know REALTORS® vigorously enforce industry standards. And they know the board's Professional Standards Committee reviews and rules on all alleged violations of the National Association of REALTORS® Code of Ethics—the ethical standards that distinguish board members from ordinary real estate licensees.

REALTORS® offer advantages unavailable from other real estate licensees. Using a REALTOR® gives buyers and sellers of real property—residential, commercial, and industrial—a competitive edge. The MLS

exposes property to 1,500 MLS members working in the vast market spanning Simi Valley, Moorpark, and the Santa Rosa Valley.

Required continuing education classes, seminars, videotapes, and a library of research material keep board members abreast of the latest trends in financing, marketing, and home security systems designed to monitor prospective buyers as they enter a home.

Since its inception, members of the Simi Valley-Moorpark Board of REALTORS® have embraced a special leadership role in the community. The board has led efforts to contain rising property taxes, endorsed cityhood for Simi Valley, fought for freeway improvements, opposed a property transfer tax, screened candidates for public office, and sought increased funding for area schools.

Even as they tend to the needs of 80 percent of all valley residents who own a home, members of the Simi Valley-Moorpark Board of REALTORS® also volunteer thousands of hours and dollars annually to several charities.

Care & Share, a local food pantry serving the hungry and homeless, annually ben-

efits from board fund-raising projects. Every year since the early 1970s, the board rallies community support for a "CanTree" food drive. What started as a modest charity project now involves thousands of area residents and collects more than 60,000 cans of food. More than 30 other local organizations and charities every year receive contributions or volunteer support from board members.

As the community prospers, so too will the Simi Valley-Moorpark Board of REALTORS®: Its headquarters will expand to 11,000 square feet to allow for a larger library, more meeting rooms, and more services. The 1990s will see increased computerized capabilities, new educational standards for REALTORS®, political activism, and an awareness of the REALTORS® duty to fight for affordable housing.

This chart, put together by the Simi Valley-Moorpark Board of REALTORS®, demonstrates the steady growth of the area's real estate industry.

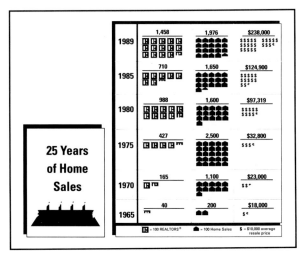

25 Years of Home Sales

1989	1,458	1,976	$238,000
1985	710	1,650	$124,900
1980	988	1,600	$97,319
1975	427	2,500	$32,800
1970	165	1,100	$23,000
1965	40	200	$18,000

= 100 REALTORS®   = 100 Home Sales $ = $10,000 average resale price

BANKS AND HUMPHRY ACCOUNTANCY CORPORATION

Although Tom Banks and Charlotte Humphry prefer jeans and sweatshirts to traditional office attire, they are far from casual in their attitude toward their accountancy.

"Our word means something. When we make a commitment, we keep it," says Humphry.

"This is a service business," says Banks, emphasizing the firm's dedication to its clients.

Banks, a Baylor University graduate, is a Certified Public Accountant (CPA) in both California and Texas. He moved to Thousand Oaks from the Lone Star state in 1976, where

Banks and Humphry offers professional accounting services paired with dedication to its clients.

he practiced for two years before coming to Simi Valley.

Humphry had a bookkeeping service and tax practice in Simi Valley since 1972 and has worked with Banks since 1980. She attended UCLA School of Business at night and became a CPA in 1986. On January 1, 1987, the two formed their accountancy partnership.

Banks and Humphry handle a full range of accounting needs, including individual, partnership, and corporate tax returns; monthly payroll and financial statements for businesses; formal financial statements for compilation and review; construction statements for contractors; consultant and controllership functions for companies; and accounting for the oil and gas industry.

Through their management advisory services they help companies achieve success. Their management professionals survey operations, helping companies maximize profits and run smoothly.

Banks, Humphry, and their associates use state-of-the-art computer programs and attend frequent seminars to keep up with the latest tax laws and regulations. One of the keys to their successful practice is their down-to-earth attitude and accessibility to their clients.

"We communicate with clients on a level they understand. We don't use buzzwords," says Humphry. "We return phone calls promptly. We don't keep people waiting—it's our job to be ready for them."

Both partners emphasize that Banks and Humphry Accountancy Corporation is "choosy" about its clients and will not involve itself in "creative bookkeeping" or any dishonest dealings.

The partners and their staff of five are a close-knit group who vacation together yearly after the busy tax season.

In addition to being proficient with ledgers and calculators, Humphry and Banks are handy with hammers and nails. The two finished the interior of their 2,600-square-foot office at 1736 Erringer Road in four evenings while doing their regular accounting each day. Banks also helped Humphry rebuild her Simi Valley home, which was gutted by fire in 1985. When doing accounting for construction firms, they often don hard hats and visit the sites when necessary.

Banks and Humphry belong to the California Society of CPAs, the American Institute of CPAs, the North American Petroleum Accounting Society, and the Texas Society of CPAs.

BUGLE BOY INDUSTRIES

new owners and the Securities and Exchange Commission.

Mow was eventually vindicated of all charges by a California appeals court, but the entire affair is basically what brought about the evolution of Bugle Boy Industries. In order to fight his case, Mow needed legal representation. In order to hire attorneys, he needed funds, which he generated by starting his own clothing business.

In 1977 Mow pulled together $200,000 from a Taiwan investor and put up his house to finance a line of bank credit. The company he then called Buckeroo International opened for business. That first season, the company lost $300,000.

The first few years of business were difficult—as tough as earning his doctorate,

---

LEFT: Dr. William Mow, founder, chairman, and chief executive officer.

BELOW: Vincent Nesi, president.

Given that Simi Valley is only a heartbeat away from the trend-setting city of Los Angeles, it seems only natural that a major clothing manufacturer would want to locate there—and that is exactly what happened when Dr. William Mow moved his Bugle Boy Industries headquarters to Simi in September 1989.

Bugle Boy Industries produces and markets casual slacks, dress slacks, and jeans for men, women, and children under the Bugle Boy and Vincente labels. BBI is among the largest privately held apparel companies in the country, selling its products to more than 2,500 department stores and specialty retailers. The Bugle Boy label is considered the nation's leading brand of casual slacks for young men and boys, and its more recently introduced women's wear and men's wear are gaining in popularity.

EVOLUTION
Mow, chairman and chief executive officer, founded Bugle Boy in Woodland Hills in May 1977. Originally conceived as a collection of better young men's merchandise, Bugle Boy was redirected towards the market for moderately priced fashion in 1981, following the appointment of Vincent Nesi as president. Today Mow owns 90 percent of the company and Nesi owns 10 percent.

Mow was born in China, the son of a Chinese diplomat later assigned to the United Nations. His family immigrated to the United States when he was 12 years old. As a student he excelled in mathematics and pursued related fields.

Although he eventually became a clothing mogul, Mow began his career in electronics, and he holds a Ph.D. in electrical engineering from Purdue University in Indiana. As a young man in the early 1970s, he founded Macrodata and helped build it into a successful company. Unfortunately the sale of that company resulted in some legal problems for Mow, who was wrongly accused of fraud by the

comments Mow. By 1981 the company had lost $750,000 on sales of $4.1 million.

Undaunted, Mow figured that he had maybe two more seasons to save his fledgling clothing company. That year he changed the name to Bugle Boy—in honor of the Yankee boys who played their bugles during Civil War battles. He also put Nesi in charge of sales.

The choice paid off—Mow and Nesi made a powerful pair, and Bugle Boy started to grow. But the company almost collapsed in 1984 when a clothing fad fell flat. At the time nylon "parachute pants" were the rage, and Mow put everything into making them. But the finicky fashion world turned around, making the pants obsolete and giving Bugle Boy a negative net worth of $5 million.

The company worked fast to recoup its losses, delivering a new line of clothing only four months later. Eager to come back from their parachute pant losses, department stores filled their shelves with the new stock. By then Bugle Boy's name had been in the public enough that the brand finally caught

on, and with that season the company turned the corner. And Mow learned a hard lesson about following whims and fashion fads.

"We never stay on one trend too long. The trick is to keep fresh and never get too set in the trends of the day," reflects Mow. "We pick up trends from all over the world. And it's not by just shopping—it's by sitting at an outdoor cafe, seeing what's going on with the young kids. You want to pick up the environment, not just the style."

STRATEGY

After years of struggling with the intricacies of the rag trade, Bugle Boy has developed an effective sales strategy that combines innovative fashion with affordable prices. Bugle Boy offers maximum value to the consumer while optimizing profitability for the retailer.

"We bring that guy who might be earning between $15,000 and $30,000 a year a branded label at a private-label price. We bring the department stores the ability to retain mass market consumers they would

Bugle Boy got its start in 1977 at this Woodland Hills facility.

otherwise lose to up-and-coming mass merchants," says Nesi, who manages and coordinates merchandising and sales. "Our goal is really to penetrate mass America. We design a product that says 'buy me,' and price it so you don't have to wait for it to go on sale."

Keeping its hands on the worldwide fashion pulse enables Bugle Boy to anticipate and capitalize on changes in consumer taste and demand. In the mid-1980s when designer jeans started to lose their popular appeal, none of the other companies were prepared to give youthful consumers an alternative—but Bugle Boy did. The company captured the popular look of fast-changing styles, creating "cargo pants" with the extra belt loops, jumbo pockets, and "as many zippers and buttons and snaps as you can find," says Mow. Indeed, those ornamentations have become Bugle Boy's signature.

Bugle Boy products are now recognized for their comfort and style. They are extremely popular with today's fashion-conscious generation.

EXPANSION

With high visibility in popular retailers, Bugle Boy has become a household word in family clothing. Throughout its evolution, BBI has embarked on marketing ventures that have made the company an important supplier in virtually every apparel classification.

Young men's dress slacks were introduced under the Vincente Nesi label in 1983, and the Bugle Boys and Junior divisions were formed in 1984. Men's and girls' products debuted in 1987, followed in 1988 by the launch of jeans, VN Men's and Vincente Missy divisions. Bugle Boy tops,

RIGHT: Cargo pants have become a fashion staple for young men thanks to Bugle Boy.

BELOW: Bugle Boy is headquartered at 2900 Madera Road in Simi Valley.

hosiery, underwear, swimwear, children's activewear, infant and toddler apparel, neckwear, footwear, and other products are distributed through licensees.

Bugle Boy has more than 800 employees on its payroll, with offices in New York, Los Angeles, Dallas, Atlanta, and Chicago. The Simi Valley facilities employ more than 500.

Bugle Boy is a multinational company, with recent sales expansions in Japan, Canada, and Australia. The clothing is manufactured in 22 countries worldwide, and Mow is constantly searching for new sources of production. In fact the company planned to add 10 new manufacturing locations in 1990. Indeed, Bugle Boy is able to deliver low price points without sacrificing the quality of the garments because of Mow's ability to identify the capabilities

of different countries' resources and to utilize and channel those resources to provide the most value for the consumers in the United States.

Bugle Boy advertises in many media, including network television spots, cable television, newspapers, radio, magazines, and billboards.

SIMI VALLEY

One of the biggest moves for the company was its September 1989 relocation to the Simi Valley. Before moving to Simi, the company was spread among various buildings in Chatsworth. Now Bugle Boy operates under one roof.

The move to Simi was planned in 1986. Mow was particularly attracted to the area because he needed land that could accommodate the projected expansion of his company, and the growing community of Simi Valley provided him with the space he needed. Mow also chose Simi for its natural beauty and serene environment. He also recognized the high level of community

commitment shown by Simi residents and businesses, and he wanted to become an integral part of the area.

Bugle Boy became involved in the community even before it moved to Simi Valley. To alleviate any increase in traffic, the company helped fund construction improvement on the 118 Simi Valley Freeway and purchased a stoplight for the Madera Road offramp. Bugle Boy also participates in local United Way campaigns, and Mow intends for the company to continue to increase local involvement in the future.

Mow invested $22 million in the 215,000-square-foot Simi Valley headquarters, located at 2900 Madera Road. The modern architecture is striking, with glass-lined archways and atrium. A glass bridge also connects the office complex to the distribution warehouse.

The Simi Valley headquarters handles all the distribution of Bugle Boy products, which come from manufacturing plants worldwide. Employees at the Simi Valley facilities promptly check, package, and

ship the merchandise to thousands of U.S. retailers. Most of the products leave the warehouse almost as fast as they come in, usually within two days.

"Goods don't stay in our warehouse more than 36 hours. It's like sushi [fish]—the longer you keep it, the more it stinks," jokes Mow.

The Simi Valley headquarters also handles all of the company's administrative and marketing functions. Product design, sales, and merchandising is done at the New York City offices.

By 1990 Bugle Boy Industries had achieved success by keeping its styles fresh, maintaining reasonable prices for consumers, and by providing retailers with above-average margins and sales. The company's future looks bright for the years to come.

More than 500 people are employed at Bugle Boy's Simi Valley location. A glass bridge connects the company's offices and warehouse.

LAMB REALTY CO., INC.

Recipe for success: Start with one home-grown boy from a firmly established Ventura County family. Sprinkle liberally with a healthy respect for the community's history and traditions. Add a pinch or two of humor. Stir in increasing portions of uncanny real estate savvy and expertise. Top this unique mixture with a philosophy based on dedication to meeting the real estate needs of the community. Light a fire under it and watch it rise to become one of the most successful, fastest-growing real estate companies in California—Lamb Realty Co., Inc.

In 1978 Ray E. Lamb founded Lamb Realty on the principle that to properly satisfy the real estate needs of a growing community, one must do more than just hire agents—one must train professionals. To this end, Lamb developed one of the most innovative training and recruitment programs in the real estate profession—programs that have become industry standards and have gained national recognition.

The results speak for themselves. Lamb Realty Co., Inc., has emerged as a most dynamic company in the competitive California market, with more than 350 sales professionals covering offices in Ventura and Los Angeles counties. A new Lamb Simi Valley office building is one of several dramatic facilities currently under development within the company's marketing area.

"Our philosophy is to enjoy people," says Ray Lamb. "We are a people-oriented company with a sense of humor. Because we're an independent firm that was founded and has grown in the area we serve, we know the communities and their needs. We know the neighborhoods, the homes, and the businesses. We create and foster confidence with our professionalism and our personal attention to people's needs. To put it simply, we never lose sight of why we are here in the first place . . . to serve the community. We will be here tomorrow—we are building for the future."

Real estate's Ray Lamb, outstanding in his field.

TRAVELODGE

When Travelodge opened in Simi Valley in April 1986, it was the second lodging facility in the area.

"At that time Simi Valley was in the beginning of a strong growth mode, both industrial and residential, that indicated a need for hotel/motel facilities," says general manager Marge Moore.

The 96-room property has been a success ever since it opened its doors. The motel was planned by the Siva Partnership as an upscale facility, and indeed it is, with large suites and airy rooms, 36 of which have built-in Jacuzzis large enough for two people.

The hotel can accommodate many needs. It has rooms for nonsmokers and handicapped guests, two honeymoon suites, and six one-bedroom units, often used by families who are relocating to the area. As large as many one-bedroom apartments, the family suites have two rooms, with two fold-out couches, two queen-size beds, and two bathrooms. Families staying more than a week get an extra television in the bedroom, as well as a free refrigerator in their suite. All of the rooms have free HBO television as well as pay-per-view movies.

About half of Travelodge's business is comprised of pleasure travelers, while the rest are corporate guests. Business travelers are upgraded to Jacuzzi rooms when available, and businesspeople have access to facsimile machines. Travelodge also has

Thirty-six of the 96 rooms at Travelodge have in-room Jacuzzis large enough for two people.

a fully equipped fitness room, laundry facilities, an indoor redwood sauna, and a heated pool. By special arrangement, guests may also play tennis and racquetball at the nearby Oakridge Athletic Club.

Most guests take advantage of the free continental breakfast served in the sunny, comfortable lobby, as well as the round-the-clock hot coffee and tea. Moore says guests enjoy visiting the lobby and chatting with the friendly staff.

"We try to make this their home away from home. I believe we're succeeding—most of our business is repeat customers and referrals," says Moore.

In addition to its plush rooms and lodging facilities, Travelodge also has a 1,600-square-foot meeting room that can be used for gatherings of up to 230 people. Weddings are convenient at Travelodge, as the honeymoon couple can make an easy retreat from the reception to their honeymoon suite, where flowers and champagne await them.

The Simi Valley Travelodge is located at 2550 Erringer Road, near the on-ramp to the 118 Freeway. Owned by the Siva Partnership, the hotel employs more than 20 people, some of whom have been at Travelodge since it opened. The staff is constantly involved in improving and upgrading the facilities.

Travelodge is an international company with both corporately owned and franchised facilities. There are more than 450 Travelodges nationwide and in Europe.

Travelodge's meeting and banquet rooms can accommodate such events as business seminars and wedding receptions.

KAISER PERMANENTE

The Kaiser Permanente Medical Care Program began in the 1930s with the premise of providing affordable care and keeping people healthy. Today the program has become the nation's largest health maintenance organization, with more than 13,000 members in Simi Valley.

The roots of the Kaiser Permanente Medical Care Program can be traced to 1933, when Dr. Sidney Garfield established a prepaid medical and hospital services plan for construction workers who were building an aqueduct in the desert outside of Los Angeles.

The contractors agreed to pay five cents per day per worker to cover any work-related accidents, and employees voluntarily paid a similar amount to cover nonindustrial care. The revolutionary health care program proved profitable for everyone: contractors experienced a reduction in lost work hours, employees had a readily accessible source of medical care, and physicians were assured of a steady source of income during construction.

In 1938 industrialist Henry J. Kaiser heard about the innovative program and asked Dr. Garfield to establish a similar program for Kaiser workers and their families in the Grand Coulee Dam construction site in Washington. Once again the program was successful.

The plan was revolutionary from both the administrative and clinical viewpoints. Administratively, the financial risk of illness and injury was spread among all the enrolled families at a cost they could afford. And the plan's "fixed-revenue" approach meant that the program's physicians could design, organize, and budget facilities and services effectively.

Clinically, the program had a significant impact on the way medicine was practiced. Until that time, doctors relied on sick and injured patients to make a living; with the Kaiser plan, doctors had a vested interest in keeping them well. The fact that Kaiser Permanente Health Plan members could get care without worrying about the cost profoundly affected the general health of the community. Members sought medical attention earlier in their illnesses, resulting in more effective and less costly treatments. That "wellness" philosophy helped make the Kaiser Permanente plan an effective health care system for decades to come.

When the United States entered World War II, Kaiser and Dr. Garfield again joined forces to establish what would later be known as the Kaiser Permanente Medical Care Program to serve workers at the Kaiser steel mill in Fontana and the shipyards in Richmond, California. (The name Permanente is derived from one of Kaiser's early business ventures, located near Permanente Creek, California.)

After the war many of the doctors were committed to remaining in the prepaid practice group, and many Kaiser employees wished to retain their membership, so the decision was made to open enrollment

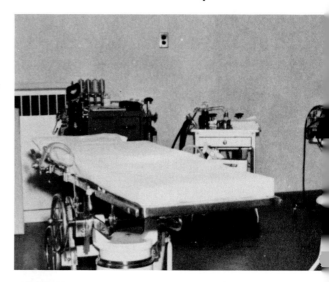

ABOVE: State-of-the-art medical equipment, circa 1940.

LEFT: His attention diverted, a young patient receives care from a Kaiser Permanente physician in the early days of the health plan.

to community residents in those areas. From its small beginnings in Fontana, the Southern California region continued to grow. In 1950 the Kaiser Foundation Health Plan extended its Southern California services to the Los Angeles area, and opened its first of many medical offices.

In 1953 Kaiser Permanente constructed new medical centers in Los Angeles and Fontana. During the 1960s it built major medical centers in Panorama City and Bellflower. A new medical center opened in West Los Angeles in 1974 and one in San Diego the following year. In 1979 Kaiser

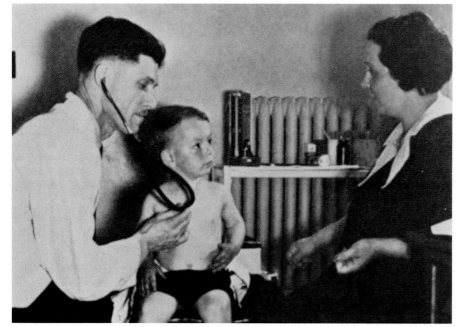

Kaiser Permanente's Simi Valley office provides a variety of medical services for local members.

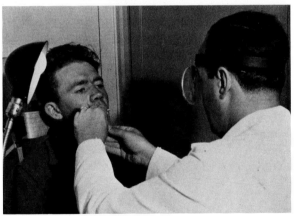

A Kaiser Permanente physician treats a health plan member in the 1940s.

Permanente purchased a large facility in Anaheim for its Orange County members.

In 1986 Kaiser Permanente opened a large medical center in Woodland Hills (frequently used by Simi Valley residents). With a staff of more than 1,600 (including more than 160 doctors), the Woodland Hills medical center provides a full range of outpatient medical services as well as acute inpatient care.

Because of the geographic distribution of health plan members, the program now operates more than 40 outlying medical of-fice facilities, one of which is located in Simi Valley. In August 1989 Kaiser Permanente opened temporary medical offices at 1633 Erringer Road. The facilities provide adult and pediatric urgent care, as well as pharmacy, laboratory, X-ray, and social services. A permanent 12-provider medical office is planned to open in Simi Valley in the near future, with expanded services including an allergy injection clinic, optometry, optical dispensing, and physical therapy.

In addition to keeping its Health Plan members healthy, Kaiser Permanente's non-profit foundation also is concerned with the welfare of each community it serves, and it has been involved with Simi Valley since the mid-1980s. Kaiser Permanente is committed to the success of its communities as well as the success of its organization and understands that it and the communities it serves are interdependent. Kaiser Permanente invests human and financial resources in its communities and encourages members of its health care team to take an active role in their home communities. Community service grants to local health and human service agencies, such as the Simi Valley Free Clinic, demonstrate that commitment.

Kaiser Permanente also helps train students at Simi Valley Adult School's nursing and medical occupation programs and offers scholarships to local students at area colleges. Kaiser Permanente also supports local adopt-a-school programs, and its Professor Bodywise and "Secrets" programs provide health messages to local schools. In addition, Kaiser Permanente was instrumental in developing the Radiology Technician Program at Moorpark Community College. Kaiser Permanente provided funding for this program and also offers its Woodland Hills medical center as an internship facility to the program participants.

The Kaiser Foundation Health Plan has 12 regions across the United States, with more than 6 million members nationwide. Kaiser Permanente serves more than 2.2 million Kaiser Foundation Health Plan members in the Southern California region, including more than 25,000 members in Ventura County.

SIMI VALLEY LANDFILL

When most people put out the bags on trash day, they don't think much about where their garbage will go. More than 1,000 tons of trash produced daily in Simi Valley end up at the Simi Valley Sanitary Landfill.

Located approximately two miles northwest of the Simi Valley Freeway at Madera Road, the landfill started in the late 1950s as a dumpsite for Simi's trash and as a private dumping area for Unocal. In the early 1970s Ventura County operated it briefly before turning it over to the state-governed Regional Sanitation District. Waste Management of California, Inc. (WMC), purchased the landfill in 1982 and continues to operate it today. WMC is a wholly owned subsidiary of Waste Management of North America, Inc. (WMNA).

The Simi Valley Landfill stretches over 274 acres northwest of the Simi Valley Freeway at Madera Road. The landfill employs several environmental and civil engineers who constantly monitor the site's compliance with environmental standards. Photos by Amy Seidman-Tighe

Established in 1965, WMNA is the world's largest and most experienced solid-waste management company. The company leads the waste transfer and disposal industry with more than 125 landfills on three continents and has been in California since 1972.

The Simi Valley landfill has more than 40 employees, including several environmental and civil engineers who monitor the site constantly to make sure that all environmental standards are strictly followed. The landfill accepts only nonhazardous wastes and is working continually to preserve the environment.

Every day landfill workers use the latest equipment to cover hundreds of tons of trash with fresh dirt. Heavy clay soils protect the groundwater from pollution. Traffic volume is estimated to be approximately 250 round-trips per workday.

The landfill is expected to reach its 274-acre capacity by the year 2004, at which time the company intends to close the site and cover it with approximately four feet of earth. Native grass, shrubs, and small trees will be used to reclaim the area, which may be turned into a public recreation area.

"We're working with local government agencies to find another site environmentally and economically feasible to develop a new landfill for the future," says general manager Mike Williams.

The Simi Valley landfill services the eastern portion of Ventura County, including Simi Valley, Moorpark, and Thousand Oaks. The landfill operators support the community and give free-use passes for area cleanup activities, amounting to thousands of dollars in donations each year. Landfill administrators also conduct community education and awareness programs.

"We are educating people to understand this is not a 'dump.' We're a high-technology sanitary landfill," says Simi site manager Paul Spencer.

Concerned with both the future and the past, WMC participates in a variety of resource recovery and recycling programs and also sponsors scientific research on the land. In the late 1980s paleontologists discovered fossils on the Simi landfill site and continue to dig for more. In 1989 the landfill installed a gas collection system and hopes in the future to generate electricity from methane gas (a by-product of decomposed trash).

Simi Valley Landfill
A DIVISION OF
Waste Management of California, Inc.

FAMILY HEALTH CARE, INC.

In 1969 the founder of Family Health Care, Dr. Otto Austel, was impressed with the need for family physicians in what was then the bedroom community of Simi Valley. With only 10 general practitioners in a town that had approximately 30,000 children, Dr. Austel felt that more such doctors were needed, so he founded Family Health Care, Inc.

As the practice outgrew the initial office in Mid-Valley Medical Center, several moves were made until Family Health Care (FHC) moved into its present office at Simi Hills Medical Center in 1986, occupying the entire first floor and part of the second floor. The practice, which started with only one physician, grew to 11 physicians, most of

Family Health Care, Inc., is located at 2876 North Sycamore in the Simi Hills Medical Center.

The doctors of Family Health Care, Inc.: (standing, from left) J. Koh, G. Carbone, M. Kang, O. Austel, V. Gupta, J. Kurohara, (seated, from left) W. Allen, J. Pattanachinda, A. Bosko, and T. McNicoll. Not shown is Dr. C.N. Lee.

whom are specialized and board certified in family practice, with others in surgery, obstetrics and gynecology, pediatrics, and cardiology. Outside consultant specialists also use the FHC facilities to care for the patients referred to them, in addition to a nutritionist and clinical psychologist who help the FHC doctors serve approximately 20 percent of the local population.

What started with two employees grew to 42 by 1989, and served growing practices in three offices in Simi Valley and one in Moorpark. Some employees have worked loyally with FHC for more than 17 years. FHC stands not only for Family Health Care, but, more significantly, for "Friendly, Helpful,

and Courteous," and this has remained the goal and motto of the organization.

FHC is unique in that it is neither a medical group nor a partnership, but an independent physicians' organization that is incorporated to allow the physicians to work as independent doctors—caring for their patients personally and individually—yet sharing the office and equipment. The doctors also cover for each other.

FHC doctors comprise a multilingual, international group. In 1990 FHC doctors included family practitioners Jonathan K. Kurohara, William Allen, George Carbone, Tim McNicoll, Otto Austel, and Allan Bosko; cardiologist Vinod Gupta; surgeon Mark Kang; obstetricians Chung Lee and John Koh; and pediatrician J. Pattanachinda.

The physicians of FHC actively serve the community and are members of various service organizations. They are frequently called upon by community groups for informative talks. They also have "adopted" local schools to attend during crisis situations, and they serve as volunteers for the free clinic, the board of directors for the Boys and Girls Club, and the Foundation for the Homeless.

Dr. Austel, who has served on the school board, was named Man of the Year by the Simi Valley Chamber of Commerce in 1973 and was nominated for the title several times since. He helped found several community organizations, including the Boys and Girls Club and Foundation for the Homeless. He has received awards from numerous service clubs, including Rotary's prestigious Paul Harris Fellowship. Prior to establishing Family Care Clinic, Inc., Dr. Austel was a missionary linguist for 10 years among the primitive Caraja Indians in the jungles of Brazil, where he wrote *The Caraja Culture.*

RADISSON HOTEL

With a panoramic view of beautiful Simi Valley, it seems appropriate that the Radisson Hotel is situated on a street called Enchanted Way. With its southwest architecture, lush landscaping, and breathtaking view, the Radisson is indeed enchanting.

The hotel, located off the First Street exit of the Simi Valley Freeway, opened on February 1, 1989, under the direction of David B. Commons and the County Bank of Santa Barbara. It is managed by Sterling Hotels Corporation of San Luis Obispo.

Originally a Ramada Hotel, the hotel converted to the Radisson chain on July 1, 1989. The change was made because hotel management felt that the needs of Simi Valley could be better met by the amenities that Radisson had to offer.

"There was a need for an upscale luxury hotel in the Simi Valley area. With the change to Radisson, we continued to upgrade our standards even more," says general manager Ray Burger.

Tastefully decorated, the 195-room hotel has six suites, including the Presidential Suite, which has two bedrooms and a large parlor. Each room is equipped with a mini-

RIGHT: Guests at the Radisson can expect high quality, friendly service from the hotel's staff.

BELOW: The 195 rooms at the Radisson are ideal lodgings for corporate travelers.

bar stocked with liquor, soft drinks, and snacks. The rooms have remote-control color television with free cable programming and additional pay-per-view movies. Each room also has a coffee maker and individually controlled air conditioning. The hotel has a heated swimming pool and a Jacuzzi.

About two-thirds of the Radisson's lodgers are business travelers. For corporate travelers the hotel offers two-line telephones and conference calls. "Throughout the hotel's operations, guests are the top priority," says Burger.

"Service is the most important thing any hotel can offer. A bed is a bed—the

ABOVE: The Radisson Hotel in Simi Valley offers upscale, luxurious accommodations.

difference is a warm, friendly staff. That's what we've given to Simi Valley."

In addition to lodging facilities, the Radisson also has its own catering and banquet services and 6,800 square feet of banquet and meeting rooms. Its scenic courtyard provides a nice background for weddings.

In addition to room service, the Radisson also has a full-service restaurant, Christopher's, which offers a variety of delectable entrees. The restaurant is popular with the community as well as hotel guests.

Also on the premises is Splash, a high-energy nightclub that has become a local weekend hot spot for entertainment. Along with its disc jockey and dancing, Splash sometimes features live bands and special promotions. The club has four big-screen television monitors for music videos and sporting events.

The Radisson hotel chain started in the 1940s in Minneapolis, Minnesota. It slowly expanded across the country, with tremendous growth in California between 1985 and 1990. With California leading the pack, there are now more than 200 Radisson hotels in the United States and 50 internationally.

ANDERSON DISPOSAL SERVICE

Today Anderson Disposal Service serves Simi Valley with 25 employees and more than 18 vehicles.

Anderson Disposal Service is the result of years of hard work by Robert and Sue Anderson, who wanted to provide a future for their five children: Barbara, Ronda, Stephanie, Chuck, and Lorenn. Unfortunately, Bob Anderson passed away on November 17, 1989, just when he was beginning to enjoy the fruits of his labor. He was a man of character and had a great devotion to his family. Bob will always be remembered by those who knew him as a kind, compassionate, respectable person.

Simi residents since 1956, the Andersons started their disposal company in 1964, with one truck and some barrels. At the time there were only four tracts of houses in Simi, but they knew the area would grow and the need for their services would increase.

The early years were tough; today, however, Anderson Disposal is thriving, with 25 employees and more than 18 vehicles. The company is divided into several divisions including commercial, residential, roll offs, and compactor services. Anderson Disposal Service has piloted some recycling projects and intends to do more. In addition to Anderson Disposal Service, Sue and Chuck are partners in Moorpark Disposal Service.

Even when times were tough, Bob Anderson always helped others, giving free trash service and employing people in need, even if he couldn't afford it. "He was

a very generous man," says Jim Safechuck, Bob's son-in-law.

"We were told quite a few times that we wouldn't survive. Now we're the only company still operating under the original family ownership, and doing quite well against the big companies," says Sue Anderson. "I give God the glory and Bob the credit for that."

For the Andersons, perseverance was the name of the game. Until the late 1970s Bob also held a full-time night job as a technician at Rocketdyne, and operated the disposal company during the day. Along with picking up the trash and the routine duties of running a company, Bob, a mechanical whiz, saved maintenance costs by doing all of his own vehicle repairs.

When son Chuck Anderson, daughter Lorenn Kouri, and son-in-law Jim Safechuck came into the company, much of the work load was taken off of Bob and Sue. This gave Bob the opportunity to pursue additional commercial business. Bob's talents enabled him to acquire most of the new business.

Sue did the bookkeeping and office duties. She sometimes drove the trash routes in a pickup truck and added a personal touch by putting ribbons on the trash barrels she delivered to new customers.

Bob Anderson is remembered as a kind, generous man who was always willing to help others.

She had several other jobs, eventually becoming a successful real estate broker. Sue Anderson opened her own business, SEA Realty, in 1975. For several years she was a director, served as secretary, and was second vice president on the local board of realtors as well as director on the state level for four years. In 1979 she was chosen Realtor of the Year by her peers. Through the years she has continued to be active in the community, and she recently was appointed as commissioner to the Area Housing Authority.

SEA Realty and Anderson Disposal Service share offices at 2789 Tapo Street. Anderson Disposal Service will continue to expand under the guidance of Sue Anderson, with the management team of Chuck Anderson, Lorenn Kouri, and Jim Safechuck. *This article is dedicated to the memory of Robert Anderson, 1928-1989.*

ROCKETDYNE

Over its 35-year history, Rockwell International Corporation's Rocketdyne Division has been a leader in applied power, from the world's most sophisticated rocket propulsion systems to space-borne electrical power.

Rocketdyne was established in 1955 as a separate division of North American Aviation, Inc., which later became a part of Rockwell International Corporation. The division was chartered to build rocket engines in support of national defense and U.S. involvement in space, which led to the creation of the Redstone, Navaho, Atlas, Thor, and Jupiter engines—all luminaries in the early years.

A key element in the development of Rocketdyne's propulsion and power system has been the Santa Susana Field Laboratory, a remote testing facility in the hills between the company's Canoga Park manufacturing facilities and the Simi Valley. The site was actually founded in the late 1940s, long before Rocketdyne's arrival, when the United States took its initial steps into the

infant science of rocketry. Prior to that time, early North American Aviation researchers tested engines in a parking lot in El Segundo near what is now the Los Angeles airport, but it soon became apparent that a larger test area was needed.

In 1948 NAA set aside a secluded por-

LEFT: A Space Shuttle Main Engine is readied for a static test in which it will generate about a half-million pounds of thrust. The test stand and surrounding natural beauty give the Santa Susana Field Laboratory an unparalleled flavor of rugged terrain blended with high technology. The location of large rocket engine test stands in the many canyons creates a built-in muffler for the test, which is augmented by a flow of water to further suppress the low engine rumble. Longtime workers at the site tell many tales of wildcats, bears, raccoons, foxes, deer, and, of course, rattlesnakes, which over the years have shared the rocky domain with engine tests and their producers. North American Aviation, Inc., a Rockwell International predecessor company, selected the remote site for rocket engine testing in 1947.

ABOVE: A very rural Simi Valley in 1956 is seen from the hilltops of Rockwell International's Santa Susana Field Laboratory while a Thor engine is put to the test in the foreground. During peak test activity, the Rocketdyne field lab had 18 large engine test stands and more than 65 engine component test areas and research facilities. The human population reached as high as 3,000 during peak Apollo program days for conducting tests, manning the instrumentation control centers to measure thrust, pressure, temperature, valve operation, and other engine performance characteristics. To support these activities there were, and in some cases, are, complete functional groups like the cafeteria, the photo lab, a fire department, protective services, a machine shop, an instrumentation lab, an equipment lab, bus service, the environmental group, and an analytical chemistry lab. The test site, in fact, was virtually a self-contained small city for some years.

tion of the Santa Susana mountains; a deep depression separating a circular arrangement of hills became the site of Rocketdyne's first test stands. Later the site was expanded to include more than a dozen separate areas, each with specific designated functions and separate facilities for control and observation. The Santa Susana Field Laboratory is now known worldwide as one of the premier testing grounds for rocket engines. It is there that engines capable of producing as much as a half-million pounds

of thrust have been tested, including Rocketdyne's Space Shuttle Main Engines.

But testing at Santa Susana Field Laboratory is not confined to rocket engines. It is also the site for testing other energy components at a facility called the Energy Technology Engineering Center. Known as ETEC, the center specializes in non-nuclear testing of components for commercial reac-

ABOVE: A reliable mainstay of America's space program since the 1950s, the Atlas propulsion system continues to play a vital role in placing commercial and government satellites into orbit. Today's model evolved by incorporation of the latest technical advances and improved production techniques into this and each of the predecessor configurations. Among the achievements in which the Atlas system has a key role are the historic NASA Mercury earth three-orbit mission of Astronaut John Glenn in 1962; the boosting of numerous satellites such as Rangers, Surveyors, Lunar Orbiters, Mariners, Pioneers, and Orbiting Astronomical Observatories; many Air Force payloads; and deep space probes such as the Venus-Mercury flyby mission which beamed TV coverage of these planets to Earth. The Atlas propulsion system is expected to be a part of the country's mixed launch fleet well into the 1990s.

RIGHT: The rugged reliability of the Redstone rocket engine, originally produced by Rockwell International's Rocketdyne Division for the U.S. Army, was proven by early test program consecutive full-duration, full-power runs with a single engine. The Redstone generated 78,000 pounds of thrust combusting liquid oxygen and alcohol. The first program test was conducted in 1950 and Redstone production ran through May 1960. This pioneer rocket engine holds two space program firsts: in 1958, the launching of the first American satellite, Explorer I; and in 1961, powering the NASA Mercury program's first manned suborbital flight.

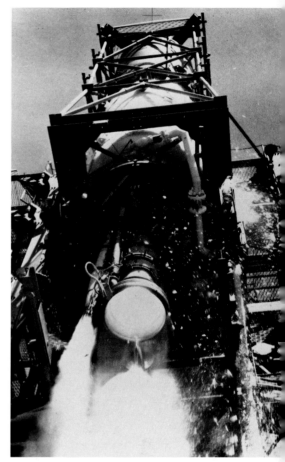

tors and other specialized energy-related work such as earthquake survival technologies. An independent government laboratory owned by the U.S. Department of Energy, ETEC has been operated by Rocketdyne since 1966. ETEC's primary focus is the development of emerging energy technologies, including solar, conservation, geothermal, fossil, fusion, and fission energy.

Until 1990 the Santa Susana Field Laboratory was used to research nuclear energy. In the 1950s Rockwell's Atomics International division produced the first nuclear reactor to generate commercial electrical energy, and for a few years provided electricity to the town of Moorpark. During the following decade the site was used to develop, assemble, and test the SNAP (System for Nuclear Auxiliary Power) series of liquid metal compact nuclear reactors. The SNAP-10A, launched from Vandenberg AFB in 1965, was the first and only U.S. demon-

stration of an operating nuclear reactor in earth orbit.

All work with nuclear materials ended by 1990, and now ETEC researchers perform only nonradioactive testing of reactor components and other energy technology programs.

Over the years, Rocketdyne had been associated with many achievements. In 1958 a Rocketdyne-powered Redstone launched the first American satellite and, in 1961, the first manned suborbital flight. Throughout the 1960s Rocketdyne built the engines that put the United States into space, from the Mercury launches to Apollo. In 1969 Apollo 11, boosted by Rocketdyne's F-1 and J-2 engines, landed the first men on the moon, and then brought them home, courtesy of Rocketdyne's lunar ascent engine.

Indeed, Rocketdyne's engines have performed well—with its SSMEs providing superb, reliable propulsion in every Shuttle mission to date. The space shuttle main engine has been a primary Rocketdyne business since 1971, and the company continues with innovative propulsion designs, paving the way for space flight well into the 21st

century. Equally important, Rocketdyne will supply the electrical power system for America's Space Station *Freedom* when it becomes operational in the late 1900s.

For all of its contributions to the United States and its space and defense programs, Rocketdyne is also actively involved in the communities which surround it, including the Simi Valley, home to a large portion of the company's 9,500 employees. Community activities include working with public education at the elementary school, high school, and college levels, providing both people and materials. The division also sponsors scholarships and arranges for NASA astronaut visits to local schools for motivational purposes. Additionally, Rocketdyne supports all of the local chambers of commerce and provides financial support to various community activities such as the YMCA's child care program, the Simi Valley Historical Society's centennial celebration, and Bottle Village.

THE ENTERPRISE

While its roots go back to the 1912 beginning of a struggling weekly newspaper to serve the handful of residents in Simi Valley and Moorpark, it's clear *The Enterprise* is also a modern pioneer.

Since 1977, *The Enterprise* has grown from a three-day weekly to a daily newspaper—one of less than 900 in the United States. In only its second year as a daily, it won the prestigious "General Excellence" award from the California Newspaper Publishers Association.

The newspaper only recently put three smaller buildings on its Easy Street site under one roof in a major renovation that boasts 19,030 square feet of multilevel working space.

Employment at the newspaper has grown progressively over the years as well, from fewer than 10 people to more than 130 full-time and part-time employees. Additionally, *The Enterprise* utilizes the "little merchant" system, giving nearly 400 youngsters a chance to earn money by delivering the daily newspaper.

One of the turning points for the struggling weekly newspaper, which was first housed along High Street in Moorpark, came in the early 1960s when the publishers of three local newspapers—the *Moorpark Enterprise,* owned by Bob Cribb; the *Simi Valley Sun,* owned by John P. Scripps Newspapers; and the *Simi Valley News-Advertiser,* owned by Frank Schroeder— merged to form *The Enterprise Sun and News.*

John Jenkins helped put the merger together and was named the local publisher for the consolidated newspaper, but he died shortly after his dream became a reality. Cribb, also publisher of the *Camarillo Daily News,* became publisher of *The Enterprise,* and later sold all his interests to Harris Enterprises, Inc., of Hutchinson, Kansas.

Ownership of the newspaper today is a unique arrangement in the world of publishing. Two major news-paper groups, Harris Enterprises and John P. Scripps, hold equal shares of stock.

The decade of the 1970s was one of major growth and maturity for the newspaper and the community. The arrival of a major department store in town and that store's desire to advertise on Mondays prompted the newspaper's expansion to a fourth day and the addition of state, national, and international news from United Press International in October 1977.

But the trend toward growth had only begun. Barely six months later, *The Enterprise* added both a fifth and sixth day of publication, and the following year, the newspaper moved into a modern plant and cranked up a new offset press.

Less than 10 years later, population in Simi Valley soared to about 100,000, which didn't go unnoticed by the giant metropolitan newspaper in Los Angeles. To keep up with the growth, maintain a competitive edge, and provide readers timely coverage of prep sports events, *The Enterprise* added its seventh day of publication, a Saturday, December 5, 1987.

By 1990 the circulation of *The Enterprise* had grown to more than 18,000, with more readers in Simi Valley than its two metropolitan competitors combined.

According to Wayne Lee, editor and publisher, the basic philosophy of the newspaper hasn't changed since that 1912 beginning.

"We're here to serve the public with the latest news and advertising," Lee said. "We strive each day to be the kind of well-rounded newspaper in which the people of Simi Valley and Moorpark can take pride.

As strong as its commitment to excellence is the newspaper's commitment to the community, evidenced by various newspaper staff members' volunteer involvement in clubs and organizations. Through the years, the newspaper has also been a quiet contributor to many local charities and organizations.

While it remains one of the newest daily newspapers in California and, in fact, the United States, *The Enterprise* has already been recognized with numerous state and national awards, including writing, editing, and photography awards from UPI, the Associated Press, Suburban Newspapers of America, and the CNPA. It once won 16 of 18 regional awards in UPI competition.

The Enterprise advertising staff also has a fine record for quality, sweeping the state's coveted silver cup sweepstakes award for four years running.

Looking ahead to the 1990s and the twenty-first century, Lee says he expects *The Enterprise* will continue in its role as a modern pioneer and grow to meet the needs and challenges of the ever-changing Simi Valley.

About 18,000 readers turn to The Enterprise *for the latest local news and advertising. The offices of the award-winning daily newspaper are located at 888 Easy Street.*

KNJO/KMDY

Simi Valley receives two pioneering radio stations: KNJO-FM, the first stereo station in Southern California, and KMDY-AM, the first to feature an all-comedy format.

Broadcasting on 92.7 FM, KNJO (a 3,000-watt station) signed on the air on April 1, 1963. Primarily geared to local interest, the station featured extensive area coverage as well as a beautiful-music format.

Over the years, programming and technology evolved to provide the current automated format of adult contemporary music. The goal of the station has always been to keep locals aware of "what's happening in their backyards," says general manager Peter J. Turpel. An integral part of the community, KNJO still emphasizes local coverage and has retained some of its early trademark features, such as lost-and-found pet reports and business-sponsored blocks of holiday music at Christmastime.

Although the studios are in Thousand Oaks, KNJO is dedicated to serving Simi Valley.

"We want people in Simi to know that this is their radio station," Turpel says. "Our studios are in Thousand Oaks, but our airwaves are everywhere."

KNJO provides full coverage of Simi Valley—from governmental actions to community happenings. KNJO is the only radio station to broadcast live from the Simi Valley

The KMDY studio.

Days Parade and to cover all events so fully. The station donates thousands of advertising dollars annually to support local events, and dedicated a live broadcast to the Corriganville restoration effort.

KNJO was one of the original tenants in the Park Oaks Shopping Center, the first shopping center in Thousand Oaks. The radio station met with disaster when part of the mall burned down Saturday night,

One of the KNJO/KMDY-sponsored Summer Concerts in the Park. Performing is Al Stewart.

September 4, 1986. Employees worked throughout the night to salvage equipment, and the station returned to the airwaves on Monday, broadcasting from an empty storefront in another section of the mall. In January 1987 KNJO moved to new offices with its current sister station, KMDY, at 3721 Thousand Oaks Boulevard.

KNJO was founded by a group of five investors, including major league baseball player Sandy Koufax. Dr. Irving Schaffner, a local general practitioner, bought the station after the first nine months and owned it for five years. In 1969 he sold it to John Poole and Alan Fischler, who kept it for 10 years before selling it to Palomar Broadcasting in 1979. In 1987 it was acquired by Comedy Broadcasting Co., which owns KMDY.

KMDY, an all-comedy AM station, brought laughter to the airwaves on April 4, 1984. Its signal, 850-AM, was formerly KGOE, a local station that had been on the air since 1969.

KMDY was the first all-comedy station in the world. The station features comic routines, interviews with comedians and classic radio theater, complete with original commercials. The comedy station was the brainstorm of several entertainers including actors Michael Douglas and Danny De Vito, who are some of the limited partners in Comedy Broadcasting Co.

SIMI VALLEY ADVENTIST HOSPITAL

The opening of Simi Valley Community Hospital in the mid-1960s represented a victory for area residents and physicians who wished to establish a medical facility in the town of Simi Valley. When local financial resources proved to be insufficient, the Seventh-day Adventist Church agreed to construct and operate the hospital as part of its worldwide health care system. Begun as a 50-bed general care facility in 1965, it became Simi Valley Adventist Hospital in 1967.

With significant growth in the 1970s and 1980s, the hospital added numerous services, including pediatrics, cardiac care, intensive care, and rehabilitation. In 1984 a multi-million-dollar addition was built to expand and remodel the existing space for emergency services, radiology, laboratories, physical therapy, and other patient services.

By 1990 Simi Valley Adventist Hospital had grown to a 215-bed main hospital boasting a staff of more than 235 physicians and 600 medical professionals. The hospital also encompasses three additional facilities offering specialized in- and outpatient services such as mental health care, transitional care, and outpatient surgery.

Within the main hospital, a maternity unit with four private LDR (labor, delivery, recovery) suites forms a part of a larger Women's Services Center. Other specialized services include an intensive/cardiac care unit, a medical/surgical unit, and a pediatric unit. The regional Paramedic Base Station, located in the hospital's emergency department, provides 24-hour emergency care to the over 100,000 Simi Valley area residents. The Oncology Institute, adjacent to the hospital, extends treatment to cancer patients, including radiation therapy.

Just two-and-one-half miles from the main facility, Simi Valley Adventist Hospital/ South contains the adult psychiatric and chemical dependency recovery units. Two

SVAH's new wing provided space for expanded emergency services, radiology, laboratory, physical therapy, and other patient services.

blocks from the main hospital is the Aspen Center, where a full array of diagnostic technology, mammography, radiology, and magnetic resonance imaging (MRI) services complements state-of-the-art outpatient surgery suites. Across the street from the main hospital is the Transitional Care Unit, a 44-bed skilled nursing facility, and a 13-bed rehabilitation center, with in- and outpatient physical therapy, occupational therapy, and communication disorders therapy.

Simi Valley Adventist Hospital sponsors many other health services and educational programs for the community as well. Ask-A-Nurse is a 24-hour health care information hotline staffed by registered nurses. In conjunction with the Seniors' Council of Simi Valley, a program called LifeLine allows senior citizens and handicapped or disabled persons to live independently with immediate, around-the-clock access to emergency help. Home health care is provided by West HealthCare. Through individual and group therapy, the Child Development Center, and the Family Connection, an employer-sponsored child care center, serves the needs of developmentally delayed children and their families.

Simi Valley Adventist Hospital is one of 18 hospitals comprising Adventist Health Systems/West, a not-for-profit, multi-institutional health care system affiliated with the Seventh-day Adventist Church. As a community-oriented facility operated primarily for the benefit of Simi Valley residents, the hospital helps fulfill the church's medical mission to humanity—a mission to carry on the healing ministry of Jesus Christ by emulating the values of His life and teachings.

Today's leaders at Simi Valley Adventist Hospital carry forward the vision of its founders—to keep pace with the dynamics of health care and an expanding population by developing more and better services for the people of Simi Valley. The hospital seeks to provide the highest quality acute medical care, including the most advanced technologies appropriate for its size and resources.

Committed to meeting the community's needs in future development, the administrators of Simi Valley Adventist Hospital have actively sought the frequent and consistent input of community leaders and organizations. In return, the hospital regularly participates in community events and interacts with local service organizations. Simi Valley Adventist Hospital is also actively in-

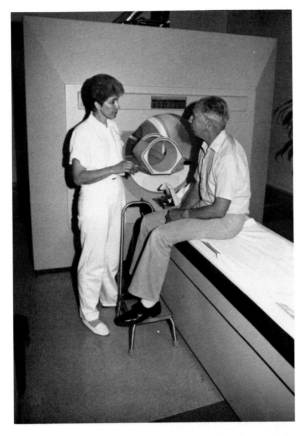

Magnetic Resonance Imaging (MRI) technology is one of the many services housed at the Aspen Center.

volved with area physicians who seek to meet the community's needs for specialized care. In addition, a strong Volunteer Guild, numbering more than 100 members by 1990s, donates thousands of volunteer hours to assist the hospital in providing services to the community.

"We can best show our commitment to meeting the health care needs of our community by enabling our clients to realize their optimum state of well-being," says hospital president Alan Rice, "whether that is through inpatient, outpatient, or educational services."

In this spirit, one unique thing about Simi Valley Adventist Hospital is its fundamental commitment to overall "wellness"—a state of spiritual, mental, physical, and social well-being as a way of life. To encourage this state of wellness, the hospital offers a full lineup of community health education classes designed to promote a life-style that can reduce the need for hospitalization.

Some of the most popular classes have been aerobic fitness, stress management, weight control, prepared childbirth, sign language, and smoking cessation.

As Simi Valley Hospital moves into the decade of the 1990s, it works toward becoming a complete health care center, with a full range of top-quality services for all ages of Simi Valley residents. Hospital administrators say that their long-range plans have two principal objectives: to render the highest quality care possible and to increase cost-effectiveness by developing additional alternatives to hospitalization. While working to achieve these goals, Simi Valley Adventist Hospital strives to be the health care center of choice for the residents of Simi Valley and the surrounding area.

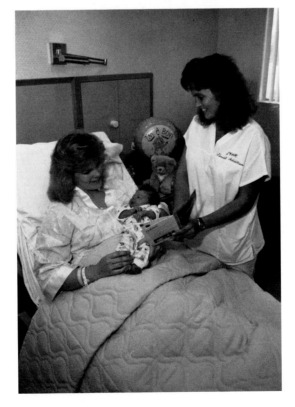

A Special Addition nurse explains postnatal care as mother and baby rest in one of the labor, delivery, and recovery suites.

MADJAR COMPANY

After many years of working in planning and development in both the public and private sectors, Fred Madjar opened his own consulting and development firm in Simi Valley in 1983.

Born in Bulgaria, Madjar emigrated with his parents as a child to Israel, where he attended school and served in the army. After his service, he won a scholarship to the University of Arizona, where he subsequently received a bachelor's degree in civil engineering and a master's degree in urban planning.

Finding life in the southwestern United States to his liking, Madjar decided to stay in that part of the world. He began his career by working for McCulloch Properties in Arizona while in graduate school, and later he was a planner for Maricopa County, which encompasses the Phoenix area. In 1975 he came to California as the chief coordinator of the general plan of the City of Eureka. After two years he came south to Simi Valley, joining the city's planning

department as an associate planner, where he worked for a little more than two years.

After his years in city planning, Madjar decided to return to the private sector. He worked for a Woodland Hills company for three years prior to opening his own company in Simi Valley.

Madjar Company is a progressive company with two distinct areas of operation: a consulting wing for planning and development and a development wing for the company's own projects. The consulting wing offers services encompassing total develop-

ment processing and project management from land feasibility through engineering, architecture, and construction.

Since the company was founded, it has successfully completed numerous consulting and development projects in and around Ventura County. One of the early consulting projects was with Ahmanson Developments Incorporated, a residential project encompassing more than 800 acres. As developer of its own ventures, Madjar Company completed several commercial and residential projects and the 30,000-square-foot Executive Center office building at 1919 Williams Street, where Madjar has his corporate offices. In the future Madjar plans to continue to develop custom residences as well commercial ventures.

In addition to his work, Madjar has been involved with several community organizations since he came to Simi. He has been the president of the Rancho Simi Foundation and has

A custom home completed by the Madjar Company.

chaired several neighborhood councils and community planning and zoning committees. Madjar joined the Simi Valley Rotary Club in 1984.

An art aficionado, Madjar is very active in the Simi Valley Cultural Association. As a member of the board of directors, he helped acquire a $32,000 grant from the city for a feasibility study for a performing arts center. Madjar also served on the advisory board of the Ventura County Art Alliance. In 1989 Madjar was appointed to the Simi Valley Family YMCA Board of Managers and to the board of directors of Ventura County Marketing Group. Composed of business and community leaders, the marketing group was formed that year to responsibly promote Ventura County as a rich environment in which to live and work.

From left: Mayor Greg Stratton, Bill Carpenter, Fred Madjar, and Bonnie Carpenter at the ribbon-cutting ceremony for Madjar's Executive Building (left).

Patrons

The following individuals, companies, and organizations have made a valuable commitment
to the quality of this publication. Windsor Publications and the Simi Valley
Chamber of Commerce gratefully acknowledge their participation in
Simi Valley: Toward New Horizons.

Anderson Disposal Service*
Banks and Humphry Accountancy Corporation*
Blakeley Western*
Lloyd Boland, D.C.*
Robert N. Brown, Jr., M.D.*
Bugle Boy Industries*
The Callahan Family*
Century 21 Tabor Realtors*
Certified Auto Glass*
Gary D. Chaffee, D.D.S.*
City of Simi Valley*
Comcast Cablevision Corporation*
Dantona and Associates*
Dataquik Corporation*
Dave's Club Service*
The Enterprise*
Family Health Care, Inc.*
Farmers Insurance Group*
GI Industries*
P.W. Gillibrand Company*
Green Acres Market*
Hirose Electric (USA) Inc.*
Robert O. Huber*
Jack's Shoes*
Kaiser Permanente*
KNJO/KMDY*
Lamb Realty Co., Inc.*
Lederer Development Group*
Moshe Litman, C.P.A.
Madjar Company*
MICOM Communications Corp.*
Charles Neault, D.C.
  Southern California Back Centers*
Oakridge Athletic Club*
Peter Quinn, D.D.S.*
Radisson Hotel*
Rancho Sequoia Veterinary Hospital*
C.A. Rasmussen, Inc.*
A Refrigerator Repair Service
The Roberts Group, Inc.*
Rocketdyne*
Scribner's Electronics*
Simi Valley Adventist Hospital*
Simi Valley Bank*
Simi Valley Landfill*
Simi Valley-Moorpark Board of REALTORS®*
Melvin Simon & Associates*
Spectrum Land Planning, Inc.*
Travelodge*
The Voit Companies*
Wangtek*
Whitney Auto and RV Care Center*
Whittaker Electronic Systems*

*Partners in Progress of *Simi Valley: Toward New Horizons.*
The histories of these companies and organizations appear in Chapter 7,
  beginning on page 129.

Bibliography

PERIODICALS

Conejo News
Daily News
The Enterprise
Enterprise Sun & News
Los Angeles Times
The Mail Cart (Published by the Simi Valley Historical Society
Moorpark Enterprise
Simi Valley News
Star Free Press

OTHER SOURCES

Bandurraga, Peter, David Hill, and G. Belden Holland. *Ventura County Yesterday and Today: Looking Back at Ventura County.* Ventura: Anacapa Publishers, 1980.

Biolchino, Louis M. "From Rural Village to Metropolitan Suburb: Community Action in Simi Valley, California in the 1960's." Thesis, CSU Long Beach, 1980.

"California Indians." *California Historical Society Quarterly* (1962).

Cameron, Janet Scott. "Early Transportation in Southeastern Ventura County." *Ventura County Historical Society Quarterly* X (1964).

———. "Newspapers in Southeastern Ventura County." *Ventura County Historical Society Quarterly* XI (1986).

———. *Simi Grows Up.* Anderson, Ritchie, & Simon, 1963.

———. "Simi's First Farmer." *Ventura County Historical Society Quarterly* IV (1956).

Cowan, Robert G. *Ranchos of California.* Los Angeles: Historical Society of Southern California, 1977.

Coy, Owen G. *California County Boundaries.* California Historical Survey Commission, 1973.

Goldman, Leslie. *A Stagecoach History of Los Angeles and the Santa Susana Stage Road.* Santa Susana Mountain Park Association, 1973.

Hadingham, Evan. "A Man Obsessed with Ancient Stargazers." *Science Digest,* August 1984.

Haigh, Gerald. *Straw Roads: A Story of Simi Valley from 1908 to 1960.* Simi Valley Historical Society, 1975.

Harrington, Robert E. *Early Days in Simi Valley.* N.p., 1961.

Hart, James D. *A Companion to California.* University of California Press, 1987.

Havens, Patricia. *Simi Valley From Many Sources: A Comprehensive Study of Ventura County, California.* Oxnard: M & N Printing, 1979.

———. *Local History Booklet No. 1.* Simi Valley Historical Society, 1989.

History of Simi Valley. Simi Valley Unified School District, n.d.

Hudson, Travis. "Cristoval Manejo: A Nearly Forgotten Man." *Ventura County Historical Society Quarterly* XXVII (1981).

Meagher, Thomas H. "Island Indians." *Ventura County Historical Society Quarterly* (1967).

Miller, Crane S. *Changing Agricultural Landscape of Simi Valley from 1795 to 1960.* Ventura County Historical Society, n.d.

Percy, R.G. "The Los Angeles to San Luis Obispo Road, 1860." *Ventura County Historical Society Quarterly* (1958).

Robinson, W.W. *Story of Ventura County.* Title Insurance & Trust Company, 1955.

Santa Susana Depot. Rancho Simi Foundation and Santa Susana Model RR Club, 1989.

Shiner, Joel L. "A Fernandino Site in Simi Valley, California." *The Masterkey* XXIII (1949).

Shumway, Burgess McK. *California Ranchos: Patented Private Land Grants.* San Bernardino: Borego Press, 1988.

Simi Valley Chamber of Commerce. *Community Economic Profile.* 1972, 1990.

Smith, Leon. *Hollywood Goes on Location.* Los Angeles: Pomegranate Press, 1988.

Snider, Ann D., ed. *Ventura County & Coast Almanac.* Ventura: Gold Coast Publications, 1988.

Spaulding, Edward S. *Adobe Days Along the Channel.* Schaver Printing Studio, Inc., 1957.

Starr, Kevin. *Inventing the Dream: California Through the Progressive Era.* Oxford University Press, 1985.

Thompson and West. *History of Santa Barbara and Ventura Counties.* Oakland: n.p., 1883.

Walker Art Center. *Naives and Visionaries.* E.P. Dutton & Co., Inc., 1974.

Roziare, Charles E. "Pictographs at Burro Flats." *Ventura County Historical Society Quarterly* IV (1959).

Ventura County and the Valley of the Simi. California Mutual Benefit Colony of Chicago. ca. 1887. Reproduced by Simi Valley Historical Society, 1986.

Facing page: One of the many television series shot in Simi Valley during the late 1950s and early 1960s was the popular "Gunsmoke." The series' stars, seen here on set at Big Sky Ranch, were (from left) Milburne Stone, Dennis Weaver, Amanda Blake, amd James Arness. Courtesy, Viacom Enterprises

*Early Simi settlers cavort by a campsite in this
late-nineteenth-century photo. Courtesy, Simi
Valley Historical Society and Museum,
Strathearn Historical Park*

Index